THE ILLUSTRATED HISTORY OF WELSH RUGBY

6

THE ILLUSTRATED HISTORY OF WELSH RUGBY

J. B. G. Thomas

PELHAM BOOKS

First published in Great Britain by
Pelham Books Ltd
44 Bedford Square
London WC1
1980

British Library Cataloguing in Publication Data
Thomas, J. B. G.
The illustrated history of Welsh Rugby.
1. Rugby football – Wales – History
I. Title
796.33'3'09429 GV945.9.G7

ISBN 0 7207 1268 8

Set, printed and bound in Great Britain by
Fakenham Press Limited,
Fakenham, Norfolk

CONTENTS

For my family

PREFACE

Having always wanted to prepare an illustrated history of Welsh rugby as a result of saving records and pictures of players and matches for over fifty years, the Welsh Rugby Union Centenary and my publishers provided the opportunity. Yet this book would not have been possible without the ready assistance of the managing director of the *Western Mail and Echo Ltd*, David Thomas, my editor Duncan Gardiner, my colleague John Billot and secretary Jill Mathias.

Down through the years the paper has financed my many trips abroad in search of the game and I am especially grateful to Thomson Regional Newspapers and the *Western Mail*, as well as other sources, for permission to reproduce the many pictures which highlight this history.

My many friends in the game, players past and present and long-serving officials alike, have helped unknowingly by relating many stories and by trusting me with their confidences.

Although I have been privileged to observe only the second half of the Welsh Rugby Union's century, the wonder of the ten decades remains an absorbing interest. The game in Wales will go on through its second century which will prove every bit as colourful and glorious as the first.

Cardiff 1980 — J. B. G. THOMAS

ACKNOWLEDGEMENTS

To my friend Vivian Jenkins for his foreword.

To the works of Revd F. Marshall, O. L. Owen, John Billot, Charles Arthur, D. E. Davies, J. Townsend Collins, J. Davies, E. D. H. Sewell, W. W. Wakefield, Rowe Harding, Danie Craven, Gwyn Nicholls, D. Gallaher and W. J. Stead for many references. Also to the Rugby Football Annual, Playfair Annual, Rothman's Annual, the Welsh Brewers' Annual and Welsh Rugby Union Handbook for records.

The majority of the photographs in this book are reproduced by kind permission of the *Western Mail and Echo Ltd*, Cardiff.
The pictures on the following pages appear by courtesy of those named:

Belfast Telegraph 104
Marcel Besson 135, 177 *below*
British Library 67, 73
Cape Times, South Africa 174 *above*
Central Press Photos Ltd 93, 172 *above*
Fox Photos 166 *below (2)*
Keystone Press Agency Ltd 101 *above*
E. D. Lacey 179 *below*
Gwyn Martin 33
H. W. Neale 175
Sport and General Press Agency Ltd 18, 100, 102–3, 129, 163 *above*
Thomson Organisation Picture Service 137
Welsh Folk Museum 58, 77, 152
J. Weston 15

FOREWORD

It has been said that the history of a nation is the history of its great men. Some, no doubt, will dispute that – the small men, too, play their part! – but it is the great ones, for better or worse, that are usually remembered. They get all the publicity!

Thus, when we look back over a hundred years of Welsh rugby, it is the names of the great players that immediately spring to mind. Hero-worship is not a modern growth. When I was a boy at school my father was always reminding me of the *really* great days of Welsh rugby, i.e. when he was a boy himself! Billy Bancroft, Willie Trew, Dickie Owen, Gwyn Nicholls, Teddy Morgan, Rhys Gabe, Percy Bush – the names rolled off his tongue like a litany to the saints; and I, at his feet, could only wonder, and feel bereft – as I do to this day – that I never saw them play.

The next best thing, for there were no films of them or TV re-plays in those days, was to hear about them and my Dad, a born story-teller, regaled me with tales of many a wondrous deed. Billy Bancroft, the one and only 'Bankie', was one of his special heroes. Had he not, after all, played thirty-three times for Wales? – against the three home countries only, a record which no-one but Gareth Edwards has equalled, and which even the great 'J.P.R.' failed to reach by two. There were no fixtures against France, or Dominions' teams, in Bancroft's day; nor were there any short tours abroad. So his record is still a remarkable one.

He held undisputed sway in Wales's team for twelve seasons, from 1890 to 1901, which takes him back to within a decade of the foundation of the Welsh Rugby Union itself. I mention this because he is my own nearest verbal contact with the beginning of the century we are now celebrating. I knew him personally, and first saw him when he came up to Llandovery to play against us at cricket, at the age of fifty-one. I seem to remember, too, that he scored over fifty runs, many of them with delicate late cuts, a stroke which has almost vanished today. He was, it so happens, a Glamorgan cricketer also, in their minor county days; but it was as a rugby player that he became a legend. The tales about him were innumerable – how he used to run opposing forwards off their feet, from one side of the field to the other (he was, it seems, extremely fast), or kick goals, in practice, from the corner flag or from a yard in front of the posts, right below the cross-bar. The rugby equivalent, as it were, of Joe Davis's trick-shots at snooker.

It fell to me many years later, when he was seventy-nine years old, to accompany him to Lord's to see his cricket protégé, Gilbert Parkhouse, play his first game for England, against the West Indies in 1950. It was my big opportunity to catch up with the past, and we talked, I am afraid, far more about rugby than cricket. Who was the greatest centre he had seen? 'Arthur Gould, without a doubt.' And who the greatest fullback? 'H. B. Tristram, of England, out on his own.' I must be honest, I had hardly heard of Tristram, except as a name. Had you? It only goes to show that there are no players, for anyone, like those of their own day!

I *had* heard of H. Gamlin, however, 'The Octopus', the deadly tackler, of Devonport Albion and England fame. 'What about Gamlin?' I asked him. 'Oh, we knew how to deal with him,' was the reply. 'Any Swansea player who kicked to the right side of the field against him was dropped for the next match.' Gamlin, it seems, was a right-footed kicker only. Who said players didn't *think* about the game in those days!

A few years later I met 'W.J.' again. Swansea had just played the All Blacks and I asked him what he thought about Bob Scott, the touring team's fullback, then the talk of the British rugby scene. 'Not bad', he said, 'Not bad at all, though I'd like to see him under a bit more pressure and when you see him next, ask him if he can kick a goal from 60 yards, *with either foot*'. It was the 'either foot' that amused me! The implication was that 'W.J.' could have done it standing on his head!

My last memory of that day at Lord's is of helping 'W.J.' across the road, just outside the Grace Gates, as the traffic roared by. He was a shade unsteady on his feet by then. 'I used to be so proud of my legs,' he said. A touch of pathos there, I thought. Old Father Time had done his work again. 'W.J.' was eighty-six years old when he died. He was born on 2 March 1871, ten years and ten days before the Welsh Rugby Union was founded – one of the 'immortals', without a doubt.

I should say here, though, that Horace Lyne, a Newport lawyer, played for Wales even before Bancroft did. He was capped five times, as a forward, from 1883 to 1885, but became much more famous later as an administrator. He was President of the Welsh Rugby Union for forty-two years, from 1906 to 1947, an unparalleled record in any country. I remember him well, a tall, silver-haired, extremely dignified figure, at the post-match dinners in my own day. Since then the Presidents of the various Rugby Unions have to go away for a rest cure after only a year in office! Horace Lyne, incidentally, signed the minutes of the first meeting of the International Board ever held, and was a member of it from 1887 to 1938, attending sixty meetings. What an infinity of work for the game his lifetime contribution represents.

Gwyn Nicholls I first saw in the flesh when he attended the post-match dinner after our Wales v All Blacks game in 1935. As captain of the team that had beaten the All Blacks in the famous 1905 match, he was called on to say a few words, and I well remember thinking 'what a lovely man'. He seemed modesty personified, in spite of all the great things he had done in the game, and I can well understand why the gates at Cardiff Arms Park were named after him. Willie Llewellyn and Rhys Gabe, two other leading lights of the first 'Golden Era', were equally charming and delightful men. Willie Llewellyn was a chemist at Bridgend, in the days when I was growing up in the game with the local club, and no-one could have been kinder or more helpful to a young player.

Percy Bush was a character all of his own, the great sidestepper from whom no-one ever knew what to expect next, either on or off the field. I had heard how, once, after a champagne lunch, he scored seventeen points for Cardiff in the first twenty minutes and then walked off saying 'That's enough, boys, I'll leave the rest to you'. Another story about him came to me from Oliver Piper, an Irish international forward of the day. 'I played against him, for Cork Constitution against Cardiff' he told me, 'and we were being given a hammering. But the worst moment of all came when Percy ran clean through the lot of us and then, after crossing the line, ran back into the field again without touching down before waltzing through the lot of us a second time and finally scoring.' Oh, to have seen Bush play!

The first international match I ever saw was Wales against England at Cardiff Arms Park in 1926, a 3–3 draw. It was a tempestuous match, very rough, as I thought (I was only fourteen years old at the time) and two memories stand out. They are of scrum-half Bobby Delahay (a real bundle of tricks, eighteen times capped, and tough as teak) 'squaring up' to Tom Voyce, the England wing-forward, twice his size, and of 'Wakers' Wakefield scoring what I still rate the greatest try by a forward I have seen. From somewhere near halfway he ran clean through the Welsh team without a hand being laid on him – he was an 'even-timer' – and grounded the ball about half-way out. Luckily England failed with the kick, and Wales were able to draw when George Andrews, the Newport wing, scored an unconverted try in the corner near the end.

Rowe Harding, one of my first rugby heroes and a great friend since on many Crawshay tours, captained Wales in that match. But it is the players of one's own time, of course, that one remembers best of all. Wilfred Wooller and Cliff Jones, in the thirties, were every bit as much of a sensation as the players of the last ten years have been. Cliff made the openings, with his devastating sidestep and scorching pace over the first fifteen yards, and Wilfred finished them off with his seven-league stride and big outward swing that left opponents standing. Howard Marshall, the leading rugby writer of the time, once described him 'like the sacrificial car of Juggernaut, leaving a trail of prostrate figures in his wake.'

Claude Davey, our captain, and none better, had the smile of an angel, but tackled like an avenging Fury – a marvellous player for any fullback to have in front of him. Then there was Idwal Rees, all style and polish, and Geoffrey Rees-Jones, a 'smiler' on the wing, who scored two of our three tries when we beat the All Blacks in 1935. It was Haydn Tanner's first match for Wales, as a schoolboy of only eighteen years of age, against the All Blacks, of all people. Yet he played like a master, and his gym mistress from Gowerton County School, as it then was, was the happiest young lady in Wales that night. She had been sent with him from Penclawdd that morning, to make sure he did not lose his way! In those days most of the Welsh players, except those from a distance, spent the Friday night at home before joining the rest of the team on Saturday morning. Times have certainly changed.

I wish I had space to write more about my contempories – Watcyn Thomas for instance, who captained us to our first win over England at Twickenham, Arthur Rees, my old Llandovery schoolmate, who led the Welsh pack like some wild man from Borneo and had them ready to follow him anywhere, big Jim Lang, of Llanelli, and many more. But there have been more than forty years of Welsh international rugby since. There were the great days, for instance, of Cliff Morgan, Jackie Matthews and Bleddyn Williams, not to mention Ken Jones, of the forty-four caps, and forwards like John Gwilliam, Roy John, Rees Stephens and the rest. Was there ever, again, a more exciting player than Lewis Jones, who under the captaincy of Malcolm Thomas, for the Navy against the Army at Twickenham, kicked the longest goal I have seen by a player in this country. From five yards inside his own half it was, and a yard in from the touchline, right in front of us in the Pressbox, yet it would have been a goal from another ten yards, at least. Years later, when I asked him about it, he said 'I only took it to waste time. I didn't think I had a chance.' What a man!

Great players, great names. Dozens more occur to me as I write – 'Wick' Powell, 'Bunner' Travers, Bryn Meredith, Denzil Williams, big Rhys Williams, Billy Cleaver, Clem Thomas, Alun Pask, Dewi Bebb, Delme Thomas, Brian Price and many besides. How can one mention them all! Nearly eight hundred players have worn the red jersey, all equally proud, I am sure, as I am, to have done so. It was the thrill of our young lives, and still brings a glow however many years have passed.

I have left the *pièce de résistance* till the end. The last decade of the Welsh Rugby Union's centenary has produced, for Welsh rugby, a second 'Golden Era', fit to be matched with the first, when Trew and Gwyn Nicholls were in their prime. From 1900 to 1909 Wales won the Triple Crown five times, and did so again in 1911. Now they have won it five times again in the seventies, as well as once just previously in 1969. Even the first Golden Age men could not manage it four years in succession, as our latter-day heroes have done. J. P. R. Williams, Gerald Davies, John Dawes, Barry John, Phil Bennett, Gareth Edwards, Mervyn Davies – great names all – and many more are legends already. They will be talked of in years to come with the same adulation, almost reverence, that my father reserved for his Bancroft and Trew.

A hundred years is a long time; if I have dwelt on the distant past rather more than the immediate present, it is because it is a whole century we are celebrating, not just the last ten years. What has happened more recently has been amply recorded, and lauded to the skies, by a multitude of scribes, and by none more faithfully and devotedly than our own 'J.B.G.', the author of this book. He and I have travelled the world together, gathering unforgettable memories in pursuit of the 'bladder' (as my grandfather used to call it!) and I can vouch for his total love of the game.

This is his 28th book on rugby in all its aspects – a staggering output. Billy Bancroft or Trew, Gareth Edwards or 'J.P.R.' or a dozen more could be put up as Wales's 'Player of the Century' but the 'Recorder of the Century', where Welsh rugby is concerned, is indisputably 'J.B.G.'. It is fitting that he should be the man to write this book.

VIVIAN JENKINS
Bridgend, London Welsh, Wales, British Lions;
formerly Chief Rugby Correspondent of the *Sunday Times*.

1 THE GAME

Where did it all start in Wales? Was it at the Roman Camp at Caerleon (Isca) and played as Harpastum, or later? Surely it must have been before the audacious and legendary William Webb Ellis caught the ball and ran at Rugby School in 1823. Perhaps it was first played in one form or another with a pigskin bladder through the villages on Shrove Tuesday.

The rugby world is till theorising as to the origins of the game and the quest for a satisfactory solution to the mystery has continued as fiercely as ever from the rolling waves of Lands End to the long heavy swell of Cape Wrath, from the shelter of Fishguard Harbour to the fish quays of Great Yarmouth and deep into the heart of Limerick, and south to Skibbereen and north to Portrush.

For myself, after many years of research, I am prepared to accept that Harpastum was the original form of rugby football, a handling game without kicking but with some form of tackling; one of the few certain facts about the Roman game was that it was extremely violent in character. Morris Marples in his splendid work *A History of Football*, highlights the

Rugby in the raw! An early form of rugby at an army barracks, published in 1827. The ball appears to be a pig's bladder.

Did it all start here with Harpastum at the Roman camp at Caerleon (Isca)?

very nature of the ancient game most vividly and from his research one can detect the very beginnings even of backs and forwards. He also points out that there was some wrestling, some handling, some throwing and some running without throwing.

One could almost apply such references to the modern game and, furthermore, they sold the 'dummy' in Harpastum by showing it to one player and passing to another, just as Percy Bush and Dickie Lloyd did so effectively early this century and as did more speedily in a later generation A. L. Gracie and Len Corbett not to mention the memorable 'dummy' run by Barry John at Wellington in 1971.

Harpastum was popular with Greeks and Romans for 800 years and must have been played by Roman occupation forces in Britain inside their forts, beneath the walls of Caerleon (Isca), Usk (Burrium), Abergavenny (Gobannium), Monmouth (Blestium) and Caerwent (Venta). When the Romans left Britain in about AD 410, not only did they leave a network of roads and a new way of life behind them but what most sporting historians now accept as the original game of rugby football.

Many years later there is well-recorded reference to Cornish 'hurling' by Richard Carew in 1602 and Welsh 'knappan' by George Owen of Henllys in 1603. It is also recorded in the records of Medieval Oxford, that a student died at Oxford in 1303 and was found by his brother Adam Salisbury to have been killed by Irish students, it is alleged, 'whilst playing ball in the High Street towards Eastgate'. In 1314 Edward II issued a proclamation banning football in the streets of London. In 1576, one hundred persons 'assembled themselves unlawfully to play a certain unlawful game of foote-ball'. In 1634, there was a great frost and 'fourteen young men, presuming to play at football on the River Trent, near Gainsborough, coming altogether in a scuffle, the ice suddenly broke, and there were eight of them drowned'. It could well have been the most disastrous 'maul' in the history of the game.

In Richard Carew's description of 'hurling' there is much akin to rugby football – although that game is, perhaps, a little wilder and more dangerous, and it is interesting to read that the ball could not be thrown forward, a principle which is the very basis of the modern game. Strange to relate these early 'hurling' matches were played, generally, at weddings where the guests used to 'undertake to encounter all-comers'. Such occasions would be rare but in those days there were few other such gatherings in the countryside and another comment by Carew brings a wry smile to the reader, recalling some of the more vigorous of modern matches, 'when the hurling is ended, you shall see them retiring home as from a pitched battle, with bloody pates, bones broken and out of joint, and such bruises as serve to shorten their days; yet all is good play, and never attorney nor coroner troubled for that matter'.

Welsh 'knappan' was similar to Cornish 'hurling' and the villagers were encouraged to exercise by playing it or engaging in pursuit of it. It was rough and vigorous, demanding stamina and spirit, as many would return home with broken heads, black faces, bruised bodies and lame legs, yet laughing and jesting on arrival at their homes, bearing no grudges against their opponents.

Oliver Cromwell, when an undergraduate at Sidney Sussex College, Cambridge, was an enthusiastic footballer and no doubt this served him well on his march through South Wales en route to Ireland. He may well have started the long-standing rivalry between the English and the Welsh in the game!

The Shrove Tuesday annual affair was traditional at Derby until 1840 and was said to celebrate a victory there over the Romans in AD 217 and as one S. Glover recalled in 1829, 'The shops are closed and the town presents the aspect of a place suddenly taken by storm.' The sight of hundreds of men in the River Derwent ducking each other with a thousand supporters on each bank cheering them on must have been something. It would have made good television.

In 1823 it is recorded that William Webb Ellis 'with a fine disregard for the Rules of Football, as played in his time, first took the ball in his arms and ran with it, thus originating the distinctive feature of the rugby game'. In 1895 the Old Rugbeian Society published a report on the Origin of Rugby Football and it reveals that at Rugby School occurred the major conversion of association football, such as it was then, into rugby football, with the handling code being encouraged. Quoting from the Society's Report (p. 22):

'It may, we think, be fairly considered to be proven from the foregoing statements, that (1) in 1820 the form of football in vogue at Rugby School was something approximating more closely to Association than to what is known as Rugby Football today, (2) that at some date between 1820 and 1830 the innovation was introduced of running with the ball, (3) that this in all probability done in the latter half of 1823 by Mr W. Webb Ellis, who is credited by Mr Bloxham with the invention and whose "unfair practices" were the subject of a general remark at the time. To this we would add that the innovation was regarded as of doubtful legality for some time, and only gradually became accepted as part of the game, but obtained a customary status between 1830 and 1840 and was duly legalised.'

The former headmaster of Rugby School, Matthew Bloxham, wrote in December 1880:

'In the latter half of 1823, originated though without premeditation, that change in one of the rules which more than any other has since distinguished the Rugby School game from the Association rules. A boy of the name of Ellis, a town boy and a foundationer while playing Bigside at Football in that half year, caught the ball in his arms.

'This being so, according to the then rule, he ought to have retired back as far as he pleased, without parting with the ball, for the combatants on the opposite side could only advance to the spot where he had caught the ball, and were unable to rush forward until he had either punted it or placed it for someone else to kick . . . Ellis, for the first time disregarded this rule, and on catching the ball, instead of retiring backwards, rushed forward with the ball in his hands towards the opposite goal, with what result as to the game I know not, neither do I know how this infringement

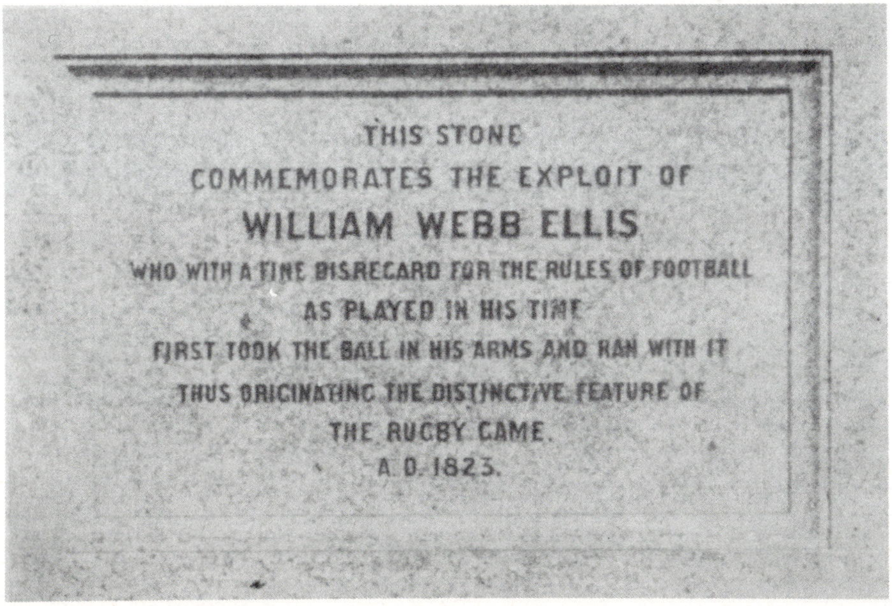

Rugby School plaque to commemorate William Webb Ellis, 1823.

The 1923 Rugby Centenary Match at Rugby School between an England and Wales XV and a Scotland and Ireland XV. W. E. Crawford (Ireland) is seen converting a try on the famous school ground.

of a well-known rule was followed up, or when it became, as it is now, the standing rule.'

So there can be little doubt that it *was* at Rugby School and it *was* William Webb Ellis who launched the change in the game of football and so created Rugby Union Football. He became a clergyman, and died in Menton, France in January 1872, where his grave is cared for by proud Frenchmen and bears a head stone inscribed with life details and his claim to sporting fame. One would almost suggest that it is a 'heavenly game', as Welshmen now treat the game that Ellis launched because of his indulgence in 'unfair practices' as a second religion.

There is reason for the 'religious' approach, for the game was launched by a schoolboy at Rugby School destined to enter the church after being an exhibitioner at Brasenose College, Oxford. Thus did the clergy in later years help to take the game into Wales and teach the younger members of their parishes the gentle art of running and handling. One believes that in the early nineteenth century they already knew all about kicking!

Vital years in the game's early development were between 1830 and 1840, for in 1839 a famous Old Rugbeian, Arthur Pell, who was to become a member of Parliament, formed the first rugby club with fellow students at Cambridge University, and the games were played at Parker's Piece, that magnificent green park that can be viewed with such pleasure from the dining-room of the University Arms in Cambridge. Matches continued to be played on the historic turf until 1881. Four years after the formation of the Cambridge University Club the medical students at Guy's Hospital formed a club and so the game got away to a healthy start, in charge of academics and medics. Scotland made a start in 1858 through Edinburgh Academicals and the first match played in the country was between Edinburgh Academy and Merchiston Castle School. Who then brought the game to Wales and why were the Welsh late developers in that the Welsh Rugby Union is the youngest of the four Home Unions? The game in its various forms was played in certain areas of Wales and pursued with enthusiasm.

The returning clergy and students brought the game, as established at the schools, Cambridge University and Guy's Hospital, into Wales and one must believe that the leading public schools in Wales did a considerable amount of pioneering work to codify the new game and in encompassing the laws or rules as laid down by Rugby School and Cambridge University. One believes that each area engaged in some form of modification which embraced local traditions and at Llandovery, Monmouth and Christ College, Brecon much was done by staff and pupils to promulgate the new form of rugby football.

When the pupils left these schools or Welsh pupils at leading English schools returned to their homes in the various parts of Wales, they encouraged their fellow villagers to engage in the hurly-burly of a game that slowly and surely was becoming more scientific. Because educated young men were the precursors, the game had a special appeal in that it was soon established that brain played an equal part alongside brawn, and

Llandovery College v Christ College, Brecon, 1979. The two leading Welsh public schools started playing each other in 1879.

the village bully who may have dominated for years found himself outwitted by the returning schoolboy or student, fully acquainted with the more sophisticated manoeuvres.

Hacking, tripping and charging were still very much in vogue and injuries were still prevalent while those young men forced to work at an early age in the various industries and trades initiated by the industrial revolution sweeping through Wales like a prairie fire in the first half of the nineteenth century, obtained no small pleasure from 'laying down' a returning student or schoolboy in the many 'pick-up sides' matches that were played. Schoolboys often invaded the fields of local farms to engage in 'modern' rugby and frequently were chased from their make-shift pitches by irate farmers long before their matches were completed.

One has searched long and hard to find a beginning but there is no one special field or blasted heath in Wales where it all began. There were small groups in many places and they battled on through the middle of the nineteenth century and after 1850 there was considerable progress, although little was reported in the newspapers of the era. The *Western Mail*, launched in 1869, did not carry many details of the game's early days in Wales but the villages were busy, like Blaenau Gwent who formed a club in 1869, and there must have been other sides who merged with their neighbours, disbanded or became senior clubs.

There is a misty haze shrouding the 1860s until the Neath Club was formed in 1871 followed by Llanelli and Swansea in 1872, Newport in 1874 and Cardiff in 1875–76. Neath rightly claims to be the senior major club in Wales and for its launching credit must go to a Scot, Dr T. P. Whittington, who, like many of his fellows qualifying in medicine in Edinburgh, brought more than the power to heal the sick with him to South Wales. He became Neath's first international player in 1873 and the first produced by a Welsh Club, as Wales had yet to form a Union and field a national team. Dr Whittington deserves far more homage than many Welsh players for it was he who launched, as an Old Merchistonian, a glorious tradition by becoming the first player in Wales to win a cap . . . still a major honour in Welsh sport. There were twenty a side in his first international for Scotland and the celebrations afterwards were as strenuous as the game for the early menu cards demanded that players possessed stomachs as well as muscles of steel. Whisky and haggis was a traditional course at every major after-match dinner and one is glad that it has journeyed safely down the years to present times.

There were other medical men, members of the clergy, schoolmasters and iron and coal masters, all unheralded and unsung, who helped feed the game to willing young Welshmen and the 1870s saw it firmly established. It was ideally suited to the temperament, the physical approach, and the native cunning of the Welsh, who proved to be every bit as enthusiastic about the codified game as they were about 'knappan'. There was a genuine 'hywl' about the game; it was basic, it was for proud hearts supported by strong arms and legs.

Early in the 1870s clubs started to meet each other and in October 1874 the code of laws or rules drawn up at Cheltenham College, where many Welsh pupils were boarders, was adopted by the game and accepted in Wales. The major public schools in Wales, having played the game for several years before the newly-formed clubs, experienced no difficulty in playing against them. Pontypridd was formed in 1875, Aberavon in 1876, Bridgend in 1878 and Penarth and Ebbw Vale in 1879. Some of the present smaller clubs had been formed before the major ones. Chepstow, for example, was launched in 1870 and played an important part in forming the Welsh Rugby Union ten years later.

The list of smaller clubs is impressive. Llandaff, Haverfordwest, Merthyr, Pontypool, Carmarthen, Abergavenny, Ely, Roath, Blaenavon, Cowbridge, Aberdare, and the colleges at Lampeter, Llandovery, Brecon and Cowbridge, all played their part in spreading the rugby gospel that was to be adopted with the forming of the Welsh Rugby Union in 1880–81 although even its formation provided a source of rivalry and contradiction, not to mention controversy; an atmosphere often not far from that of many matches in Wales at the time. It is said that the Welsh enjoy a good argument and the early days of Welsh rugby in an organised form produced much dispute.

The Welsh were quick to notice that England and Scotland had launched international rugby and were impatient to emulate them, but they had no firm ideas about the establishment of a governing body; local rivalries, especially those between East and West, engulfed all. However, by the mid-1870s a special club was formed, the South Wales Football Club, with the suggestion that it should be composed of leading players from clubs already in existence and make itself strong enough to challenge the leading English clubs – which had been playing for ten years or more. Again, the opportunity to play against better players would provide a means by which Welsh standards could be raised. The Club then launched a challenge cup competition in 1877 which aroused interest and controversy, and continued for ten hectic seasons before the senior clubs retired from a competition hampered by rough play and refereeing disputes, but its origin, launching and colourful ten years of existence must be examined as an integral part of the game's development in Wales.

In October 1877 representatives of the interested existing clubs met in the Castle Hotel at Brecon to discuss ways and means of developing the game and encouraging closer co-operation between their clubs. One can imagine that this almost casual meeting, assisted in its enthusiasm by good old fashioned ale from the wood was, in its way, the beginning of organised Welsh rugby and sowed the seeds of the Welsh Rugby Union yet to be born. By the time the evening's discussion had ended the representatives had agreed upon one thing, the launching of a knock-out competition. The prize would be a challenge cup worth fifty guineas, a large amount in those far-off days when a week's wages for most working Welshmen, as soldiers in the industrial revolution, was hardly a pound a week. It would

Richard Mullock – the father of the Welsh Rugby Union and its first secretary 1881–92.

cost clubs £2 annually to enter the competition and eighteen clubs quickly paid their dues and were thirsting for battle, but little did the club representatives realise at their Brecon meeting how seriously the competition would be taken and how fierce and argumentative would be the football produced.

Newport won the trophy in the year of launching, beating Swansea by a goal to nil in the final, and again in the next year before Swansea, Cardiff and Llanelli followed in turn as victors. In the ten years of its existence, the South Wales Cup was won by one of these four clubs who came to be known as the 'Big Four', an image that has remained with them and which was to be celebrated in Centenary Year by their being allocated a match apiece against the touring New Zealand All Blacks. These four do not overlord Welsh club rugby as they did 100 years ago, yet their influence is still powerful. They stand like four major bastions from East to West, veritable meccas for sporting visitors, starting at Newport and moving through Cardiff and Swansea into Llanelli.

Now there are other clubs, equally successful, like Bridgend, Pontypridd, Aberavon, Neath, Pontypool, Maesteg and Ebbw Vale but it is the big four that remain as the symbols of early greatness in the game in Wales and, Newport still having a foot in both camps, as members of the Rugby Football Union and the Welsh Union. A link between two great rugby nations, reluctant still to declare full allegiance to either country and strangely feudal in its constitution.

The South Wales Football Club had set the ball of organisation rolling and the momentum of the movement continued apace, the next year it was replaced by the South Wales Football Union which required the clubs rather than players to form its membership. The result was a rapid increase in the number of club fixtures and the formation of the Welsh Rugby Union. Records suggest that the Welsh Rugby Union was formed on two occasions, once in Swansea and once in Neath, and although this does not matter in Centenary Year since the Swansea meeting was in the Tenby Hotel in March 1880 and the Neath meeting in the Castle Hotel in March 1881, the Welsh Rugby Union, proceeding with traditional caution, have decided upon the 1881 date.

Many will feel that its true launching was in the formation of the South Wales Club some years previously and, as the first international was played at Blackheath against England in February 1881, there are some who feel that the 1880 date was the meeting that spurred one particular official to take the initiative, gather together a side and set off into England to challenge the originators of the contemporary game. The official was Richard Mullock of Newport who is deserving of the title 'Father of the Union'.

At the Swansea meeting representatives of Cardiff, Chepstow, Haverfordwest, Llandaff, Llanelli, Neath, Newport, Pontypridd and Swansea attended and whatever decisions were taken, the imaginative Mr Mullock set about the task of selecting his side to meet England at

Opposite:
The first Welsh XV, selected by Richard Mullock, which played England at Blackheath in 1881.

FIRST WELSH TEAM.

WALES v. ENGLAND,

1881.

W. D. Phillips, Cardiff. G. F. Harding, Newport. R. Mullock, (Hon. Sec). Newport. F. S. Purdon, Newport. G. Darbishire, Bangor. E. Treharne, Pontypridd. R. G. D. Wlliams Abercamlais.

T. A. Rees, Llandovery. E. Peak, Chepstow. A. J. Bevan (Capt.) Grosmont. B. E. Girling, Cardiff. B. B. Mann, Cardiff.

L. Watkins. Llandaff. C. H. Newman, Newport. E. J. Lewis. Llandovery. R. H. B. Summers, Haverfordwest.

Blackheath. On the day the result was not unexpected. A much superior English team won by seven goals, one dropped goal and six tries to nil; the heaviest defeat ever suffered by Wales, and in modern scoring values a 69–0 defeat.

The defeat did more good for Welsh rugby than many would imagine as it rallied all those clubs who did not have a representative in the heavily defeated national XV to protest and seek another meeting where a Union of clubs could be set up without personal prejudice. Some clubs accused Mr Mullock of taking upon himself too much power (a cry that remains ever true in amateur Welsh sport!). If it was a private team, then who cares, the names are recorded and they are recognised as capped players. They set Wales along the road towards international fame, if somewhat ashamedly!

Yet the second meeting had only two more clubs in attendance and the eleven were Bangor, Brecon, Cardiff, Lampeter, Llandeilo, Llandovery, Llanelli, Merthyr, Newport, Pontypridd and Swansea and thus the big four were prominent in both meetings and their influence, evident in those early meetings, has never wavered in the corridors of Welsh rugby power, prompting on occasions accusations of aloofness. Mr Mullock may have been called to task, as were many pioneers in the days of Victorian sport, but he remained undaunted as if seeing into the future. He wanted a Welsh Rugby Union because there was much to be done in pursuit of the other three home countries. The meeting forgave him the audacity that was more imagination than a search for power and elected him the first honorary secretary of the newly-formed Welsh Rugby Union.

Mullock was to hold the post for eleven years and the first president, Mr C. C. Chambers, came from the West in an attempt to bring harmony to the cause. As only one West Walian had been invited by Mullock to play at Blackheath, unknowingly he created a rivalry between East and West rugby that has remained active throughout the 100 years, sometimes overpowering but now more sporting and enjoyable. In one hundred years there have been only five secretaries of the Union. One of these, Walter Rees, reigned for fifty-two years, and Bill Clement, who retires when the Centenary season ends, will then have completed twenty-five years.

By the time Mullock retired in 1892, Welsh rugby was on the verge of international success, about to win its first Triple Crown, and he had guided the Union and the national team through the most difficult years to earn the title of 'Father of the Union', while his initiative and imagination also played an important part in fostering the cause and reputation of the Newport Club. He was the first of many colourful officials who have steered Welsh rugby through the hundred years and, in Centenary Year, the Union could pay tribute to him and place a small plaque to his memory in the Committee Room at its Cardiff headquarters. Of all early rugby leaders in Wales he remains the most fascinating.

A Welsh cap of 1884.

Much happened between 1881, when the Welsh Union was formed, and the winning of the first Triple Crown twelve years later. Tactical develop-

The first Welsh XV to achieve victory. In Dublin against Ireland in 1882 captain C. P. Lewis (with ball) and secretary Richard Mullock sporting a smart bowler hat.

ments were to have an important impact upon the game generally, and for these Welsh ingenuity will be remembered. The first match against England was lost (in Chapter Two the international record is described in detail) and Ireland first beaten in 1882, Scotland in 1888 and England in 1890. However, in 1886 the Welsh team took to the field with four three-quarters and eight forwards, instead of the traditional three and nine, against Scotland at Cardiff and lost by two goals and one try to nil. It was a pioneering effort in the game, following the introduction by Cardiff of the four three-quarter system.

This system started with the Cardiff Club in 1883–84, when they brought in a young reserve, F. E. Hancock, to play against Cheltenham College at the College ground because a regular was unable to travel, and he played so well that the Wiveliscombe-born member of a famous family of brewers that settled in Cardiff could not be dropped for the next match. Thus against Gloucester at Cardiff on 23 February 1884, four three-quarters were played by Cardiff. It is recorded that neither side scored but Cardiff were pleased with their new formation and it was to have a considerable influence upon the young Hancock who became a devotee of the system, eventually turning an experiment into a set formation that was to change the very pattern of rugby football.

F. E. Hancock who launched the four three-quarter system in 1886.

In 1885–86 Hancock was elected captain of Cardiff, only one of three Englishmen to lead the club, and they played the four three-quarter system throughout to enjoy their most successful season. The club lost only one match, its last, at Moseley and it is remembered as Hancock's year. Wales decided to give the Hancock formation a trial against Scotland in 1886, with six Cardiff players in the side. One other member of the side, A. J. 'Monkey' Gould, gave it great thought, as he was selected as one of the original four three-quarters but was moved to fullback by Hancock

A. J. 'Monkey' Gould, the greatest of all Welsh rugby players and personalities, who led Wales to their first Triple Crown in 1893.

himself and Harry Bowen, the fullback, moved into the pack to make nine forwards in an effort to match the Scots but without success. For three seasons the idea was cast aside before it was reintroduced against the New Zealand Native Team, wrongly called the Maoris, in December 1888. Norman Biggs appeared on the wing, at the age of eighteen years one month the youngest Welsh international player, and Wales won by a goal and two tries to nil.

Arthur Gould did not favour the four three-quarter system after his experience of 1886 and was not in the Welsh team against the Maoris but took his place against Scotland in 1890, the match in which W. J. 'Billy' Bancroft made his debut as a replacement for the selected Tom England of Newport who was injured a week prior to the match. Bancroft went on to play thirty-three consecutive matches at fullback and poor Tom England never won a cap. If Gould became the first 'player personality' then Bancroft was the second. Two weeks later against England in a gale of wind at Dewsbury, Wales defeated their rivals for the first time and set another seal upon their development as a rugby country.

Playing four three-quarters against England's three and eight forwards

W. J. Bancroft, the brilliant fullback, who shared early triumphs with Gould.

The First Welsh Triple Crown XV of 1893. *Standing:* N. Biggs, W. M. McCutcheon. *Second row standing:* T. C. Graham, F. Mills, H. T. Day, A. F. Hill, C. B. Nicholl, F. Wilkins (touch judge). *Seated:* A. W. Boucher, W. H. Watts, A. J. Gould (capt.), J. Hannan, G. H. Gould, W. J. Bancroft. *In front:* H. P. Phillips, F. C. Parfitt.

against England's nine, Wales succeeded because half-back 'Buller' Stadden scored the winning try through a clever ruse. Shortly afterwards Stadden became the first Welsh player to turn professional, as he joined Dewsbury who played for expenses that were considerably more than he had received while playing for his Welsh Club, Cardiff. Thus the match will be remembered for two milestones and when, in 1891, the James brothers, Evan and David, appeared for Wales as a pair against Ireland at Llanelli most of the Swansea Club's members travelled to Stradey Park to watch their two heroes help Wales to victory.

The two brothers turned professional in 1892 and played in the Northern Union before returning to Wales to be reinstated and appear against England in 1899, but their appearance brought forth strong protests from England and despite a Welsh victory they ended their careers as international players. In 1893 Wales achieved the final accolade to set themselves up as a team comparable with those of the other three home countries. The Triple Crown and Championship were won for the first time. This provided a certificate of merit for the four three-quarter system. England were beaten at Cardiff, Scotland at Raeburn Place, Edinburgh and Ireland at Stradey Park, Llanelli. All three opposing countries employed three three-quarters and nine forwards but the eight Welsh forwards held their own and the backs both outwitted and outnumbered their opponents. It was a major revolution in the game and in 1894

England fielded four three-quarters for the first time and handsomely defeated Wales on a frozen ground at Birkenhead Park. Scotland and Ireland also acknowledged the value of four three-quarters and chose them. A new era had been launched.

The first Welsh Triple Crown produced a number of players whose names became household words but none more so than Arthur Gould who played on until 1897, through the 'Period of Promise' to set Welsh rugby up for the twentieth century. As player, captain, selector, referee and administrator he had an exceptional influence upon the game in Wales. The year 1900 saw the Triple Crown return again and launch the first 'Golden Era' that lasted until 1911 and is still spoken of as the greatest period in Welsh rugby history, though matched by the last decade.

W. M. Llewellyn, the first of the great wings.

Wales had produced rare skills in the 1890s but not enough physical hardness, especially at forward, and a search throughout the land brought forth the Rhondda type of forward; a man who worked hard manually at the coal face and was able to scrummage and wrestle for possession of the ball. His job was to get the ball for the backs to use and he was not expected or indeed allowed to interfere with the fast-moving backs!

There was almost a class distinction between the two units and the captains of the Era invariably told their forwards to 'win the ball and no more'. The personalities who led in the 'Golden Era' were notables like Bancroft, Gwyn Nicholls (one of the greatest of leaders), Willie Llewellyn and W. J. Trew. They were shrewd performers; tactical thinkers who developed a distinctive style of back play that placed Wales at the top of the rugby world. Trew was one of the shrewdest of tacticians and on the fourteen occasions he led Wales victory was achieved a dozen times.

There was an abundance of good players and three or four leading players could drop out of the national side through injury or other causes and be successfully replaced. There was intensive rivalry between the 'Big Four' major clubs and this helped provide a high competitive standard. New Zealand (1905) and Australia (1908) were beaten during this period and only South Africa (1906) remained invincible. The Welsh team that defeated New Zealand by a try to nil at Cardiff to this day is recalled with enthusiasm and, although New Zealand claimed that they, too, scored a try by Deans, the Scottish referee, John Dallas, ruled otherwise and the argument has raged between the followers of New Zealand and Wales ever since. The record of the first 'Golden Era' is almost a history in itself!

In twelve seasons (1900–11), Wales played forty-three matches, won thirty-five of them, drew one and lost seven, scoring 534 points against 228. They lost to England once, Scotland three times and Ireland twice, all away from home, and South Africa was the only country to win in Wales in twelve seasons, which is a remarkable record. In comparison, the last 'Golden Era', the eleven seasons from 1969 to 1979, produced fifty-three matches with thirty-six victories, thirteen defeats and four drawn matches with a ratio of 82·5 per cent success in the first era and 71·70 per cent in the second.

R. T. Gabe, a brilliant centre.

E. G. Nicholls, centre and leader 1905.

It is a coincidence that in each era England were dominated and the successful sides against Wales in the second era were New Zealand (4), France (3), Scotland (2), Australia (2) and England and Ireland once apiece. The forty-three championship matches produced seven defeats, all away from home, indicating the tremendous encouragement provided for Wales at the Cardiff Arms Park. As many opponents have suggested, it is worth at least six points to Wales. South Africa were the only side to win in Wales during the first era, only New Zealand succeeded in the latter, winning two official matches and one unofficial. Wales last defeated New Zealand in 1953 and have never beaten South Africa; the best being a drawn match in 1970. France met Wales for the first time in 1908, and achieved a first win in Paris in 1928 and in Wales (at Swansea) in 1948.

The late Willie Llewellyn, who was capped twenty times as a wing during the first 'Golden Era', said of the Welsh team when he was a sparkling ninety years of age:

'It was just like playing in a club side. We knew each other so well that we often used to choose our own captain for the day before leaving the dressing room. Again, we suggested occasionally that changes should be made and new players tried, and the selectors used to listen to our views. It was quite unusual and without wishing to appear immodest, members of the Welsh team during the period were heroes in the eyes of followers. The great custom was for young boys to touch our jerseys, much as they collect autographs in modern times. In 1905, before Wales defeated New Zealand, the backs trained together on their own initiative, and we planned and rehearsed the movement in private that led to the scoring of the winning try by Teddy Morgan. There was no coaching as such in those days, just a team talk by the captain before we took the field and, I recall, a fine address by our captain (Gwyn Nicholls) before the New Zealand match.'

The late Rhys T. Gabe, a fine strong centre of the first 'Golden Era' with twenty-four caps, provided me with many a brilliant word picture of the Era and once told me:

'We knew each other's play inside out and were great believers in support play. There was no prompting and I believe we were the first of the home countries to take the game *really* seriously in planning and preparing as we played so often together. The players put a great deal of effort into it

The historic Welsh XV which defeated New Zealand in 1905. *Standing:* T. Williams (selector), J. F. Williams, G. Travers, D. Jones, A. Llewellyn (touch judge), W. Joseph, R. T. Gabe, Sir J. T. D. Llewellyn (president WRU). *Seated:* C. M. Pritchard, J. J. Hodges, W. Llewellyn, E. G. Nicholls (capt.), H. B. Winfield, C. C. Pritchard, A. F. Harding. *In front:* E. Morgan, R. M. Owen, P. F. Bush.

and the club rivalry was so intense that we were able to maintain the peak of match fitness and hardness that fitted us for international matches.

'Again the after-match celebrations were amusing and magnificent. There was a meal big enough to feed a family in those days and everyone enjoyed themselves. There was considerable comradeship and leg-pulling between the sides, with no ill-feeling. In 1905 against Scotland, I went down on the ball to save before a rush and the Scottish captain gave me a heavy boot in the back-side. As a result, I was not able to sit down properly for six months and took all my classes at school standing up. For ever will I remember, "Feet, Scotland, Feet!" and after that only remained on the ground when it was absolutely necessary at Inverleith!

'However, behind the scrum, once you beat a man in midfield, the way to the fullback was clear and once you drew him in to the tackle, you could send your wing away to score. Nowadays (1950s) it is so different, the back-row forwards are as fast as three-quarters, especially in defence where they form a second line of tacklers and spoilers. If my Welsh team had to play now they would still be a good side, for they had skills but would have to adjust their approach to meet the specialisation at forward and the stronger covering defences. Yet, I believe we handled better in those days and especially our passes which we timed accurately. Of course, the forwards today are bigger and faster, if not stronger. Our forwards were expected to provide the ball and then not interfere with the intricate manoeuvres of the backs.

'One fine forward, Jehodia Hodges of Newport, went out on to the wing against England at Swansea when Tommy Pearson was injured in a tackle by the powerful English fullback Gamlin, and scored three tries. He was up with me to take the final pass and did it all well. Clearly, all the players of the era were skilful, dedicated in a way, yet always enjoying themselves and quite determined to win.'

The first 'Golden Era' was spectacular and gave to the game at large the delights of fast-moving back play with power moving away, at last, from the grip of the forwards and although this was to return after World War II, classical three-quarter play behind clever half-backs was continued by England after the Welsh Era faded just before World War I and into the years afterwards until the Welsh revival of the 1930s. During the Era the forwards scrummaged hard and wrestled at the mauls to win the ball. They were non-specialised, being first up and first down at the set scrums although George Travers, a long-legged, strong Newport forward, father of an illustrious rugby family, could move his leg and foot rapidly in the front-row, and he became the first specialised hooker with his twenty-five caps (1903–11) revealing how important he was to the side.

Yet the back-row forwards were never organised as a defensive unit and it was in the late 1920s that Scotland and Wales really accustomed themselves to the brilliant play of the England trio of Wakefield, Blakiston and Voyce who, under Wavell Wakefield's admirable direction as pack leader and captain, were outstanding and dominated the pattern of play in their matches.

As Rowe Harding says:

'In the late twenties, the blind side wing-forward in the 3–2–3 formation stopped the scrum-half moving round the blind side and creating an extra man, while the open side wing-forward (now called flanker) drove the opposing outside-half across field. The lock (now called No. 8) broke from the scrum and moved across behind his backs as an extra defender. As a result back play was cramped unless the whole side was balanced and possessing speed and skill. It forced backs to move the ball along the line more quickly to give the wings a chance. Again, fullbacks rarely came into the line in attack as they do now and, of course, one could kick out on the full from anywhere.'

Judge Rowe Harding, skilful player and observer of the 1920s.

W. J. 'Billy' Bancroft, who led Wales into the first 'Golden Era', was quick to tell me when recalling his playing days, that individual players trained and practised very hard. 'I used to spend hours punting and place-kicking at St. Helen's with both right and left foot. The halves, Owen and Jones, or Owen and Trew, would work hard together so that they could play together almost blindfolded. They rarely dropped a pass and had an uncanny understanding. At the end of the Era, Swansea developed the first genuine Welsh loose forward in Ivor Morgan.'

The heralding of the end of the first Era came with England's victory over Wales in the first international played at Twickenham in 1910 and the inspiring Englishman was the Harlequin, Adrian Stoop, who took over from Owen, Trew and Nicholls as the game's leading tactical thinker and shrewd director. He was captain of England, as he was of his club and, like the Welsh before him, added a new dimension to back play and to the game.

It was the first 'Golden Era' that gave the rugby union game an art form, a new exciting beauty of combined movement, with players working like a machine yet without the monotony or predictability of a machine. The human element always dominated and sparkled when least expected with an individualism that brought the roar from the crowd in appreciation. The powerful running of Rhys Gabe, the play (as if one) of the centre pair of Gabe and Nicholls, the delicate and intricate running or even scurrying of the two fleet-footed wings, Willie Llewellyn and Teddy Morgan, the native cunning and resourcefulness of the indestructible yet diminutive Dicky Owen at scrum-half, often called the 'artful dodger' by opponents but possessing a rugby brain as sharp and as bright as the early morning sun, and his two partners, first Dicky Jones, as careful, accurate and responsible as a housemaster and then the electric, pyrotechnical Percy Bush, overflowing with creative ideas and always wanting to be the 'originator' of attacking ideas. Bush directed, others followed, and he did it brilliantly with the casualness of a genius, although there were occasional lapses!

There was a clash of temperament and ambition on the part of Owen and Bush, two brilliant players neither of whom wanted to be the deputy when in partnership. They only played together three times although Bush won eight caps. They did not enjoy playing together, preferring their club partners, and made this fact known. Bush played well with Tommy Vile, his British Lions tour partner of 1904. Owen preferred Dicky Jones at outside-half and later the brilliant, all-purpose W. J. Trew. Bush was a student and Owen a working man, and the personality clash was strong, apart from the deadly rivalry of East versus West. Yet their first pairing, and Bush's first cap, produced the most historic move in Welsh rugby history to bring about the defeat of the 1905 All Blacks team. Owen feinted to pass to Bush from a scrum moving right and sent the ball back across the scrum and Wales scored through Teddy Morgan in the left corner; a try that highlights the wonder of the first great era.

Billy Trew had a special magic in his play which tempted Gabe to assess, years later, that the Swansea player was the most complete footballer of all, and there were many great ones. Modern times have produced few players of equal ability and magnetism, and although Trew's approach was not flamboyant, he could play anywhere. Gareth Edwards proved himself admirably gifted in all facets of play, strong, confident and elusive with the basics completely mastered, but it must be players like Alun Thomas of the 1950s and the brilliant Phil Bennett of the 1970s who were the modern Trews because they could play anywhere with equal grace and skill. Edwards would have done well in other positions but he made himself the best player seen in the scrum-half position.

After the legendary W. J. Bancroft at fullback – peerless Billy – small and dapper and immensely talented, there followed a mixture of fine players in John Strand Jones, George Davies, Bert Winfield and Jack Bancroft, younger brother of W.J. All were purely defensive, able to tackle, catch and kick. Jack Bancroft was the best place-kicker and points scorer of the group but Winfield was the most able and Strand-Jones the most tenacious tackler.

The forwards were a group apart but strong and hard-working and in the period were respected and enjoyed the adulation of their own supporters even if it was the backs whose names linger in the memory. Yet Alfred Brice, C. M. Pritchard, Harry Watkins, A. F. Harding, W. T. Osborne, George Travers, Dai Jones, Will Joseph, J. J. Hodges, George Boots, Billy Neill, J. F. Williams, Watts, Webb, John Brown, Tom Evans and Ivor Morgan were genuine stalwarts who gradually specialised as their careers progressed. Nowadays, forwards are highly specialised; dominating and involved throughout in most matches and one plays at loose head prop *only* at top level, rarely moving to the tight head, and in the left and right lock positions, or the number eight or flank position, and then left or right flank! Such specialisation would have been laughed at by the heroes of the first Era when the first-up and first-down principles were applied and every forward 'had to do his bit' as Will Joseph, another hero of 1905, told me after watching a club match in the 1950s in which several forwards performed in 'seagull' style. Yet specialisation was inevitable, as was the four three-quarter system, and Wales suffered considerably before it was accepted and indeed understood by administrators, players and selectors, who did not want to change that which had served their 'fathers' well.

The last match played by Wales before World War I was one of the hardest, against Ireland at Balmoral, Belfast, and became known for a time as the roughest ever, until the France v Wales match of 1930. Wales won by eleven points to three and the two packs of forwards, Wales led by Revd Alban Davies and Ireland by Dr William Tyrell, later Sir William and president of the Irish Union in 1951, hammered each other on the field but the moment the final whistle was sounded they were friends again and many remained so for the rest of their lives.

The War spelled disaster for Wales in many ways but especially economically as oil superceded coal, and Welsh rugby lost the magical touch that had made the years 1900–14 so memorable. International rugby restarted in 1920 and Wales won three matches out of four, sharing the Championship title with England and Scotland, then won it outright in 1922, remaining unbeaten while sharing a draw with Scotland. Sadly, it was nine seasons before Wales headed the table again and these nine years are known as the 'dark era' of Welsh rugby.

The doleful 1920s found Wales bereft of ideas and imagination, of skills and confidence, and subject to poor administration and even worse selection. Club rugby was hard and often querulous. Indeed, the game reflected the times in Wales and, as a schoolboy during the period, I found few contemporary heroes to cherish and had to formulate visions of players I had never seen in action but about whom my father and uncles told me, describing the wonders of the 'Golden Era' with flashing eyes. Thus I could but ask myself, where are the modern Nicholls and Gabes, the Bancrofts and Bushs, the Owens and the Trews? There were a few I cherished and still admire as friends, in Rowe Harding, Ivor Jones, Windsor Lewis, Tom Arthur and Ned Jenkins, happily still alive and interested in the game.

Players arrived on the international scene as quickly as they disappeared and it was ten years before Wales defeated England after the 1922 victory; indicating that each country does well in the Championship when the other is weak and, in some matches in the 1920s, Wales were very weak! I blame attitude more than anything else on the part of clubs and the national selectors. Rowe Harding highlights the situation admirably in his outstanding book *Reminiscences and Opinions* (1929). He wrote then, a year after his retirement from the game and with seventeen caps behind him, bravely, accurately and with keen technical knowledge:

'Rugby in Wales is essentially the game of the people, and although Welsh rugby players are drawn from all classes of society, the majority of them are working-men, miners, steel workers, tinplate workers; and most first-class rugby players in Wales are products of village clubs, whence Welsh first-class clubs draw most of their players. Most of them have no training other than that which comes from practice and experience, so that it is true to say that, in the main, Welsh rugby is village rugby, and its exponents have inherited the traditions of their predecessors in the village teams. As long as those traditions were good, Welsh village rugby and first-class rugby maintained a standard hard to beat anywhere. Welshmen, like Basques, have a natural aptitude for rugby, because they are quick-muscled and quick-witted, but unfortunately Welsh rugby traditions are no longer abreast of the scientific thinking of modern theorists. Welsh village rugby is fastbound in the rusty fetters of obsolete tradition, and it is to the public schools that Welshmen must look for the revival of Welsh rugby.'

That was the cry from the heart of a brilliant player with a legal mind who cared a great deal for the game and for his country. It is a brilliant summary of the situation in the 1920s and, as a schoolboy who wondered why Wales did so badly after the brilliance of the pre-war years I came to appreciate the words of my now good friend Judge Rowe Harding. He recommended that everyone aspiring and eager to acquire a working knowledge of modern forward play should read the book of the time on the game by W. W. Wakefield and Howard Marshall. I was awarded it as head boy of my high school, was enthralled by it and have not read a better thesis on basic forward play.

Wales in the 1920s was old-fashioned at forward play; refusing to accept the advent of scientific specialisation and, because of this basic weakness, with a slow delivery to the backs and no swift heeling from the loose, the backs suffered and were constantly changed by inconsistent selectors who possessed no appreciation of modern methods. Consequently, Wales were hammered in turn by England and Scotland, and no one in authority attempted to analyse the situation. The cry, often unheeded, was for better, faster and more intelligent forward play and combined elusive back play.

Rowe Harding believed that in the 1920s England had the best system of forward play in the world. The Welsh forward approach was out of date because they would not accept the modern back-row system, for better, for worse, that created the wing-forward as the decisive man in mid-field. They did not realise that unless the ball could be transmitted smartly to the far wing before the wing-forward arrived, all was lost. Welsh passing and running in the 1920s was too slow and the game in Wales had not speeded up overall to counter the destructive wing-forward. This may appear as 'old hat' now but it produced a crisis in Welsh rugby.

The Welsh believed that the 'good old days' and the heroes of yesteryear would return and ride over the common enemy. It was like expecting old-fashioned infantry to conquer the machine-gun and the tank. Wales had no chance and selectors were not prepared to go outside their native clubs to bring in players better acquainted with English methods and the teachings of Wavel Wakefield. They stuck to the pattern of Welsh club play and although Llanelli and Newport, in their way, were successful, the selectors could not blend a national side. They refused to bring students from the universities into combination with the working men of the local clubs.

J. A. Bassett, Welsh captain 1931–32.

In Welsh rugby, it was the era of class war and, as a result, the game suffered. Defeats were heavy and frequent, players were often given only one chance to establish themselves, and a new group of players emerged, known as the 'one cap wonders'. Many players moved to the Northern Union or into rugby league with its regular employment hard to obtain at home. The 1921 and 1926 miners' strikes made life difficult for all. However, by 1927 there were shafts of light as if pointing the way to success. In that year Windsor Lewis and Wick Powell played at half-back against a Triple Crown-seeking Irish XV, with three Cambridge blues at three-quarter, including Harding, helping to bring a notable victory. Eight months later, the whole side was changed and Lewis forced to play with a scrum-half unknown to him while only one Cambridge blue remained with Lewis. In the next match the selectors mixed the rival groups and then plumped for seven of the successful Llanelli club side for a first win at Murrayfield.

By the beginning of the 1930s the lesson was slowly being learned and a group of talented players began to put it all together under a shrewd police-sergeant captain, Jack Bassett of Penarth. By 1931 Wales had a championship side with Jack Morley, Claude Davey, Tommy Jones-Davies, Ronnie Boon, Frank Williams, Harry Bowcott, Dickie Ralph and Wick Powell, with Bassett behind the scrum. At forward were hard, experienced players like Archie Skym, Tom Arthur, Jim Lang, Arthur Lemon, Ned Jenkins, Watcyn Thomas, Tom Day and a lively intelligent flanker in Norman Fender. At long last, the Welsh back-row had made the breakthrough with Arthur Lemon as a hard blind-side flanker, Watcyn Thomas and Jim Lang as the number eights, and Norman Fender fast about the field in attack and defence.

Wales should have been champions in 1932 but failed against Ireland in the spring sun at Cardiff. They gained a first win at Twickenham in 1933 but were still hampered by poor selection and injury right through to December 1935. Then came the second victory over New Zealand at 13–12 in a memorable match and the undergraduate era had arrived. The seven Welsh backs were past or present students, five from Oxbridge and two from University College, Swansea, while the pack leader was from Cambridge. The tide had turned as the 1935–36 season produced another championship for Wales with four victories and a draw in five matches. Yet all three matches were lost in 1937 and one apiece in 1938 and 1939.

Wilfred Wooller, King of the 1930s.

However, there were signs that a more intelligent approach was being adopted in schools, clubs and at international level as players were thinking more about the game. There were brilliant backs in Jenkins, Wooller,

The Welsh XV which defeated New Zealand 13–12 in the exciting 1935 match. *Standing:* G. H. Gadney (referee), T. J. Rees, T. Williams, J. Lang, A. M. Rees, E. Watkins, D. J. Tarr, M. Moses (touch judge). *Seated:* V. G. J. Jenkins, H. Payne, G. Prosser, E. C. Davey (capt.), J. I. Rees, W. Wooller, G. Rees-Jones. *In front:* C. W. Jones, H. Tanner.

Davey, Rees, Jones and Tanner, and the need was for forwards who, though lacking nothing in courage and strength, were just that little more adept at winning the ball from the loose. The Cardiff club adopted the 3–4–1 formation in the set scrum of the 1931–32 Springboks tour. In the immediate years before World War II the club enjoyed considerable success, mainly because their forwards were more urgent ball providers for clever backs. Swansea, Newport, Llanelli, Cross Keys and Aberavon were powerful club sides but the national pack of forwards was still at a loss as to how to win a good ball in the loose from the rucks and mauls. It was still a 'wrestle and boot on' rather than a quick heel back despite the fact that Haydn Tanner at scrum-half rapidly acquired the stature of a 'great one' as World War II engulfed the game.

In the 1930s the idea of all-embracing back-row defence was finally accepted in Wales and in many instances it was carried to the extreme in club as well as international football and the cold hand of concentrated cover engulfed many a brilliant pair of halves and mid-field backs. Three-quarter lines stood up in defence; wing-forwards stood out from the lineout and often at the scrum, opposite the opposing outside-half!

Four great players appearing regularly in Welsh club football in mid-field before the War were Haydn Tanner and W. T. H. Davies for Swansea and Cliff Jones and Wilfred Wooller for Cardiff, and having to contend with a considerable amount of spoiling, they did remarkably well to survive. Jones often suffered nasty injuries and was forced to retire at the end of 1938 when only twenty-three years old although he was contemplating returning to the game when the War broke out in 1939. Obviously, all four players would have added many more caps to their collection but for the War and it is interesting to recall that when Swansea or Cardiff played away from home, many spectators would wait outside their club grounds until it was confirmed that Tanner and Davies or Wooller and Jones were playing.

In the late 1930s Cardiff dominated Welsh club rugby, especially from 1936 to 1939. During 1936–37 under the captaincy of Les Spence they won thirty-six out of forty-four matches and scored 553 points against 173. In 1937–38 under A. H. Jones they won thirty-eight out of forty-six with 580 points for and 260 against and under Wooller in 1938–39, they won thirty-one out of forty-two with six drawn. Wooller was also captain of Wales at the time and at the height of his short but remarkable career with the club. In the 1938–39 season he collected a record 163 points. Cliff Jones had retired and five players turned professional during the season but Wooller shone like a remarkable, resilient beacon, brightly and effectively, and while he was proving himself one of the greatest of match winners, an illustrious former captain of Cardiff and Wales, Gwyn Nicholls, passed away. The traditions continued to be maintained in Cardiff, as in many other Welsh clubs, and the memory of the 1930s is full of hard matches, stern defences, and not a great deal of 'love lost' between the senior clubs. Many Welsh rugby players lost their lives during the War and many were taken prisoner, including Cardiff captains Wooller and Spence, but they survived to return and serve the game well.

During hostilities, the Welsh Rugby Union decreed that there would be no official rugby in Wales but allowed clubs and charity organisations to arrange matches to help the war effort and allowed for relaxation when circumstances permitted. Three of the big clubs, Newport, Swansea and Cardiff, staged many fixtures at their grounds for servicemen and civilians, and former rugby league players were allowed to play with Union players under rugby union laws, although not for any payment!

It was a splendid idea and England, Scotland and Wales included former league players in unofficial representative sides while the British Army played the French Army in Paris before the fall of France. A great deal of money was raised in Wales and when, in 1945–46, the pressure eased as players were being demobbed, the four home unions arranged a series of Victory international matches to revive enthusiasm before full internationals were staged in 1946–47. The Kiwis, a New Zealand Army touring side, travelled through the British Isles and proved themselves one of the most popular of all visiting sides under Charles Saxton.

In Wales they were extremely popular and did a great deal to restore enthusiasm and incentive. On Boxing Day 1945, at the Arms Park, they met Cardiff with both sides unbeaten at the time and a large crowd saw the Kiwis win (3–0); Newport like Cardiff, had carried on through the War, and they shared a draw (3–3) and Monmouthshire, with several

Newport players in their ranks, inflicted the only defeat suffered by the Kiwis in Wales, by 15–0 at Pontypool. In 1946–47 the *Western Mail* Club Championship was restored with fourteen first-class clubs competing, Aberavon, Abertillery, Bridgend, Cardiff, Cross Keys, Llanelli, Maesteg, Neath, Newbridge, Newport, Penarth, Pontypool, Pontypridd and Swansea. Three of these clubs were admitted to the select circle of eleven who formed the Championship in the years between the Wars, Maesteg, Newbridge and Pontypridd and, in the post-war years that followed, other clubs joined the group: Ebbw Vale, Glamorgan Wanderers, London Welsh, South Wales Police and Tredegar. The nineteen clubs in the present Championship table battle annually for the *Western Mail* plaque, while other tables have followed in the last decade but none can express the vital factor that makes the best for comparison, consistency. To head the *Western Mail* table is regarded as the top achievement in Welsh club rugby, and although Cardiff won the title five times in the first twelve years after the War, they have not won it since.

In the international arena, Wales shared the title with England after losing to their rivals at Cardiff in the first official international match since 1939 before 43,000 spectators at a war-damaged Arms Park. Thirteen new caps were awarded and only scrum-half and captain, Haydn Tanner, and fullback Howard Davies remained of the 1939 side that had defeated Ireland in Belfast. Yet among the thirteen were players set to achieve much fame in the game: Ken Jones became a record cap holder on the wing, and centres Bleddyn Williams and Jack Matthews, outside-half W. B. Cleaver and forwards Rees Stephens and Gwyn Evans, all became popular and successful performers.

One of the side, George Parsons, a lock from Newport, later in the season figured in an unusual incident when he was withdrawn from the party travelling to France at Newport Station on the grounds that he had 'spoken' to a Rugby League scout. Victories followed over Scotland, France and Ireland and the match in Paris, won by a penalty goal to nil, is still considered as one of the hardest played by a post-war Welsh side and ranks with the Irish matches of 1914 and 1978 as three of the hardest. The penalty goal kicked by Bill Tamplin was the most important of his career. The final match against Ireland at Swansea started half an hour late owing to a traffic jam delaying the Irish team after the match had been postponed for three weeks because of a frozen ground.

Wales had made an excellent start in the opening Championship season but the next two seasons were dismal ones although club rugby gathered pace and enthusiasm. There was a strange anomaly in that a record number of players from one club, ten from Cardiff, appeared against England, Scotland and France and nine against Ireland and in all, eleven players from the club were capped in 1948 but only one match, against Scotland, was won. The backs did not play as a normal mid-field unit, as for their club, and the pack never really settled into a compact unit. England were well-beaten at the beginning of the 1949 season but this victory was followed by three defeats and the selectors, in despair, selected four new young caps for Paris, in what was Haydn Tanner's last of twenty-five appearances for his country at scrum-half, a total only surpassed by Dickie Owen (33) before him and Gareth Edwards (53) after him, and these three players remain the greatest Welshmen in their position.

Welsh followers and the selectors looked for a genius to lead them back to their rightful position in the game as the criticism of Welsh teams was such as to suggest that selection was not always wise, and that teams were poorly prepared and rarely blended into a really effective unit. Cohesion and a sense of controlled discipline in play (not relating in any way to rough or dirty play) were rarely present in the side, and many of the victories were due more to individual brilliance on the part of certain players than to a combined effort. Cardiff were the club side of the era, disciplined and effective as a team, where individual talents were subdued to the cause of the team. Yet this approach could not be transmitted to the national XV until 1950, and then more by accident than design, when two experienced players and leaders, Bleddyn Williams selected as captain and Rees Stephens chosen as pack leader, had to withdraw on the eve of the Twickenham match against England through illness and injury.

A player less brilliant than Williams and less well-known than Stephens, and almost an exile, John Gwilliam, a lock turned number eight who had played six times for Wales, was suddenly handed the captaincy. His approach was not traditional but rather was it cool and calculating. He did not set out to inspire by example but by demanding and directing. In the side were six new caps, five of whom were to be chosen as British Lions three months later. Wales achieved a notable victory and the match was of greater significance than most followers appreciated.

What happened thirty years ago before Twickenham's record crowd of 75,500, only the second victory by Wales at the ground in forty years, set Wales along the road to the success of the 1970s. Few realised it at the time but the new-found discipline of control and organisation on the field produced a new blend of fruitful combination in the Welsh approach that had been absent, even unconsciously, since the 'Golden Era'. There was still a good layer of individual skill but this was directed for the benefit of the side. One believes that historians and critics have failed to give Gwilliam the full credit he deserved for his new but simple approach to international rugby. He just got the fifteen players to play as a unit. He told them in simple terms what was necessary, made it appear much less complicated and awarded the honours to his players while accepting all criticism himself. Quite an unusual leader of Welshmen!

Thus 1950 remains an historic year; the year of the restoration of the true image of Welsh rugby and, possibly, the most satisfying in the second half of the century of activity. It was followed by the participation of thirteen Welsh players in the overseas British Lions tour to New Zealand and Australia and then a difficult year in 1951 when the returning Welsh players, adopting New Zealand methods, were routed by a young Scottish

John Gwilliam, Grand Slam captain 1950–52, leaping at a lineout.

side at Murrayfield. By the end of the season even the selectors had turned against Gwilliam, dropping him for the French match but recalling him to lead against South Africa eight months later. The match was lost narrowly and billed as one for the World Championship.

Gwilliam led them through 1952 to another Grand Slam and this was the year that the selectors accepted the 'conversion' from average size front-row men to 'jumbo' size, another development that proceeded through the 1950s, an exciting decade that produced two of the most attractive of British Lions sides in 1955 and 1959, in which Welshmen played an important part. The brilliant players in the decade were Cliff Morgan, Lewis Jones, B. L. Williams, Jack Matthews, M. C. Thomas, Alun Thomas, Rex Willis, Gareth Griffiths, Ken Jones, D. O. Brace, Terry Davies, Lloyd Williams, Malcolm Price and Dewi Bebb behind the scrum.

Gwilliam remained in the side until 1954 and shared in the victory over New Zealand in 1953 and there was a host of long-serving forwards through the 1950s who had adjusted to the demands of the modern game, namely strength, pace, knowledge and handling ability. W. O. Williams, D. M. Davies, D. Hayward, Roy John, J. R. G. Stephens, B. V. Meredith, R. C. C. Thomas, J. D. Robins, R. Robbins, S. Judd, C. C. Meredith, R. H. Williams, R. Prosser, W. R. Evans, H. J. Morgan and J. Faull were sixteen forwards who shone during the decade and represented a new-look forward approach. It was unfortunate that W. R. Cale should have turned professional after being unwisely omitted from the 1950 Lions side and that R. T. Evans suffered a premature knee injury, for they would have played an equally important part in the decade. Half of the forwards mentioned won twenty or more caps, which suggests a consistency derived from strength, skill, enthusiasm and a tactical appreciation aided by good leadership. In all this Gwilliam played a part in launching the new approach and highlighting an important step forward in Welsh rugby.

In the 1950s Wales contributed five members of the pack that won the memorable First Test of the 1955 Lions tour in South Africa, and four members of the 1959 pack, an encouraging tribute to the all-round improvement in Welsh forward play. Again, the administration stirred and moved on to better things with the first democratic appointment of a Union secretary. The post was advertised for the first time in 1955 and former Lions and Wales wing, W. H. Clement, narrowly gained the position in 1956 from close rival Rees Stephens, an active forward leader for Wales in the 1950s.

Wales moved into the 1960s rather gently and in 1963 the selectors nominated a new cap at scrum-half in D. C. T. Rowlands and launched him on a career as player, captain, coach, selector, administrator and tour manager that has carried him through to 1980. Yet his path was not always easy and there were hard times as well as good. An emotional player, dedicated to the cause of Welsh rugby, he suffered the experience of leading Wales through South Africa with Alun Thomas as assistant manager/coach and David Phillips as manager. It was a reasonable side but unprepared for the conditions and forced to jog along like settlers in an uncharted land. The test match at Durban revealed the difference of approach between the home countries and the Southern Hemisphere. A

The Welsh XV which defeated New Zealand in 1953. *Standing:* P. F. Cooper (referee), R. C. C. Thomas, S. Judd, J. R. G. Stephens, E. R. John, J. A. Gwilliam, C. C. Meredith, Ivor Jones (touch judge). *Seated:* W. O. Williams, G. Griffiths, B. L. Williams (capt.), K. J. Jones, D. M. Davies. *In front:* Dr G. Rowlands, W. R. Willis, C. I. Morgan, G. Williams.

24–3 defeat left its mark deep in the rugby hearts of Welshmen and was to prove the turning point, although it was to be six or seven years before the Welsh were to climb their Everest.

Wales won the Triple Crown again in 1965 under Rowlands; it had taken an incredible spell of thirteen years to emulate the feat of Gwilliam's team, after a wait of thirty-nine years before 1950. Why the amazing fluctuations in fortune and dramatic inconsistency? Wales was never geared on or off the field to make the best use of its resources and the 1960s provided a decade of hit or miss selection, indifferent form, and a lack of organised coaching and training, but it also sowed the seeds of the success enjoyed in the 1970s. The lessons were bitter ones after the shining dominance of the Gwilliam era and the way to permanent success had to be planned, prepared and worked for with a combined dedication that had hitherto been absent. Rugby football, like most other games, does not stand still and past glories mean little or nothing.

There were some fine individual players in the 1960s and the Triple Crown pack of 1965 included six Lions of various vintage and the whole side contained eleven, so that Welshmen, as individuals, were still the leading performers. They just could not put it all together all of the time. It was the 1964 defeat at Durban that sent the Welsh scurrying home; players, officials and press all determined to do something about it. In a way it was the Dieppe defeat before the Normandy victory of World War II. The first had to be suffered for the second to succeed.

Alun Thomas and David Phillips knew what was required but Phillips

Clive Rowlands, Welsh captain, coach and selector.

could not fulfil his mission. He passed away soon after his return when there was still so much he wanted to do. Cliff Jones joined the cause and a Coaching Advisory Committee laid the 'blueprint' for the future. A national Coaching Organiser, Ray Williams, was appointed as a sort of professional crusader for the cause of coaching. He had to carry out a whistle-stop tour attempting to convince clubs, players and officials that it

John Dawes, Welsh captain, coach and selector.

was the 'way and the light' to rugby success. A good talker, as is coaching chairman Cliff Jones, they helped blaze the trail. Yet the Union was not really wholeheartedly behind it and 'tradition' stood like a raised drawbridge, refusing to allow the crusaders into the inner sanctum.

Strange as it may appear, a committee meeting in a Dublin hotel on the eve of the Ireland v Wales match of 1968 settled it once and for all by choosing the management of the team to visit Argentina later in the year and not including a coach. Alun Thomas resigned as a selector in protest and the Annual General Meeting of the Union did not like it. Clive Rowlands, having retired, contested a vice-president's seat and won it. The Union members, quick to compromise, revised the management for the Argentina tour and included Rowlands as team coach, with S. J. Dawes as captain. Thus Rowlands was thrown in at the deep end; the first official coach to a Welsh XV overseas and having to follow another Welshman, J. D. Robins, the official coach who was rarely allowed to coach the 1966 Lions side. Would Rowlands be coach in name only? The future was balanced on a razor's edge. Fortunately, Rowlands learned the job as he went along. He was a PE master and could put it over, simply and with emotional enthusiasm. It was hard in Argentina, suffering poor refereeing and without leading players who had been committed to the 1968 Lions tour.

In 1969 a bolder impression was made when Wales defeated Scotland, Ireland, England and drew with France to win the Triple Crown and Championship, and although the ill-chosen short tour to New Zealand in the close season provided a setback and really started all the feuding and the fighting between the two enthusiastic rugby-playing nations, Wales recovered through defeating Australia and Fiji and by avoiding defeat for the first time against South Africa. Three matches out of four were won in the 1970 Championship and by 1971 Wales had got it right. They won the Grand Slam and set off on the second 'Golden Era' with team coaching at all levels established; and, as in the launching of the four three-quarters system, the other countries followed.

In 1971, there was S. J. Dawes as captain; J. P. R. Williams at fullback; contrasting wings in J. C. Bevan and T. G. R. Davies with a sound centre, A. J. Lewis, completing the three-quarter line; brilliant individuals combining as points scorers and match winners at half-back and a pack of forwards composed of D. Williams, J. Young, D. B. Llewellyn, W. D. Thomas, M. G. Roberts, J. Taylor, T. M. Davies and W. D. Morris.

The squad system had developed a club side at international level and the game in Wales had progressed to draw ahead of that of the other home countries and level with those 'down under' as Wales supplied fourteen members of the 1971 Lions side that became the first British team to win a test series in New Zealand. Barry John scored 191 points and John Bevan collected eighteen tries while eleven Welshmen appeared in the Tests.

British rugby was a world power again and the magical affinity between the Irish and the Welsh on tour provided an even greater success in 1974 in

Welsh Grand Slam XV 1971. *Standing:* D. B. Llewellyn, T. M. Davies, M. G. Roberts, D. Williams, W. D. Thomas, W. D. Morris, D. C. T. Rowlands (coach). *Seated:* J. P. R. Williams, J. C. Bevan, B. John, S. J. Dawes (capt.), J. Taylor, G. O. Edwards, T. G. R. Davies. *In front:* J. Young and A. J. Lewis.

South Africa when the Lions remained unbeaten in twenty-two matches, creating eighteen new records and being the first British side to succeed in South Africa this century and the greatest side to visit that country. Managed by Alun Thomas, returning in triumph after 1955 as a player and 1964 as a coach, coached by Sid Millar, another former Lion, and captained by the magnificent W. J. 'Willie' McBride. Nine Welshmen were in the party and six appeared in the Tests although it was much more of a British side in the Tests with six Welshmen, three Irishmen, four Scots, and two Englishmen. All four Home Unions had got together, at last, producing the greatest side of the century since the 1924 All Blacks. It had taken Britain fifty years to catch up!

After the Lions' triumph of 1974, Gareth Edwards and Phil Bennett returned with Mervyn Davies, who took over the captaincy, and the Championship was won again, with only one defeat, at Murrayfield. The final match produced a remarkable 32–4 victory over Ireland, one point short of the record-winning margin of 1907. The successful side then visited Japan in September and laid the foundations of the 'club' that was to achieve four successive Triple Crowns in the next four seasons. None of the home countries has been able to achieve anything like such consistency and, at the end of the 1979 Championship, Wales led with sixteen Triple Crowns and eight Grand Slams.

This consistency was the result of organisation, skill, dedication, wise selection, coaching and, not least, the fact that the majority of the leading players appeared for clubs in an area bounded by Llanelli in the West, Newport in the East, and Abertillery and Ebbw Vale in the North, making life a great deal easier for the selectors and for the players to get to know

A great duo – Barry John and Gareth Edwards.

each other off the field as well as on. The combined approach is bound to be stronger where the rugby community is close together geographically.

T. M. Davies was captain in 1976 before his unfortunate illness which prematurely forced him out of the game – Phil Bennett in 1977 and 1978, and then J. P. R. Williams in 1979. The fact that five players of world class, Edwards, Bennett, Cobner, T. G. R. Davies and J. Bevan retired and that T. P. Evans and G. L. Evans were absent from international rugby before the 1979 Championship, did not reduce the effectiveness of Wales as a force in the tournament and two new young halves, Gareth Davies and Terry Holmes, played with the sang-froid and effectiveness of battle-hardened veterans. The one sad happening was the controversial defeat at the hands of New Zealand by 13–12 which appeared to stiffen the resolve of the new-look Welsh XV to emulate their predecessors. Thus the Welsh at international level were able to enter the 1980s in much the same mood of confidence and combination as they did the 1970s, and prepare themselves for Centenary Year. Success at international level is not everything in the game but it is important; it is the shop window, and the mass coverage by the media in pictures and words, and the highlighting of leading personalities must serve as a stimulus and encouragement to young players to develop their skills, enjoy themselves, and share in the success of the rugby community.

Thus Welsh rugby history is divided into several eras and in most there was development, learning and understanding and in some, adjustment.

Gareth Edwards scoring one of his twenty tries for Wales.

Barry John scores his last try in the special Urdd match of 1972.

Mervyn Davies, outstanding number eight and Triple Crown captain.

From 1880 to 1892 under Richard Mullock there was graduation; from 1893 to 1899 there was realisation under Arthur Gould and W. J. Bancroft; from 1900 to 1911 there was the first 'Golden Era'; from 1919 to 1930 there was adjustment and from 1931 to 1939, recovery. After World War II there was a mini 'Golden Era' and further adjustment in the 1960s before the second 'Golden Era' of the 1970s.

Richard Mullock would have enjoyed the 1970s as would have Horace Lyne, Arthur Gould, W. J. Bancroft and Walter Rees. They would have admired the classical pattern of the era; the thought and work that went into the making of success; the dedication of players and officials; the approach on the field, with stern forward play in the first half when opposing packs were worn down, mainly through scientific scrummaging;

Phil Bennett, world's leading points scorer and Grand Slam captain, leads Wales out on to the Arms Park ground.

the desire to score before the interval to set things up for the second half followed by the 'purple patch' mid-way through the second half with the full power of the back play unleashed and, finally, a canter to finish. Occasionally, there were close finishes and a few disappointing defeats but none more so than those by New Zealand in 1972 (19–16) and in 1978 (13–12).

A comparison of the two outstanding eras reveals that the players had confidence in themselves and in their fellow players. They appreciated what each other had to do and helped each other, while the captains were capable leaders. Maybe it was not all that difficult to lead sides bristling with skill and moving like well-oiled machines that sparkled frequently with brilliant individualism that was not harnessed or coached. In both eras there was supreme control at half-back – first Owen and Jones, Bush and Owen, and then Trew and Owen; to be followed seventy years later by first Edwards and John and then Edwards and Bennett. However, as if to indicate that Wales could produce replacements overnight, there followed the pairing of Gareth Davies and Terry Holmes. Barry John was a prolific points scorer but Phil Bennet became the world's highest individual points scorer in representative matches.

The Welsh forwards of the 1970s played together as units for several seasons at a time and there emerged smaller units within packs as exemplified by the Pontypool front-row of A. G. Faulkner, R. W. Windsor and G. Price, and the pair of locks, A. J. Martin of Aberavon and G. A. D. Wheel of Swansea. One back-row to excel during the period was that of W. D. Morris (Neath), T. M. Davies (London Welsh and Swansea) and J. Taylor (London Welsh) and, towards the end of the decade, J. Squire and T. J. Cobner (Pontypool) on the flanks and D. L. Quinnell (Llanelli) at number eight. Pontypool had five forwards in the Welsh pack on several occasions with their front-row and the two flankers as mentioned, and the club pack enjoyed a period of supremacy with their approach based on New Zealand methods which had impressed the coach, Ray Prosser, when he toured that country as a British Lion in 1959.

Modern coaching has proved successful in Wales though it still has its critics because forwards need to be ball-winners and ball-handlers while the backs have to be ball-carriers. The maul rather than the more dangerous ruck was an important facet of the forward game in Wales through the decade. Law changes and interpretations, which vary throughout the world, and the sudden change of interpretation from 1978 onwards, disturbed Welsh forward play, as Welshmen are not as expert at rucking as New Zealanders. Yet rucking reared its ugly head in Europe at the end of the decade as one of the basic reasons for head injuries and 'trampling' and 'raking' became nasty words highlighting nasty play.

Yet organised coaching was the major development of the decade, at least on the field of play, and regular courses organised by the Welsh Rugby Union enabled all member clubs to have their own qualified officials. It may have produced a great deal of 'pattern' play as the theatre has produced 'method' acting but all has helped to improve standards and pave the way for entry into the national squad. Fitness has been a feature of the last fifteen years of the century. Players are fitter and they have to be, as changes in the laws have made the game faster overall. At first-class level, an unfit player is highlighted! During the decade, attention was paid to the coaching and care of referees and, whereas they were almost 'outcasts' previously, they are now accepted and respected even if some crowd sections at some grounds enjoyed giving verbal advice to officials allegedly having only one eye!

The International Board Laws Sub-Committee chaired by Welshman Hermas Evans at its first-ever meeting in Cardiff in March 1979. *Left to right:* R. C. 'Bob' Stuart (NZ), D. H. 'Danie' Craven (SA), Hermas Evans, Dr R. Vandefield (Aust.), H. B. 'Harry' McKibbin (Ireland).

From the two umpires of the early days with Norfolk tweeds and smart cloth caps who moved at a leisurely pace up and down the centre of the field while players, in twenty-a-side huddles, almost forgot about the ball, the hundred years has seen the two umpires change into a single referee, the latter breed wearing special jerseys and shorts not far removed from bikini pants, with whistle, stop-watch, pencil and note-book, and the erudite mind of a young legal eagle. There are hundreds of points that have to be considered when administering the twenty-eight Laws of the Game.

In the one hundred years the laws have both changed and increased, and Welsh officials have played their part in the International Board's development of the laws, which have grown apace with the game.

There are many ways now of incurring penalty kicks and although some are now indirect kicks, to a great extent the game is dominated by the penalty goal. An increase in the value of the try from three to four points in 1971 helped to make totals bigger but did not see the try move ahead of the penalty goal as the most frequent scoring item. The try was originally worth one point and in turn became two and then three points before its present value of four. The conversion of two points was, for a short period (at least a season), valued at three, while the penalty goal used to be two but has been three points since 1891. Will it ever return to two points, or would that smack too much, perhaps, of rugby league? The dropped goal was three points, then four for fifty-seven years before reverting to three again in 1948.

It is not possible to compare year one with year one hundred as much has changed, for better and for worse. Yet it is possible to comment that the game is faster overall. It may not be harder or tougher; it may not even be enjoyed as much, but it is pursued with energy and enthusiasm and, whereas a few watched the first international and only a small report appeared in the papers of the next morning, now millions can watch it on TV as it is being played; scores and incidents can be played over and over again, referees and players can be 'tried by TV' for errors or misdemeanours, and millions of words are written each year by the press. In one hundred years the game has changed – but what a century it has been for Welsh rugby!

2 THE INTERNATIONAL RECORD 1880–1939

The day 19 February 1881 was a special if sad one for Welsh rugby, the day when the first Welsh team took the field, unheralded and unsung, with no publicity build-up, no 50,000 crowd to cheer and sing, and without all fifteen members of the side being acquainted with each other. It was on Mr Richardson's Field at Blackheath and Richard Mullock's Welsh 'marauders' were decisively beaten by an established and clever England side by seven goals, one dropped goal and six tries to nil and, as was said in later years of another country, Wales was lucky to score nil.

Under the modern scoring system it would have been a 69–0 defeat, the heaviest sustained by Wales, and it was this defeat that brought about the second 'formation' of the Welsh Rugby Union (as explained in Chapter One). Mr Mullock had staged a preliminary trial and matched his 'marauders' against several neighbouring English counties but this preparation was not enough to challenge the might of England, even though their first national XV had been handpicked by Mullock. Had his side been victorious, Wales might have launched the one-man selection committee and revealed a progressive attitude from the start and, as history has revealed down through the hundred years, a heavy defeat always disturbs the Welsh, especially the selectors.

If the first defeat caused confusion, it was nothing compared with the memorable Scottish victory of 1951 at Murrayfield, when John Gwilliam's Grand Slam side that included eleven 1950 British Lions was humbled by nineteen points to nil and, dare I say it, lucky to get the nil! Sack the lot, was the cry throughout the land and heads had to roll, but the selectors, always wary and sometimes mysterious, gave it up as a bad job. They nominated only ten players for the next match and left five 'A. N. Others' in the side to meet Ireland which, according to research, is the largest number of players selected from that club for a national side.

Such a playing disaster always produces a major crisis and the 21–3 defeat in South Africa in 1964 was just as important for the future as the previous heavy defeats. It started a revolution that led to organised coaching for, emotional as the Welsh may be, they are deeply moved by heavy defeats and inspired to rectify the weakness, being extremely self-critical and slightly ashamed of harsh failure.

In contrast they cannot digest the bitterness of narrow defeat in unusual circumstances and that is why the memory of such moments haunts

Welshmen and becomes a form of emotional torture. The All Blacks defeat of 1905 by a try to nil was turned into a legend by an eager correspondent of the *Daily Mail*, looking for an 'angle' on Sunday morning, 17 December, at Cardiff, for his Monday morning report. He wanted a story that was different and controversial so as to highlight what was regarded, at the time, as a match to decide the Champions of the World. When Mr Buttery's famous telegram reached Fleet Street it became an historic document and all New Zealanders believe that Bob Deans did score. The referee and Welsh team denied it and no member of the New Zealand side mentioned it during the after-match function. Mr Buttery asked Deans how near he was to scoring and Deans, in all honesty, replied, 'I thought I had scored!'

It appeared in print as 'Bob Deans says he scored against Wales!' and since that historic day, New Zealand and Wales mourn deeply when each suffers defeat at the hands of the other. Welshmen complain bitterly about the defeats of 1972 and 1978 and blame poor refereeing, not biased but poor, and there is a considerable difference. The convincing and heavy defeats suffered by Wales in other years are accepted, if sorrowfully, and Welshmen are never afraid to castigate their own players in failure and praise outstanding members of the successful opposition.

If this were not so, how then would one account for the carrying from the Cardiff Arms Park, shoulder high in triumph, of such fine players as A. L. Gracie of Scotland and Wilson Whineray of New Zealand? The Welsh rarely extend such an accolade to visitors except when truly earned and there can be few more generous in the game. In appreciating this, one can also accept the disgust of Welshmen when a New Zealand forward, in disgrace for trampling on an opponent's face in the previous match, was sent on as a replacement at half-time against the Barbarians at Cardiff in 1978. The Welsh would have no part of this. They could not accept it, whatever their own shortcomings, and one believes that such an incident and its accompanying reception will not be lost, even upon a rugby-mad nation like New Zealand, as 'one-eyed' as the Welsh, when the All Blacks make their short tour of Wales in the Centenary season.

In the first international match of 1881 Wales fielded six backs and nine forwards under the leadership of J. A. Bevan, who was an Australian by birth living near Abergavenny at the time. He was one of two three-quarters and there were two fullbacks and two half-backs plus the nine forwards. The change from twenty-a-side had been made in the 1876–77 season. Before this Welsh match England had lost only twice in ten years, justifying the claim of being the originators of the 'new and manly' game for sportsmen and, as the Revd F. P. Marshall records in his excellent work of reference, 'In 1881 Wales were thoroughly overmatched', a comment which nowadays appears as something of an understatement.

The Englishmen felt some sympathy towards the Welsh and refused to play them in a full fixture in 1882, suggesting a match against the North of England as a worthwhile substitute. It was played at Rodney Parade,

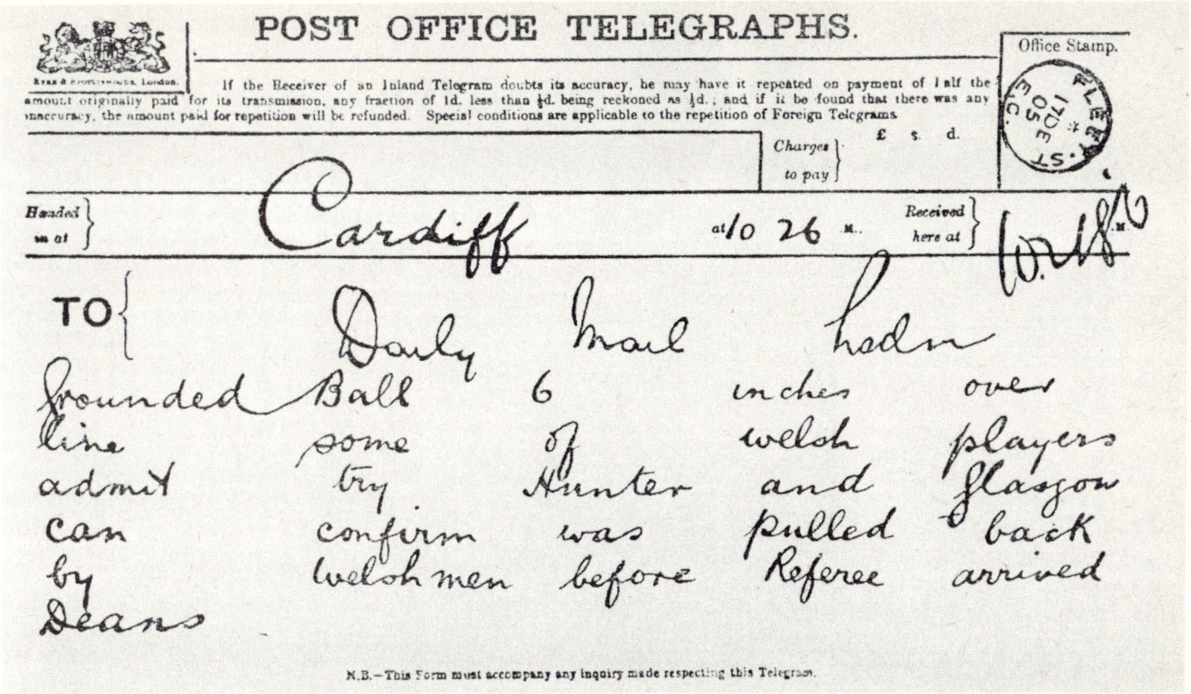

POST OFFICE TELEGRAPHS.

Office Stamp.

If the Receiver of an Inland Telegram doubts its accuracy, he may have it repeated on payment of half the amount originally paid for its transmission, any fraction of 1d. less than ½d. being reckoned as ½d.; and if it be found that there was any inaccuracy, the amount paid for repetition will be refunded. Special conditions are applicable to the repetition of Foreign Telegrams.

Charges to pay £ s. d.

Handed in at Cardiff at 10 26 M. Received here at 10.18 M.

TO Daily Mail London

Grounded Ball 6 inches over line some of welsh players admit try Hunter and Glasgow can confirm was pulled back by Welshmen before Referee arrived Deans

N.B.—This Form must accompany any inquiry made respecting this Telegram.

The famous telegram which was sent from Cardiff on the Sunday after the 1905 Wales v New Zealand match by *Daily Mail* reporter J. A. Buttery on behalf of R. G. Deans. This was a 'big story' at the time, but not confirmed in later years although it launched a legend which has persisted for seventy-five years.

Newport in January 1882 and when Wales lost only by a goal to a try, the English acknowledged the sudden improvement and agreed to field a full side at St Helen's, Swansea in December 1882 to provide an historic day with the first home international match for Wales.

One can imagine the excitement and wonder of the occasion but also the sorrow of the Welsh as they lost by two goals and four tries to nil, although a narrower defeat than that of 1881 at 28–0. Richard Mullock, as befitted an early pioneer in the game, did not castigate the losers on this occasion but pointed out the marked improvement revealed over the first match. He believed in determination conquering all, as Wales had managed a victory over Ireland at Lansdowne Road, Dublin (the oldest international ground still in use for representative rugby) in January 1882.

In this match Mullock's determination in pursuit of victory upset the Irish and they refused to meet Wales in the following season. Apparently, Mullock was one of the two umpires and the Irish players hotly disputed some of his decisions. Two of them were not sent off but left the field of their own accord, refusing 'to continue under such biased administration' and, as two Irishmen were injured as well, the side finished the match with only eleven players and a 20–0 defeat. It was an unhappy dispute but they were early days in the game and both Ireland and Wales experienced difficulty in combating the forward ball-winning capacity, sureness of hand, and pace of foot of the backs of England.

Wales first met Scotland at Raeburn Place, Edinburgh in January 1883 and only two of Mullock's original Welsh XV at Blackheath remained, the

The Welsh XV of 1885, which included the 'makers' of Welsh Rugby in A. J. Gould, F. E. Hancock, H. S. Lyne, W. H. Gwynn and others, against England at St Helen's, Swansea. The sixteenth man on the right-hand end of the front row is the illustrious Richard Mullock.

two Newport players, C. H. Newman and G. F. Harding. This time Wales fielded one fullback and three three-quarters, led by C. P. Lewis of Llandovery who converted the Welsh try. Scotland were successful by three goals to one and it is recorded that a Scot (or was it an Irishman?), Dr A. Griffin of Edinburgh University, took the field with the Welshmen who had arrived in the Scottish city a player short. This led to the time-honoured phrase in Welsh rugby, 'bring your boots, we may be short', employed by committee men to prevent players hurrying off to other clubs, or the telegram from students on holiday to club secretaries 'have boots, can travel'.

An even more interesting event took place at Cardiff in April 1884, when Ireland arrived in the city two players short, and one already capped Welshman, Frank Purdon of Newport and Swansea, and one yet to be capped, H. M. Jordan of Newport, completed the Irish side. It is said that Purdon possessed some Irish blood in his make-up, and while Wales won the match 11–0 in a drizzle before 5,000 soaking-wet spectators, relations between the two countries remained 'strained' and they did not meet again until 1887.

All was not well within Wales at the time, as the East versus West rivalry that was created at the launching of the Welsh Rugby Union was still very much alive and burning with fierce hatred. Mullock arranged a trial before the selection of the team to meet Ireland but, alas, as if to show their supreme contempt for Eastern officials, only one member of the West XV,

Goldsworthy of Swansea, put in an appearance. He, along with five others, were awarded their first caps, two of whom (F. E. Hancock and W. H. 'Buller' Stadden of Cardiff) were to play an important part in the development of the national XV.

Hancock, as reported in Chapter One, developed the four three-quarter system and 'Buller' Stadden scored the try that led to the first defeat of England with a clever 'ruse' in 1890. The first try registered against England, another milestone, was scored by Charles Allen of Beaumaris at Leeds in 1884. W. H. Gwynn of Swansea, later to become the second secretary of the Welsh Rugby Union, made his debut in grand style in this match.

Arthur John Gould made his debut in 1885 against England at Swansea, and H. M. 'Shorty' Jordan, already capped for Ireland, wore the scarlet jersey for the first time and celebrated with two tries. Hence, the sporting quiz question, who played for Wales and Ireland in Wales? England won another handsome victory but the mighty Gould was to haunt the rival countries for many a year during his twenty-seven appearances. He led Wales on eighteen occasions, more than any other player in the 100 years,

F. E. Hancock's Cardiff XV of 1885–86 which lost only one match – the last – to Moseley. *Standing:* A. Duncan, A. F. Bland, A. J. Hybart, J. A. Sant, A. Emery, G. Young, A. F. Hill, H. J. Simpson, W. H. Treatt (hon. sec.). *Seated:* W. Jones, H. Hughes, C. S. Arthur, F. E. Hancock (capt.), W. M. Douglas, Q. D. Kedzlie, A. J. Stuart. *In front:* D. Lewis, J. Mahoney, W. E. Jarman, W. Stadden.

eight times as a winning side. Newport and Wales grew to adore him, even if opponents feared him, and his admirers saw fit to collect a sum of money, £400, quite a fortune in those days, to purchase the deeds of a house for presentation to Gould. Not averse to a reward for his labours, dedicated as he was to the game off the field as well as on, he received his gift in 1897 from the president of the Welsh Rugby Union, and England objected thus causing a major dispute; but more of that anon.

After losing to England in 1886, Wales experimented with the Cardiff four three-quarter system, with Hancock paired with Gould in the centre. F. E. Hancock, born in England, the 'guinea pig' player with the Cardiff Club in the launching of the system, was made captain of Wales in the centre but co-centre Gould was 'not amused' because the experiment failed. So troublesome were the nine Scottish forwards that Hancock was forced to move Gould back to fullback where he started his career and sent the fullback, Llanelli's Harry Bowen, to join the eight Welsh forwards under seige. This traumatic experience was not lost on Gould who took some time to recover from it and to realise the considerable potential of the system. Whereas the Cardiff forwards had been taught to win the ball for their backs, the Welsh eight attempted to 'take on' the fiery Scottish nine.

Two goals and a try to nil was enough to force the Newport members of the national XV to rebel against the system of their Cardiff rivals and when Wales returned to three three-quarters in January 1887 against England at Stradey Park, Llanelli, it gave fuse to the intense Cardiff–Newport rivalry that was to follow and which has lasted until today, even if less fierce and more in words than deeds, for 'blue and black' Stanley Bowes now calls Newport 'those black and amber darlings', or words to that effect! The match at Stradey Park, which Wales should have won, was drawn on a bone-hard pitch and there followed a decisive defeat at Raeburn Place against Scotland where Gould was reported as playing poorly.

Wales won the next two matches before losing to Ireland again and entering the 1888–89 season; a season that was to prove important for the future. Against the visiting New Zealand Native touring team, Wales played four three-quarters and won the match. Gould was not selected so that the new system would not be prejudiced. The Maoris saw the value of this and adopted it for the rest of their matches in Wales while Wales never again reverted to the old system. Three more matches were lost by Wales before another milestone was reached and Welshmen should regard 15 February 1890 as a special day. England was defeated for the first time at Crown Flat, Dewsbury, and the winning try-scorer was 'Buller' Stadden, by this time a member of the local club because Dewsbury paid 'generous expenses'. Later, Stadden became the first Welshman to turn professional and it was his try that carried the day, although most members of the England side thought he had applied the art of gamesmanship excessively by resorting to sharp practice. He appeared to attempt to throw a long ball in from touch but, instead, dropped the ball short in front of the first forward, nipped in smartly to gather, dodged two surprised Englishmen

The Welsh XV which defeated England for the first time in 1890 at Dewsbury, led by A. J. Gould. *Standing:* A. Duncan (umpire), S. Thomas, A. F. Bland, W. E. O. Williams, R. Mullock (hon. sec.), W. Bowen, J. Meredith, W. H. Treatt. *Seated:* D. P. Lloyd, J. Hannan, A. J. Gould (capt.), W. H. Thomas, W. D. Evans. *In front:* C. J. Thomas, D. Gwynn, W. Bancroft, R. Garrett.

and dashed over the line before one could have said, 'Buller Stadden'. Gould was the Welsh captain and Stoddart captain of England. The day was a cold one with snow, sleet and wind, and again the Welsh eight held the nine English forwards.

Matches were lost and won in turn and it was 1893 before the big year arrived and Welsh rugby was really established at international level with the first Triple Crown triumph. It was a memorable season and Gould, by now fully convinced of the four three-quarter system, played it with consummate skill and inspired his fellows in a magical way. Helping him was a small but effective fullback, the dapper cheekie-chappie, W. J. 'Billy' Bancroft, who was to become a personality almost as memorable and famous in the game as Gould. One from Newport and the other from Swansea, rivals from East and West, and even though they did so much together for Wales they were not always ready to agree on the field of play, especially in the heat of the moment! The England match of January 1893 at Cardiff highlights this personal rivalry, for they became the first Welsh players to develop, albeit unconsciously, the player 'personality' cult.

There have been many exciting and memorable encounters between England and Wales but none more important, at least of those in Wales, than that at the Cardiff Arms Park on 7 January 1893 when South Wales was in the grip of one of those terrible winters that enveloped the land with snow and ice in Victorian times. It has been called the 'Brazier' match

The Cardiff Arms Park as it was in the 1890s. The picture shows the official opening of the first grandstand, built at a cost of £362, on Boxing Day 1885 before Cardiff played Liverpool.

because of the climatic conditions but in truth it was much more spectacular and far-reaching. The week before the match was an impossible one, reminiscent of 1947 and 1963 in modern times. Roads ice-bound and impassable, horses' hooves bandaged in sacks to prevent slipping; the poor in the land, and there were many, huddled around small fires, and boys trying to skate upon the frozen patches of the River Taff, adjacent to the Cardiff Arms Park. The pitch was frozen solid. How could the match be played? A blizzard had silenced the land almost as successfully as that of 1881. By the morning of 6 January a decision had to be made so that the England team, already mustered in London, could travel down to Cardiff.

The Welsh Rugby Union secretary was W. H. Gwynn in Swansea and he travelled to Cardiff to find club officials already covering the pitch with 'fire-devils' or coal-filled braziers in a brave effort to thaw it out for the next day. Mr Gwynn gambled and sent a telegram to the father of the modern postal system, Rowland Hill, secretary of the Rugby Football Union, stating that they were working on the ground and the match would be played.

The English party set off from Paddington at 5.45 p.m. together with the Scottish referee and went straight from Cardiff Station to the Arms Park and found something akin to a scene from Breughel with more small boys than braziers and enough smoke to suggest the second Fire of London. Rowland Hill commended the Cardiff Club and Gwynn for their action and the England party retired to their St Mary Street hotel to enjoy a hearty meal and a good night's sleep after the committee, at least, had fortified themselves against the cold. However, they had little hope, deep down in their hearts, that the match would be played, and their dreams were of another express train ride back to Paddington via the comparatively new Severn Tunnel.

In the morning, to the surprise of many, referee John Morton declared the ground playable and the players, changing in their hotel, shivered beneath their overcoats as they shuffled gingerly to the ground, amidst the cheers of equally cold admirers. In the ground were 17,000 spectators about to witness the making of a little of rugby's colourful history. Wales had seven backs and eight forwards; England six backs and nine forwards. Eight of the Welshmen were from Newport, headed by Arthur Gould as captain, while six Englishmen came from Blackheath, thereby acknowledging two of the outstanding clubs of the era.

At that time the methods of scoring in England and Wales differed. The Welsh were not aware that the International Board had amended the scoring system two days before the match and thus, when they tallied the final score they believed it to have been a draw at 14 points apiece. However, it was not so. The International Board counted the try as two points and a penalty and the dropped goal as three. Wales thus won by a converted try (5), a penalty (3) and two tries (4) against one goal (5) and three tries (6), giving a tally of 12–11.

Welshmen thought the match had been drawn, for Wales would have scored a goal (5), a penalty (3), and two tries (6) against a goal (5) and three tries (9) making 14–14. Yet it proved a famous victory and the match was won through the audacity of W. J. 'Billy' Bancroft after Wales had been awarded a penalty towards the end when England were leading by eleven points to nine.

Gould called up Bancroft to take the kick and as the fullback recalled once to me:

'Arthur asked me to place-kick for goal and I refused. We argued for a moment, as I wanted to drop for goal. The crowd grew restive and Arthur, annoyed, threw the ball down and said, "Kick it!" I retrieved the ball, took three steps back and then moved forward to drop for goal through the spot. The ball sailed on its way and I turned to Arthur and shouted, "It's there, Arthur!" and it was, straight and high between the posts. I had no idea how important a goal it was at the time but it became the most memorable dropped goal of my career and set Wales on the way to our first Triple Crown. By the end of the season the goal had become a legend!'

There were great rugby men in that Welsh side, and it was a personal battle between Stoddart of England and Gould of Wales as the respective captains, both national heroes in those early days. Wales had Gould, Bancroft, Biggs, McCutcheon, Conway-Rees, Phillips and Parfitt at half-back, C. B. Nicholl, A. F. Hill and five of the Newport pack. This side was

The illuminated address presented to A. J. Gould, captain of Newport and Wales, as a tribute to his outstanding play for club and country. It is now one of the main items in the Newport Club's museum.

destined for glory. It travelled to Edinburgh four weeks later and once again the four three-quarter system triumphed, and Gould now a converted disciple wisely forecast after the match, 'The system will probably revolutionise the game and our victory will compel the other countries to employ it'. Wales won by a penalty and three tries to nil and five weeks later, in the last international match played at Stradey Park, Llanelli, Ireland made a bold effort to prevent the Welsh ambition of the Triple Crown. The weather was perfect with the crowd of 20,000 bursting the very seams of the historic park. The play was hard, the game close. Ireland fielded only three three-quarters but changed to four at half-time. It was too late; already Wales had scored the winning try through Arthur Gould's brother Bert, and Ireland could not score in the second half.

The four Welsh three-quarters were able to create the overlap and the powerful mid-field burst of Arthur Gould was decisive. Sam Lee, the Irish captain and sole centre was a magnificent player who tackled superbly and yet, even in defeat, he was too proud to concede that the four three-quarter system won the day. Thus 1893 had been memorable for Wales, important for rugby and historic tactically. Once Gould had put his seal of approval upon it, and it had brought the dramatic triumph of a first Triple Crown for Wales, there was no turning back. W. H. Gwynn was totally convinced and even though the next few years did not bring continued success, the year 1893 and its winter of blizzard and cold laid the foundations for the 'Golden Era' that was to come. The season was, of course, the greatest hour for Arthur Gould, as well as providing many moments of pleasure for the dapper Bancroft, surely the most confident player ever to pull over his head the magical scarlet jersey of Wales, and it set the Welsh believing that rugby football could be their national game.

Gould appeared for the last time in the scarlet jersey against England in January 1897 appropriately at Rodney Parade, his beloved home ground where he was as exciting an idol for supporters as any player that followed him. Yet his appearance was not without controversy as the player who gave birth to the personality cult in the game had announced his retirement at the start of the season, in September 1896. Newport missed him immediately, then badly needed him, and eventually persuaded him to play again at the age of thirty-two.

Wales wanted him and invited him to captain the side against England in his twenty-seventh appearance when he led the team to victory at 11–0. After the match Gould really did step down from the scene he had adorned with courage, distinction, confidence and remarkable skill, and followers saw fit to reward him. A testimonial fund, the first for an international player, raised £400 and the president of the Welsh Rugby Union, no less a person than Sir John Llewellyn, a leading industrialist, presented Gould with the title deeds of the house he lived in at Newport. It was in tribute to the man and his beneficial influence upon the game he loved and served so well.

Scotland and Ireland objected strongly to what they considered to be an act of professionalism and refused to meet Wales in 1897. They went further and raised the matter at the next meeting of the International Board in January 1898, demanding that the Welsh selectors never again include Gould in their side. The indignant rugby men of Wales, ready worshippers of the mighty Gould, refused point blank to give any such

W. J. Bancroft as captain of Wales in charge of the 1899 side against Ireland at Cardiff. *Standing:* T. Williams (WRU), A. Brice, J. Blake, R. Hellings, W. H. Alexander, D. J. Daniel, E. G. Nicholls. *Seated:* F. H. Cornish, G. Boots, W. M. Llewellyn, W. J. Bancroft (capt.), H. V. P. Huzzey, R. T. Skrimshire, J. J. Hodges. *In front:* G. L. Lloyd, Selwyn Biggs.

undertaking, even though they knew Gould would not play again.

It seemed that the axe of excommunication from the rugby brotherhood would fall upon Wales but Gould issued a public statement to the effect that he would never again play for Wales although he would continue to serve the game as a member of the Welsh Rugby Union Executive and a selector. Yet it was fifteen months before Wales played their next international match, against Ireland at Limerick in March 1898, and Gould's friend and rival, W. J. Bancroft, took over the leadership while Gould consumed his tireless energy in selecting, refereeing and administrating. The first twenty years of the Welsh Rugby Union and its battle for recognition and success had found Mullock and Gould as the inspiration, both on and off the field.

Bancroft led Wales in eleven consecutive matches; the record holder is Clive Rowlands who led in fourteen successive matches, and Gould is the overall leader with eighteen. Wales moved into the 1900s in great style under the command of the little fullback; seven of the matches under his captaincy were won and the defeat he least enjoyed was the last match of the nineteenth century, against Ireland at Cardiff, which was a memorable one for the Irish, as it brought their second Triple Crown success. Poor Bancroft was roughly handled by the famous Ryan brothers of Rockwell College who shadowed him during Irish pressure, caught him in a crushing sandwich tackle, and threw him into the crowd!

This happened mid-way through the first half and the fourteen Welshmen could not hold out against the fiery Irish although they just failed to score an equalising try. Bancroft suffered fractured ribs and was most displeased with his opponents but his confidence remained unshaken, although he did not realise that the following season was to bring him his greatest triumph as captain – a second Triple Crown for Wales, to launch the first 'Golden Era'. England, Scotland and Ireland were beaten and the new players introduced to the scarlet jersey included one who was to become an illustrious name in rugby history and the darling of the crowd, W. J. 'Billy' Trew of Swansea. Small and sinewy, his dark face well-lined at an early age, he made his first appearance on the wing.

The next season saw Wales introduce more players of outstanding potential and, as Trew was unfit, Rhys Thomas Gabe of Llanelli, a publican's son from the village of Llangennech, made his first appearance on the wing. At half-back, the stylish and elusive Newport pair, Llewellyn Lloyd and Lou Phillips, gave way to the Swansea combination of the 'dancing Dicks', Dickie Owen and Dickie Jones. Wales had lost to Scotland and four new caps were introduced against Ireland at Swansea, which saw Bancroft play his last and thirty-third consecutive match for Wales. He landed the winning conversion from the touch-line with the final kick, to ensure that posterity would always remember his mastery of the art of kicking. His fullback record remained until surpassed in the 1970s by J. P. R. Williams.

R. M. 'Dickie' Owen made thirty-five appearances for Wales, which

Opposite:
Wales v Scotland at Cardiff 1902 as depicted in the *Illustrated Sporting and Dramatic News* of 8 February 1902. The pictures highlight the contrast in styles of scrummaging and lineout play.

1
2
3
4
5

The Welsh Triple Crown side of 1905 which defeated England at Cardiff, together with the other four players who appeared during the season.

remained a record from 1912 to 1955 when it was overtaken by an outstanding wing of the post World War II era, Kenneth Jeffrey Jones of Newport. Gabe, like Owen, played through the first 'Golden Era' until he retired from the field at the end of the 1907–08 season, having scored eleven tries for Wales and fifty-one for Cardiff. R. 'Dick' Jones played fifteen times for Wales as Owen's favourite partner. Having taken a teaching post at Howard Gardens in Cardiff, Gabe left Llanelli to join Nicholls, who was a few years his senior, in the Cardiff side and they established a successful if not the most successful, and skilful partnership in mid-field in Welsh rugby.

The Triple Crown won in 1902 was just missed in 1903 because of a gale of wind at Inverleith, Edinburgh where the fierce Scottish forwards carried the day in atrocious conditions and where it is recorded that few enjoyed falling before the feet of Mark Morrison and his Scottish pack. Only one match was won in the lapse of 1904, as England shared a 14–14 draw at Leicester and Wales lost in Belfast to Ireland 14–12. The critics of those days suggested that the same referee in both matches, Crawford

Findlay of Scotland, was not 'particularly fond of the Welsh'. At one stage of the match at Leicester, Owen refused to put the ball into the scrum because he was being penalised continually, and tries were disallowed in both matches. Thus complaint against referees is not essentially a modern trend!

The winning mood was recaptured in 1905 with a fourth Triple Crown and the successful season set Wales fair for the triumph over New Zealand at Cardiff in the December of that year, in a match that is still regarded as the most important, if not the most spectacular, of the hundred years. There have been many superior in attractiveness and gracious style and even in hardness, but none that can compare with it for arousing emotion and pride in the hearts of Welshmen, and in the hundred years it remains the 'greatest hour'; the match that launched a thousand memories for those who witnessed it, and the seventy-five years of intense rivalry that has existed between New Zealand and Wales and tested the patience of many!

It had such an effect because the first New Zealand All Blacks team had gone through their British tour like a devastating hurricane, carrying all opposition before them, destroying fine sides and poor sides alike with skills, inventive ideas, fitness and magnificent team spirit. Their players became household names in the mouths of British rugby men in a matter of weeks and they were led by a magnificent sportsman, if a somewhat controversial figure on the field of play as a 'wing forward', in David Gallaher, who later laid down his life bravely in the Flanders Fields of World War I. They won twenty-seven consecutive matches before they entered the Principality to meet the men in scarlet at the Cardiff Arms Park.

Scotland, Ireland and England had been overcome and only Wales could foil their bid for the Grand Slam. Their victories included a 55–4 win over Devon (many followers throughout the four countries thought the evening papers had reversed the score in error) and thirteen victories in which they scored thirty points or more. The tour was a startling rugby phenomenon and, as the tourists raced away to score try after try, opponents could only stand and stare.

Undoubtedly they were the greatest of all the New Zealand sides as their achievements outstrip all others, even though the 1924 and 1967 sides remained unbeaten in the British Isles. In thirty-two matches they suffered one defeat, that by Wales, and they scored 830 points against thirty-nine with 109 tries to five. It is a magnificent record and one wonders how they came to suffer defeat at Cardiff on 16 December 1905 when they were firm favourites.

They faced the outstanding contemporary side in the British Isles; a side geared tactically, emotionally and physically for the encounter; a side as clever and determined as themselves. The Welshmen realised that it would be a hard game; not dirty but hard, and that it would require a special ploy to achieve a score against a magnificent New Zealand defence

Wales v New Zealand in 1905. A general impression of the play taken from the north-west corner of the Cardiff Arms Park showing the well-packed ground, with a few policemen on the touch-line. The ground held just over 40,000, but as many as 100,000 Welshmen have claimed 'they were there' on the historic day of 16 December 1905!

and, once the lead had been achieved, Wales would have to defend with matching strength, pace and accuracy. It was the supreme challenge in the 'Golden Era' to the holders of the Triple Crown, something they believed could never happen again, and Gwyn Nicholls, the Welsh captain, collected his backs together for a special practice session 'in camera' at Cardiff.

It was the brain child of the 'mighty atom' at scrum-half, Dickie Owen, who believed that the tourists could be wrong-footed. The manoeuvre practised was put into operation by Wales ten minutes before the interval. Nicholls gave the signal to Owen as a set scrum was formed between the half-way and the New Zealand twenty-five yard line, slightly to the right of the posts. It was a Welsh ball and Owen put it in. It came back sharply and Owen moved to his right, with Bush and Nicholls moving up to take the ball on, as Willie Llewellyn on the right wing raced into top gear. This was part one of the scheme and the New Zealand backs moved towards their left touchline to cover. Owen, sensing they were moving into the well-laid 'trap' surprised all, except of course his team-mates, by swinging his body and sending a reverse pass across the set scrum, which broke up more slowly in those days. Wales, adopting the New Zealand forward formation and playing seven tight forwards and a 'rover' standing out of the scrum, had Cliff Pritchard ready to take the pass on the left-hand side of the scrum.

Pritchard of the sure hands took the pass readily, and moved rapidly

W. J. Wallace – the best loved of New Zealand All Blacks – who played against Wales in 1905 and scored 230 points on the tour. Here he is seen playing in the first match of the tour (against Devon and Cornwall) wearing a hat as a protection against the sun!

away. The defence now knew that it had been 'caught' and, as Pritchard set off, the defenders turned in pursuit towards their own right corner-flag. Wales had Pritchard, Gabe and Morgan while New Zealand had Deans and McGregor, centre and wing, and thus was established the classic three to two overlap. Gabe received and gave the ball smoothly while running at top speed, a maxim that remained with him for the rest of his life, and little Dr Teddy Morgan, from Guy's Hospital, scuttled away with the ball held firmly to his chest. Fullback Gillett raced across but he could not cut off the dapper left-wing who crossed the New Zealand line in the corner with a spectacular dive.

The crowd's tension was released in a momentous emotional roar and it mattered little that the try was not converted by Bert Winfield although there was still a long way to go. Tacticians have argued since that neither side was bold enough, being far too cautious and respectful of the other. Gabe once told me that it was an error to have sat upon such a small lead, and Wales should have tried for more scores, even in orthodox fashion. There were opportunities not taken, but the second half produced one incident that, at the time, had little significance, except that it was a determined last-minute tackle by Gabe on Deans to prevent a try. By the Monday morning the incident was well on its way to becoming a legend!

In the second half New Zealand attacked strongly, in an attempt to equalise the score and W. J. 'Billy' Wallace, who was to become the greatest figure in New Zealand rugby, on and off the field, went near to

The 1905 All Blacks XV v Wales. *Standing:* W. J. Stead, C. E. Seeling, R. G. Deans, J. J. O'Sullivan, F. Newton, A. McDonald. *Seated:* F. Roberts, F. T. Glasgow, D. McGregor, D. Gallaher (capt.), G. A. Gillett, G. A. Tyler, W. J. Wallace. *In front:* H. J. Mynott, J. Hunter, S. Casey.

Opposite:
The 1905 Wales v New Zealand match highlighted by a picture-page from the *Illustrated Sporting and Dramatic News* issue of 23 December 1905. The pictures are typical of the best in rugby illustrations at the time.

scoring as Wales were forced to defend desperately. Play continued, hard and exciting without being classical as the two sides matched each other play for play and Wales, apart from an attempt at dropped goal by Percy Bush, appeared content to maintain their narrow lead. Those present often related how the tension increased with the passing of each minute as the 40,000 spectators gave vent to their feelings with each saving tackle and clever kick by the Welsh defenders.

New Zealand, sensing a first defeat, made a special effort. They moved the ball sharply and Wallace was set free to run up-field. When challenged by Willie Llewellyn on the Welsh right-wing, Wallace fed Deans, supporting him on the inside, so that the young centre could put in a determined burst for the line. Rhys Gabe, to his immortal glory, sensed the situation and kept racing for Deans to get to him near the line, crashing the All Black to earth with one of his special tackles. Deans was stopped short of the line, but here let Gabe take up the story: 'I knew it was touch and go as to whether or not he had scored but, as he kept struggling to go forward, I knew he had not reached his objective. Other players joined the maul *outside* the Welsh line and then I heard referee John Dallas blow his whistle and order a scrum.'

That is the true story of the try that never was but since that memorable moment many versions have been printed and claims laid. Nothing was said after the match at the celebration dinner when the wine flowed freely and some of the game's most illustrious players set an example for after-match sportsmanship. There were no complaints, no Murdoch incidents and it was Mr Buttery who set the rugby world alight with his famous

W. M. Llewellyn, the three-quarter. H. T. Winfield, who was brilliant at back. E. T. Morgan, who scored the try.

A section of the orderly crowd of over 40,000 people.

E. Gwyun Nicholls, the Welsh captain, who defended splendidly.

1. *Wales.*
5. *Stopping a Welsh run.*

2. *A rush.*
4. *New Zealand.*

R. G. 'Bob' Deans, the New Zealand centre who claimed on the Sunday after the match against Wales that he had 'scored' the disallowed try.

telegram. From that Sunday onwards the legend of the 'try' grew and accounts varied in emotive power and accuracy. Bob Deans is reported to have uttered as his dying words, 'I did score!' It was my privilege to be presented by the daughter of the neutral referee with the whistle he used in the match and attached to it was a written statement in the hand of Mr Dallas, recalling the match and incident in concise detail . . . 'It was not a try. Deans did not score.'

Despite the hundreds of thousands of words written about this historic match since 1905, no enemies were made among the players on the field. Dickie Owen was reported as having been 'manhandled' by Dave Gallaher but, as a key man, the diminutive scrum-half was subjected to close marking. At the official dinner afterwards, Gallaher said, 'It was a real good game, played out to the bitter end with the result that the better team won'. This was a brave thing to say on the part of a disappointed captain, tasting and accepting defeat after twenty-seven consecutive victories. Gwyn Nicholls, the Welsh captain, commented as wisely and honestly as did Gallaher, 'There really was nothing between the teams. The difference appeared to be that we took advantage of our only opportunity to score.'

There were no hard feelings and when the All Blacks returned, two of their party, the captain Dave Gallaher and the brilliant five-eighth W. J. Stead, wrote a book on rugby football, *The Complete Rugby Footballer*, and no better technical book has been written since. If one regards it as a rugby 'Bible', one is paying only fair tribute to its technical soundness and understanding. Of the Welsh match, they wrote:

'It is not our place now to make excuses for this defeat that stung so much at the time. It is enough to say that the game we played did not entirely deserve a much greater reward than it was vouchsafed. The worst fear we had came true. We had of late been thinking too much about this match, and at last the thoughts went on to the field with us and paralysed the efforts of many of our men . . . When we made an ineffectual start, and the Welshmen from the beginning showed a wonderful amount of dash and fire, something very much like nervousness crept into our side and our coolness vanished . . . The Welshmen were excited too, but their passing and their play was generally very good. They were a strong side, probably just about as strong as we expected to find them, and in their ranks were contained some of the finest masters of the game.'

A splendid and modest account of the occasion by two leading New Zealand players some months afterwards gave no suggestion that Deans had scored. Had Gallaher felt that a try had been scored he would have been well within his rights to have mentioned it. The legend was created by Mr Buttery and if it was a good story angle at first, it got out of hand and merely served to give both countries grounds for unnecessary argument.

Apart from the decisive Welsh try there was another tactical ploy that may have proved even more important. Wales chose to play seven scrummaging forwards, a 'rover' and seven backs which, in effect, gave them eight backs to mark eight New Zealand backs. Few, if any, of the touring side's previous opponents had employed this formation and Wales went a step further. At each set scrum, two front-row men bound together against the New Zealand front two of their two-three-two scrum formation. On each side of the Welsh two was another forward ready to pack down to make a front-row of three, and thus have the loose-head on the side the ball was being put in at every scrum! The fourth Welsh forward would then return to the back of the scrum immediately and ensure a good shove. It was an intelligent counter to the effectiveness of the New Zealand scrum and it never allowed the tourists a spare back, with Cliff Pritchard out of the scrum as a 'rover' or eighth back. Thus it remains the most memorable of Welsh matches and the leading players were impressed enough to continue with the New Zealand eight back formation for a while.

The Triple Crown was not won in the 1906 Championship because Wales failed to overcome a very brave Irish side in Belfast. However, the season remains historic in that Welshmen accepted the fact that the scrum, at least the front-row, had to include specialised players and the agile, consistent George Travers of Newport, who was to become the head of a famous rugby family, became the first really specialised Welsh hooker and had the props of his choosing with him.

The seven selected forwards held England but were in trouble against Scotland and eight were beaten by the Irish. One sensed that for once in the 'Golden Era' it was selectorial errors as much as anything that had brought about the defeat. Two outside-halves, Trew and Gibbs, were played against Scotland, as in the New Zealand system, and it was reported that Gibbs did well and Trew poorly, so the Swansea man was dropped against Ireland and Wales returned to the orthodox eight-forward formation. The New Zealand formation was not used again until the 1924 Wales v New Zealand match and then with disastrous results. Ireland finished in 1906 with only thirteen men and it is still regarded as their outstanding victory over Wales.

The Welsh captain against Ireland, Gwyn Nicholls, retired from international rugby after this match but was recalled in the following December to lead the squad just once more against South Africa. Evidently, the selectors believed that he would revive the 'old red magic' that had defeated New Zealand twelve months previously but nothing went right that ill-fated day at Swansea in December 1906, and Wales still has to beat the Springboks after this first (11–0) defeat. Owen and Bush were together in name only and although there was some good tackling, the South Africans appeared to have all the answers to the Welsh ploys and were not caught unawares, even on one occasion, as were the All Blacks.

It was a decisive defeat and it is recorded that an injured Nicholls was too sad to attend the official after-match dinner. In fact because of injury he could not attend but he recovered in time to appear a month later for Cardiff against the tourists and play an important part in a memorable 17–0 victory in the mud. This was Cardiff's greatest hour as the First

The Welsh XV of 1907 which achieved a record victory over Ireland at Cardiff by 29–0. *Standing:* T. Evans, W. Dowell, J. Brown, Walter Rees (sec. WRU), G. Travers, J. Watts, W. Neill. *Seated:* D. P. Jones, J. Evans, C. M. Pritchard, R. T. Gabe (capt.), H. B. Winfield, J. L. Williams, A. F. Harding. *In front:* P. F. Bush, R. David.

Springboks, under the leadership of Paul Roos, lost only two matches in an outstanding tour, to Scotland and Cardiff. Thus was Nicholls able to retire at the end of the 1909–10 season having, as an Englishman, contributed much to Welsh rugby since his start with Cardiff in 1892. In the long and colourful career that earned him the title of the 'Prince of Centres' he was a British Lion in 1899, appeared twenty-four times for Wales and 242 times with Cardiff for whom he scored 111 tries, almost one every other match. His eighteen seasons with Cardiff remain a club record and a lasting tribute to his amazing consistency and modesty.

Wales recovered from the South African defeat but did not win the Triple Crown in 1907 although the final match of the winter against Ireland at Cardiff saw Gabe lead his team to a record victory margin of 29–0 over that country. Six tries were scored and Percy Bush, with his club partner R. J. 'Dickie' David for the one and only time, was in superb form directing operations. David, who was a window cleaner, had to take his ladders to Bush's home in Cardiff late on Thursday night, tap on the bedroom window where Bush lay ill with influenza, to plead with the outside-half to play or David would be replaced and the Swansea pair would play. Ever a sportsman, Bush appeared and was magnificent, highlighting the fact that for Wales it would have been wiser to have selected, at all times, either Owen and Trew of Swansea or Bush and David of Cardiff, as in those days, East was East and West was West, and 'never the twain shall meet'!

Two splendid seasons followed in 1908 and 1909 with successive Triple Crowns and Grand Slams and a season of five wins in 1909 that was not repeated until 1976. The run of nine successive victories, ten if one counts the last match of 1907, was the purple patch of the Era, and it started with a victory in the fog at Bristol City Association Football Club ground; Twickenham was yet to be. The two sets of backs hardly saw each other and the ball was followed by the noise it made bouncing on the ground! It is recorded, too, that when the game appeared likely to be cancelled before it started, the new Welsh scrum-half, Tommy Vile, having waited long for

The 1908 Welsh XV, the first side to win the Grand Slam, which played against Scotland at Swansea and won 6–5. *Standing:* W. Neill, J. Webb, J. Brown, W. Dowell, G. Hayward, J. Watts, A. Llewellyn (touch judge). *Seated:* W. J. Trew, R. A. Gibbs, H. B. Winfield, G. Travers (capt.), R. T. Gabe, J. L. Williams, A. F. Harding. *In front:* T. H. Vile, P. F. Bush.

his cap (although a British Lion in 1904), allowed the tears of possible disappointment to stream down his cheeks. When the teams took the field, his face was consumed in a broad smile and he and his Lions partner, Bush, were outstanding performers in the fog.

However, when Scotland were beaten by only a single point at Swansea, back came Owen and Jones of Swansea for the next two matches and the Grand Slam. In the next season W. J. Trew assumed the captaincy for the first time and led the team throughout the five-victory season (Australia being beaten at Cardiff) and Jack Bancroft, the younger brother of W.J., took over from Bert Winfield to continue the line of immaculate kickers at fullback. Against France in Paris, Wales achieved their biggest championship victory of 47–5, scoring eleven tries.

In 1909 there appeared no stopping the invincible Welsh and the 1910 season opened with a 49–14 victory over France at Swansea and Jack Bancroft established a new individual scoring record with nineteen points (eight conversions and a penalty goal), a record that has survived although equalled by Keith Jarrett (1967) and Phil Bennett (1976). Yet the second match of 1910 heralded two important happenings; the beginning of the end of the first Welsh 'Golden Era' and the start of a timely revival by England. It was the first international match at Twickenham and England ended a barren spell of eleven seasons against Wales with a 11–6 victory. It would take Wales another twenty-three years before they achieved a win at the spacious headquarters of the Rugby Football Union. Wales fell away as England prospered, and history reveals how each of the two countries has ruled the championship while the other struggled. Thus England and Wales must surely be the greatest rivals in the game, and their annual

Welsh XV of 1911 against Scotland. This side was the last to achieve the Grand Slam until 1950. *Standing:* T. Schofield (touch judge), G. Travers, J. Webb, R. Thomas, T. Evans, J. Birch, A. F. Coldrick. *Seated:* J. Pugsley, W. Spiller, R. A. Gibbs, W. J. Trew (capt.), L. M. Dyke, J. L. Williams, D. J. Thomas. *In front:* R. M. Owen, F. W. Birt. (The all-Cardiff three-quarter line produced seven of the eight tries scored in a 32–10 victory.)

meeting the outstanding attraction at Twickenham and the Cardiff Arms Park in alternate years. In 1910, Adrian Stoop, leading England, said, 'We were lucky to win' and Trew, leading Wales, commented, 'England deserved to win, they were too good for us'. The rugby game still retained its sporting chivalry.

The first international match at Twickenham was remarkable in many ways apart from it being the first English victory over Wales since 1898. Wales kicked off; it was Ben Gronow of Bridgend who sent the ball sailing away from the half-way line, for Adrian Stoop to gather and instead of kicking to touch in accordance with tradition, he set off diagonally before handing on to Poulton-Palmer who cross-kicked for Berry to gather and send the ball back to scrum-half Dai Gent, a Welshman who became the rugby correspondent of the *Sunday Times*. He then fed the ball out again to Solomon of Redruth who sold a 'dummy' before sending the other wing, Chapman, for the line. The big, burly Westoe wing handed off Trew and dived through a tackle to become the first player to score in an international at Twickenham and so Wales, once they kicked off, didn't touch the ball again until they restarted play a second time!

It was a poor display by Wales and halves Owen and Jones did not appear again in 1910, but Wales finished with three wins out of four and felt confident enough to take the Triple Crown and Grand Slam in 1911. It was a record-breaking season, defeating England 15–11, Scotland 32–10, France 15–0 and Ireland 16–0. The final match against Ireland at Cardiff was for the Triple Crown and both sides were in line for it, attracting a record crowd of over 40,000 which filled the Arms Park to overflowing. Mounted police had to 'repel boarders' as hundreds stormed the gates; a

Welsh XV of 1912 against France in the last international match played at Rodney Parade, Newport. Wales won 14–8. *Standing:* H. Jenkins, Glyn Stephens, A. Merry, P. Coldrick, H. Uzzell, L. Trump. *Seated:* Ewan Davies, W. Spiller, J. P. Jones, T. H. Vile (capt.), R. C. S. Plummer, F. Hawkins, H. Hiams. *In front:* W. J. Martin, H. Thomas.

scene that was to be repeated in similar circumstances in 1936. Trew and Owen played through the season brilliantly at half-back and an all-Cardiff three-quarter line appeared in the three matches following the match against England, R. A. Gibbs, W. Spiller, L. M. Dyke and J. L. Williams, to score eleven tries between them. Trew had his best season as captain and fullback Jack Bancroft did extremely well.

England won again (8–0) at Twickenham in 1912 and this marked the end of the 'Golden Era', as Owen and Trew at long last refused to play for Wales, preferring to appear for Swansea, their club, rather than against Ireland and France. Walter Martin and Tommy Vile of Newport were chosen instead and the match against France was the last international played at Newport (on a Monday). It was the thirteenth successive win at home by Wales since the defeat by South Africa in 1906, and the next match in December 1912 brought the next defeat, again by South Africa, at Cardiff.

The Springboks had lost to Newport and London and had beaten Scotland and Ireland before meeting Wales in difficult conditions and the heavier Springbok forwards managed to carry the day although both sides missed chances. Yet Wales deserved a draw, as centre Fred Birt of Newport just failed with a penalty attempt while Douglas Morkel kicked a goal for South Africa. A disappointing match that continued the failure by Wales to overcome the Springboks' challenge. Eight new caps in the Welsh XV signalled the end of the 'Golden Era' although six members of the successful Newport side failed to inspire their Welsh team colleagues in a hard, unspectacular but clean match.

The year 1913 started even more disappointingly when England won

Douglas Morkel of South Africa kicking the penalty goal that defeated Wales at Cardiff in the mud in December 1912. Wales lost 3–0.

their first match at Cardiff decisively at 12–0. An inspiring player for England was a Welshman W. J. A. Davies, destined to become one of the outstanding outside-halves of all time for his adopted country, appearing in twenty-two matches and only once on the losing side. In his first season he shared in the Triple Crown and Grand Slam and caused Welshmen to wonder for many a year why this young, Pembroke-born naval officer should play so consistently well before and after World War I, although only three times against Wales in his six seasons.

Tommy Vile lost his place and the captaincy, and Billy Trew was recalled to lead the squad to victory against Scotland and France. Trew was injured in the French match, his twenty-ninth appearance, and never played again. The frail, gentle man, who never really looked fit enough or strong enough for rugby football, became a member of the Welsh Rugby Union but died at a comparatively early age in the years between the Wars. The records state that the match at the Parc des Princes (in its original form) was played on a Thursday. The three victories in the season saw Wales finish as runners-up to England who won again at Twickenham in 1914, albeit by a single point at 10–9, and that through a last-minute converted try, before going on to gain a successive Triple Crown and Grand Slam; highlighting the fact that they had taken over from Wales as the leaders of British rugby. Wales went on to beat Scotland for the seventh successive time, ran riot against France at 31–0 and then achieved a memorable victory over Ireland at Belfast.

In 1914, Wales appointed a forward, the Revd Alban Davies of Llanelli, as captain, as strong, powerful and forthright a man on the field as he was in the pulpit and his team, especially his forwards, worshipped him. He was a man's man, enjoying every minute of the vigorous match against the Irish, and it is recorded that the rival packs promised each other a 'hard time' on the Friday night before the game. They kept their word. It was excessively hard but a Scottish referee, realising that all sixteen forwards were as bad as one another and that he could not ascertain who started what, allowed them to get on with it. They all survived and left the field, friends for life!

The Welsh pack acquired the fearsome title of the 'terrible eight' and their names and deeds were revered long after World War I ended. It was the last match before the War and completed the second stage in the history of Welsh rugby. From 1900 to 1914, the football had been exciting, occasionally disappointing, yet skilful enough to earn the admiration of the world and with enough colourful personalities to enlist a following of supporters that established rugby union football as the national sport of the Principality.

Three victories in four matches kept Wales close behind England but many of the years that followed after the War were dark and dismal. Eighty-five international players from all countries were killed in World

The 'Terrible Eight', the name given to the Welsh pack led by the Revd Alban Davies (Llanelli) against Ireland at Belfast in 1912. *Standing:* P. Jones, E. Morgan, H. Uzzell, T. C. Lloyd, D. Watts. *Seated:* T. Williams, Revd A. Davies, W. E. Rees (sec. WRU), J. Bedwelty Jones.

The Welsh XV which lost to Scotland 14–8 in 1921 when the crowd invaded the field at St Helen's, Swansea and halted play for twelve minutes as police cleared the pitch. *Standing:* W. Trew (touch judge), M. Thomas, S. Winmill, J. Williams, E. Morgan, L. Attewell, T. Roberts, W. Hodder, W. Rees (sec.). *Seated:* J. Rees, W. Bowen, T. H. Vile (capt.), P. Baker-Jones, J. Jones, T. Parker. *In front:* A. Jenkins, J. Evans.

War I and the game was not revived in championship form until 1920. It was launched with a remarkable victory (19–5) by Wales over England at Swansea with one player, Jerry Shea of Pill, Newport scoring sixteen of the points. Nine of the Welshmen were new caps and some of them were to establish reputations for their skill even during the dark days of the 1920s: fullback Joe Rees, centre Albert Jenkins, scrum-half Jack Wetter, who had played in 1914, and forwards Harry Uzzell, Tom Parker, Steve Morris and Jack Whitfield.

Wales lost to Scotland, with whom the championship was shared in 1920, before England continued the run of success at Twickenham in 1921. This proved a disappointing season, highlighted by the 'disaster' match at Swansea when the crowd stormed the field, forcing the players to take refuge in the changing rooms. Play was held up for over ten minutes and the Scottish team, rested after a harrassed period, returned to win 14–8 in Tommy Vile's last match at the age of thirty-five.

This is what that provocative but well-informed historian and rugby writer, the late E. D. H. Sewell, had to say about the disaster:

'This match is not worth describing, as it was ruined by the behaviour of the crowd, which broke into the ground and behaved as no other crowd at a rugby match has ever done before. But for the extremely sane and tactful handling of a ticklish situation by the referee, John Baxter of Liverpool (later to become chairman of the RFU selectors as well as honorary manager of the 1930 Lions and who first accused New Zealand of 'cheating'), it is certain there would have been a serious riot. He kept his presence of mind, and was very wise in playing the game through as best he could, in spite of several unavoidable cessations of play, the last of which, caused entirely by the crowd lining up along the Welsh goal line, cost Wales the match.'

He goes on to write about the resumption after the unprecedented ten minute break:

'Play was resumed and A. T. Sloan scored a final and deciding try for Scotland (to lead 14–8) just after Albert Jenkins' previously 'weak' ankle had 'given', and then to the relief of a good many people the 'no-side' whistle was sounded. It is perhaps just as well in the circumstances that the score ended in Scotland's favour as, on appeal to the International Board, the match certainly would have been given to Scotland.'

The home country or club is responsible for crowd's behaviour and if the crowd should interfere and prevent the opposition being able to play normal rugby, then the result should go to the visiting side. The Laws of the Game (No. 6) states that, 'no person other than players, referee and touch judges may be within the playing enclosure or the field of play unless with the permission of the referee, which shall be given only for a special and temporary purpose.' The instruction to referees under Law No. 9 (3) is 'When a ball strikes a spectator and if the referee is in doubt, the award shall be made to the visiting team if that team is the defending team under (1) a touch down in defence or, if that team is the attacking team under (2) a touch down for a try.'

Unfortunately, the crowd was to burst upon the pitch at St Helen's, Swansea on several occasions in international matches that followed.

The Welsh XV which defeated England 28–6 at the Cardiff Arms Park in January 1922. *Standing:* D. Hiddlestone, Revd J. G. Stephens, T. Roberts, S. Morris, J. Whitfield, W. Cummins. *Seated:* C. Richards, J. Rees, B. Evans, T. Parker (capt.), T. Jones, I. Evans, F. Palmer. *In front:* W. Bowen, W. J. Delahay.

A. L. Gracie of Scotland who was carried off shoulder-high at Cardiff in 1923.

Little was done to prevent this by the Welsh Rugby Union between the Wars and, when it happened in the 1940s, the Welsh Rugby Union eventually decided to play all matches at Cardiff after 1954. It was not the basic factor but one that strongly contributed towards the decision.

The heated controversy between the rival values and attractions of St Helen's and the Arms Park is considered in a later chapter but this 1921 match against Scotland was really the beginning of the end for Swansea as an international ground even if the decision was delayed for thirty-three years. The next match in 1921 was at Cardiff and because the ground was completely full by 2.55 p.m., the scheduled kick-off time of 3.15 p.m. was brought forward to 3.08 p.m., to avoid any possible repetition of the St Helen's scenes. B. O. Male was a late replacement for Joe Rees at fullback and won his first cap while a member of the Cross Keys side, although he was later to appear for Cardiff. Changes were made in the winning Welsh side before the final match against Ireland and the cracks in the selection approach, highlighting a lack of confidence and understanding, first appeared.

The following year, 1922, was to hide this falling away, at least for a season, since Wales won the Championship again and would have had the Triple Crown and Grand Slam but for a drawn match in Edinburgh. Yet it was to be the last championship for nine long and painful years. England were crushed in the mud at the Cardiff Arms Park by eight tries (two converted) to two (28–6) and one Welsh forward, Dai Hiddlestone, making his first appearance in the scarlet jersey at the age of thirty-two, was an outstanding player. For the first time Wales played two lively forwards with pace on the flanks of the back-row of the scrum. However, overall Welsh weaknesses in technique were hidden in the mud.

Scotland were winning at Inverleith before centre Islwyn Evans dropped an equalising goal for Wales (9–9), and Ireland were beaten at Swansea 11–5 due to the forwards. Then France were beaten in Paris 11–3, again on a Thursday, when the forwards mastered the French to complete the season as an unchanged eight. Four of them were new caps when the season started and it was to be some time before such consistency was to occur again. Welsh packs became inconsistent and the backs totally lacking in cohesion, mainly as the result of poor selection, indifferent form, little imagination and a lack of appreciation of the post-war changes in tactical approach.

The Championship season of 1923 brought little cheer with it for Welshmen with only one victory in four matches, yet it produced a spontaneous demonstration of the natural love of the Welsh for the true skills of the game and the greatness of individuals. England won again at Twickenham to give birth to the belief that the ground nurtured some sort of bogey for the Welsh. England scored direct from the kick-off, as in 1910, without their opponents touching the ball. With several men injured, Wales lost 7–3. The players recovered to face Scotland at Cardiff in the next match and were winning 8–6 until the last minute. Scotland

Wales v Ireland in 1924 at the Cardiff Arms Park. Welsh forwards engaged in a short passing movement but Ireland achieved their first win in Wales in twenty-five years by 13–10. David Parker (Swansea) in possession and Jammy Clinch (Ireland) with head-band.

moved away from a scrum and outside-half McQueen missed out centre McLaren by lobbing the ball over his head to the Scottish captain, A. L. Gracie, who, with a sharp burst disturbed the Welsh defence. He slipped by the centres, swerved past fullback Male and was over at the corner. Then he turned in towards the posts to make it easier for Dan Drysdale to convert in case Wales should score again. Drysdale kicked the goal and the final whistle went for a memorable 11–8 Scottish victory. The crowd swarmed on to the field and several members lifted Gracie to their shoulders. He was a hero, a Scottish hero and the Welsh recognised a true touch of fighting genius, a player of quality. It was a moment to savour in the game and Wilson Whineray was to receive a similar accolade in 1964, as Welshmen respect great New Zealand players as much as those of other countries.

Wales defeated France (16–8) at Swansea in a tough, vigorous match that was to speed the termination of fixtures which came eventually in 1931. The French cast skill and pace aside for vigour in their struggle against the heavier Welsh side. Ireland defeated Wales in Dublin by a point (5–4); the first victory for Ireland since 1912 and it left Wales holding the Wooden Spoon they were not to lose during another quite desperate season in 1924. The three defeats, England (17–9), Scotland (35–10) and Ireland (13–10) were not erased by the lone victory in Paris (10–3). For the last match, the selectors changed their team en route to Paris and fullback Male was replaced having defaulted by playing in a midweek match before the international.

The year 1924 was a sad one for Welsh rugby. The invincible All Blacks decisively defeated Wales at Swansea (19–0) and avenged the loss of 1905. Wales fielded an ill-assorted side and so poor was the form, skill and confidence of the national team that any group of fifteen Welsh players

Wales v New Zealand 1924. The Welsh XV were defeated 19–0 by New Zealand at St Helen's, Swansea in November 1924. *Standing:* T. Schofield (touch judge), M. Jones, S. Morris, C. Williams, J. Gore, D. Parker, Col J. Bruton (referee). *Seated:* W. R. Harding, D. Hiddlestone, T. Johnson, A. R. Stock, J. Wetter (capt.), C. Pugh, A. Jenkins, E. Finch. *In front:* E. Williams, W. J. Delahay.

would have stood no chance against one of the most efficient teams to leave New Zealand. It was not a spectacular match and a front-row forward in the 2–3–2 formation, W. R. 'Bull' Irvine, scored two tries. The Welsh experiment of two five-eights was a disaster and one of them, the captain, Jack Wetter of Newport, suffered an injury and played with the forwards in the second half.

The third Wooden Spoon was suffered in 1925 and these three years of disappointment represented the lowest period of the hundred years. Only France were beaten, and perhaps the man best suited to judge the situation is Rowe Harding who played in those days and like so many other players, suffered from appearing in teams at the whim of selectors who created several 'one cap wonders' and never allowed the national XV to settle and work out its own salvation. This period is a complete contrast to the other extreme of the 1970s, when everything was done to build a successful side. There were some splendid players in the 1920s, as they proved when playing for their clubs, but they were different men when they donned the scarlet jersey; confused and striving individuals lacking cohesive skills and teamwork.

After his retirement, Rowe Harding wrote in *Reminiscences and Opinions*:

'Although Wales produced, season after season, big strong forwards, the quality of our back play was uniformly dull and uninspired, partly, I am sure, because there was so much chopping and changing of players behind the scrum that no Welsh back division was able to settle down into a cohesive whole. It is not that we did not have the players. They were there but they were picked sporadically, dropped, and picked again, as we

The invincible New Zealand team of 1924/25 which narrowly defeated Newport 13–10 in an exciting finish. *Standing:* S. S. Dean (manager), J. Steel, M. Nicholls, C. Brownlie, I. H. Harvey, A. H. West, M. J. Brownlie, A. White, W. R. Irvine. *Seated:* G. Nepia, Q. Donald, C. G. Porter (capt.), A. E. Cooke, H. W. Brown. *In front:* J. Mill, K. Svenson.

lurched from one defeat to another. Secondly, the depradations of the Rugby League in what were hungry days for so many working men, also took heavy toll of our best players. The last and perhaps most important factor in the failure at international level was our refusal in Wales to recognise that the basic strategy of the game had changed beyond recognition since the 'Golden Era'.'

Rowe Harding went on to emphasise the need during the 1920s of intensive specialisation at forward in the manner of England, since while the Welsh legislators, players and critics still worshipped the 'Golden Era', all things round them were changing rapidly. As a result Wales was left behind, a land wallowing in golden memories and, Harding continues: 'The other art the Welsh forwards never mastered in the 1920s was the quick heel from the loose. They still relied on the foot rush to make ground and it was foreign to their temperament to heel the ball back rather than kick anything higher than a daisy. Technically, therefore, we were at a disadvantage as compared to the other countries.'

Having played much of his rugby in England, and especially at Cambridge during that University's halcyon period, Harding had a great respect for the English theorists but he was a lone voice in the wilderness of disbelief since it was hard for the indigenous Welsh to accept that W. J. A. Davies, W. W. Wakefield and their English colleagues had done so much to change the course of the game. It was hard to accept after the 'Golden Era' especially among the men who had played in and legislated during it.

During the dark years, from 1920 to 1929, Wales played forty-two matches, won seventeen and lost twenty-two with three drawn, but if one subtracts the wins against France, then Wales won only eight matches of

The 1926 Welsh XV which prevented Ireland achieving the Triple Crown at St Helen's, Swansea, by winning 11–8. *Standing:* J. Newton Jones (touch judge), S. Hinam, D. Jones, J. H. John, S. Lawrence, D. M. Jenkins, E. Watkins, R. C. Herrera. *Seated:* T. E. Rees, R. A. Cornish, C. F. Rowlands, W. R. Harding (capt.), W. J. Delahay, T. Hopkins. *In front:* W. C. Powell, W. H. Lewis.

the thirty played for the Triple Crown with only 28 points for and 300 against. This was called the dark era, the least successful apart from the opening period of the hundred years. It did improve, however, in the 1930s with fifteen victories in thirty matches and 228 points for and 178 against.

During this period Wales improved in defence and the team enjoyed two years of Championship success in 1931 and 1936 but, as the Welsh captain of 1938, Welsh Rugby Union doyen Cliff Jones, points out: 'I was still begging my forwards to try and heel from the loose. We had the backs to score the tries but very little good possession from the loose where it was most valuable.'

Returning to the 1920s, Wales improved in 1926 with a drawn match against England at Cardiff and victories over Ireland and France. The victory over Ireland at Swansea was notable in that it introduced a purely attacking outside-half, Windsor H. Lewis, formerly of Christ College, Brecon, a member of the brilliant Cambridge University attacking machine which in the four seasons, 1925–28, scored ninety-nine points against thirty-two by Oxford in an era when, generally, scores were not particularly high.

During this period, the following Cambridge backs played for Wales, if in and out and off and on: Rowe Harding, B. R. Turnbull, Guy Morgan, Windsor Lewis, John Roberts and Harry Bowcott. They should have been the inspiration of a brilliant Welsh back division but a lack of appreciation on the part of the selectors, a belief that undergraduates were not hard enough, and with forwards who could not win quick possession in the loose, meant such brilliant backs were wasted.

Harding and Lewis were in the side that prevented Ireland winning the Triple Crown in 1926, and against England at Twickenham in 1927, with Roberts and Turnbull, who was made captain at the age of twenty-two. England were fortunate to escape defeat as Wales lost a forward after fifteen minutes and Powell was concussed. At last there appeared a light at the end of the long, dark tunnel even though defeats were suffered against Scotland and Ireland and Wales finished with one victory. At the end of 1927, against the New South Wales 'Waratahs', poor selection brought defeat by a cleverer side. At half-back Lewis was partnered by a man he had not played with and who was completely different in temperament and approach, although ideally suited to inter-club rugby in Wales, Tal Harris of Aberavon. In 1928 the selectors attempted to blend the undergraduates with members of the successful Llanelli side.

Rowe Harding suffered an early injury and once again Wales were unlucky to lose to England, but Scotland were beaten at Murrayfield to record the first Welsh victory on Scottish soil since 1913. Llanelli provided six members of the side and when the 'magnificent six' returned to Llanelli station on the Sunday evening they were met by the town band and thousands of supporters. Yet in the very next match, Wales disappointed against Ireland at Cardiff and this marked the end of the career of Albert Jenkins.

In 1929, Wales won two and drew one and were beaten only by England at Twickenham, something the Welsh had grown to expect as inevitable,

Wales v Waratahs at Cardiff in November 1927. The beaten Welsh XV (18–8) against New South Wales. *Standing:* D. Hellewell (referee), J. Roberts, D. R. Jenkins, Iorwerth Jones, H. Phillips, A. E. Broughton, E. M. Jenkins, T. Hollingdale, A. E. Freethy (touch judge). *Seated:* D. Jones, R. Jones, T. E. Rees, Ivor Jones (capt.), W. H. Lewis, E. Finch. *In front:* F. A. Bowdler, T. Harris.

and the improved form that induced a revival of sorts was helped by players like J. A. Bassett, a policeman from Penarth, at fullback, who was to prove one of the strongest in a long line of defenders, Harry Bowcott, J. C. Morley, Guy Morgan and Frank Williams, playing outside W. C. Powell, with forwards strong enough to hold their own. However, it remained only for Wales to slip back tragically in 1930 with defeats by England and Scotland before Ireland were prevented from winning the Triple Crown at Swansea and France were beaten in Paris in the roughest match of the years between the Wars.

Fists and boots were busy and often the ball was forgotten as the French battled in an attempt to win their first championship. Casting aside skill in favour of muscle, they lost 11–0 and virtually signed their warrant of excommunication, as 1931 was to be their last season in the championship until 1947. The allegations of rough play and professionalism at club level cost them sixteen years of exile from the brotherhood of five nations. Happily for all, their return in 1947 was a wise reprieve as they are now members of the International Board and a progressive world power in the game.

So the 1920s ended on a rough note but opened the doors to a new wonderland for Wales, a championship in 1931 and, but for a drawn match at Twickenham (11–11), the Triple Crown and Grand Slam. Wales led 11–8 at Twickenham with three minutes left for play and then a penalty for a scrum infringement saw South African-born Brian Black, a lock forward with the 1930 Lions, land a fifty yards penalty to draw the match. The referee had earlier overruled the touch judges to award a conversion that eventually proved decisive.

Wales v Scotland at the Cardiff Arms Park 1931. Watcyn Thomas, the Welsh number eight forward, crashes over the Scottish line for a try despite a broken collar-bone.

Welsh XV v England at St Helen's, Swansea, 1932. *Standing:* W. Davies, A. Skym, W. Thomas, A. Lemon, E. M. Jenkins, T. Day, D. Thomas. *Seated:* J. C. Morley, E. C. Davey, J. A. Bassett (capt.), F. A. Bowdler, F. L. Williams, R. W. Boon. *In front:* W. C. Powell, A. R. Ralph.

There were fine backs in Bassett, Morley, Davey, Williams, Bowcott, Boon and Powell, who were joined by Newport's A. R. 'Dickie' Ralph, to give a splendid display against Ireland for the Championship. The ten forwards, too, are worthy of mention as forming one of the best packs of the 1930s – A. Skym, D. R. James, T. Day, T. Arthur, E. M. Jenkins, A. Lemon, Watcyn Thomas, J. Lang, N. Fender and H. C. Day. This side went into action against South Africa at Swansea in December 1931 and but for the torrential rain would have beaten the powerful tourists. Unfortunately, Wales endeavoured to play a running and handling game while the Springboks under their shrewd leader, B. L. 'Bennie' Osler, engaged in nothing more than kick and rush. It was close, it was hard and the Springboks won 8–3. Even so, Jack Bassett produced the outstanding performance of his fifteen-match career, which was to end sadly in the last match of that season with Wales poised for the first Triple Crown since 1911, against Ireland at Cardiff on a beautiful spring afternoon in March 1932.

On a firm ground with an over-inflated ball, the Irish scored four breakaway tries, and errors by Bassett contributed to defeat as did those of the referee, who allowed one blatant offside try. Even near the end, when Bassett had to place a conversion for a draw and the championship, his kick veered just wide. As in many cases of leading Welsh players during the 100 years, Bassett's few errors in defeat are remembered more than his many moments of triumph. When he eventually retired a few years later, Bassett left the rugby scene as if in disappointment but remained a cheery

The Welsh XV which achieved victory (by 7–3) for the first time at Twickenham in January 1933. *Standing:* B. Evans, V. G. J. Jenkins, W. Wooller, I. Isaacs, T. Arthur, D. Thomas, W. J. Llewellyn (touch judge). *Seated:* A. H. Jones, R. B. Jones, R. W. Boon, W. Thomas (capt.), E. C. Davey, E. Jones, A. Skym. *In front:* H. M. Bowcott, M. Turnbull. (Seven of the side were new caps.)

police officer and then a smiling bailiff before retirement. Few better fullbacks played for Wales when tackling and sure touch-finding were the main requirements.

The year 1933 was memorable, despite two defeats, as the lone victory was long-awaited and much cherished; the first win at Twickenham after twenty-three years of endeavour to lay the 'bogey'. The Welsh players of that day remain heroes. Led by Watcyn Thomas, a strong, intelligent number eight, the side included seven new caps in fullback V. G. J. Jenkins, wing A. H. Jones, centre Wilfred Wooller, scrum-half M. J. Turnbull and forwards Bryn Evans, Iorrie Isaacs and R. B. Jones. With them were established players in R. W. Boon, E. C. Davey, H. M. Bowcott, A. Skym, E. Jones, D. Thomas, T. Arthur and, of course, the captain.

Thomas, forthright, experienced and humorous, made an inspiring pre-match speech and another pep-talk at the interval. It was a keen match and seven points from Boon, named as the 'cheekie-chappie' of his era, a try and a dropped goal, to a try by Elliott the English outside-half, was enough to lay the bogey and satisfy Welsh followers. All the new caps did well and Bowcott kicked immaculately with Davey tackling tremendously hard. Of this side four members had played, or were to play county cricket for Glamorgan.

A successful season was anticipated but injuries produced enforced changes and the season ended in extreme disappointment and 1934 started similarly as the selectors really excelled themselves in nominating thirteen new caps against England at Cardiff! They had a complete clear-out, as if their 'lease' was about to terminate, and only two players, E. C. Davey, and D. Thomas of Swansea, remained from the previous season. Such a selection deserved the wrath of followers and a sound beating by England, while it taught one of the new caps, C. W. Jones at outside-half (later to select in the post-war period for twenty years), that panic selection never pays. It was the 'tunnel' match and Jones rarely received a pass throughout it, although his 'baptism' launched him on his career as the most brilliant attacking outside-half of the 1930s. The scrum-half and six forwards were promptly dropped, and five more new caps introduced against Scotland when the side won handsomely by 13–6 at Murrayfield before demolishing Ireland in the final ten minutes at St Helen's by scoring thirteen points, with V. G. J. Jenkins becoming the first Welsh fullback to score a try; followed many years later by Keith Jarrett and J. P. R. Williams.

The next year was not quite as successful with one win, one defeat and a drawn match and the 1935 season marked the end of the long and colourful career enjoyed by W. C. 'Wick' Powell, of whom it is said, 'his reverse pass was stronger and more accurate than his normal pass'. He made twenty-seven appearances between 1926 and 1935 and was indestructible; a hard man to play against who once employed a long safety-pin to ward off the over-eager attentions of an Australian wing-forward when playing for London against the Waratahs in 1927!

Yet the sorrow of the season passed into oblivion when in December 1935 Wales achieved a second victory over New Zealand in the most thrilling of circumstances. A tremendous match, with the lead changing hands throughout, ended with a victory by a mere point for Wales at 13–12, and the final scenes remain with the author as the most memorable in his lifetime. All the Welsh players were heroes but Wilfred Wooller became the 'Dragon of Wales' as it was he, more than anyone, who snatched the victory cup from thirsting New Zealand lips.

J. E. Manchester's Third All Blacks were a happy, running side and as they lost their unbeaten record early on to Swansea by 11–3 in a fascinating tussle, they were not inhibited by safety methods. Although not fully appreciated by their own followers at home, they toured the four home countries when overall the game was much stronger than in 1905 and 1924. They lost only three matches in twenty-eight played – to Swansea, Wales and England.

Only against England were they indifferently selected and played below par; in the Welsh match they made a special effort and led 3–0 at the interval with a try by Nelson Ball. Early in the second half, Wales produced a purple patch to claim fine tries through E. C. Davey, the Welsh captain, and wing G. Rees-Jones, both converted by V. G. J. Jenkins for a 10–3 lead before a couple of defensive lapses allowed New Zealand to go ahead again. Fullback G. Gilbert dropped a splendid goal, and then kicked wide attempting a second one for Nelson Ball to snap up

J. E. Manchester, the popular captain of the 1935–36 New Zealand team in the British Isles.

Wales v New Zealand at Cardiff, December 1935. Jim Lang, the Welsh number eight, kicks the ball back from a lineout in the exciting 13–12 Welsh victory. The forwards are (left to right): S. T. Reid (NZ), J. E. Manchester (NZ), T. J. Rees, T. Williams, E. Watkins (W), A. Mahoney (NZ), J. Lang (W), D. Dalton (NZ), A. M. Rees (W) and W. E. Hadley (NZ).

the awkward bounce and race over for his second try. Gilbert converted and New Zealand led 12–10. The Welsh hooker, D. J. Tarr, suffered a broken neck in a maul and referee Cyril Gadney saved his life by leaving him face downwards until the stretcher arrived. Sadly, Wales faced certain defeat.

In desperation the remaining fourteen players launched one further effort and the seven forwards won the ball at a scrum for Tanner to send Jones bursting away and he fed Wooller behind inside-centre Davey. Wooller raced up the field and, when confronted by fullback Gilbert, punted over his head, only to find the ball bounce high and back over his own head on the New Zealand goal-line, as in the scoring of the second Welsh try. Horror of horrors, he thought, New Zealand saved by the bounce, and then he heard the almost deafening yell of victory burst from fifty thousand throats, as Rees-Jones on the right-wing, not as fast as the long-striding Wooller and following in the big man's wake, gathered the ball, as he had done in scoring his first try, and crossed for the vital one. Jenkins did not convert but no one cared; it was a thrilling end to a magnificent match and Manchester's team, although disappointed, accepted it all like sportsmen.

The Welsh team was V. G. J. Jenkins; G. Rees-Jones, J. I. Rees, E. C. Davey (captain), W. Wooller (who exchanged places with a slightly unfit J. I. Rees before the interval); C. W. Jones, H. Tanner; T. J. Rees, D. J. Tarr, H. Payne, E. Watkins, T. Williams, A. M. Rees, J. Lang and G. Prosser.

Without doubt, it was the best match as a spectacle between the two countries and launched the spectacular and effective Jones–Tanner partnership as well as highlighting Wooller as one of the outstanding match-winning centres of the 100 years. Haydn Tanner of Gowerton was an eighteen-year-old schoolboy and had shared already in Swansea's triumph over New Zealand with another equally-gifted player, his cousin W. T. H. Davies, and while Tanner went on to win twenty-five caps between 1935 and 1949, the longest career in Welsh international rugby, Davies won six caps and became a brilliant rugby league player.

In 1936, Wales were held to a draw at Swansea by a defensive England (the same side that had beaten New Zealand by Prince Obolensky's two tries), and then won handsomely at Murrayfield before narrowly defeating Ireland at Cardiff. England's fullback, and South African test cricketer, H. G. 'Tuppy' Owen-Smith, tapped Wooller's heels in desperation as the centre pounded for the line and a try that would have earned the Triple Crown. However, as the Editor of the *Rugby Football Annual* (the genial O. L. Owen) commented in reviewing the season, 'Wales were entitled to end the season on distinctly good terms with themselves . . . as they well deserved their success'.

Yet, as often happened during the 100 years until the four consecutive Triple Crowns of the 1970s, a highly successful season was followed by a poor one. The 1937 season was a disaster as Wales fell from grace; from Champions to Wooden Spoon holders in three defeats, mainly through ill-advised selection and poor form. The forward play proved extremely disappointing, highlighted by sluggish heeling, and the opposition was able to successfully snuff out the sporadic Welsh attacks. Tanner was badly concussed in a trial match and this affected his form, Wooller and Davey were never properly fit and Jones was out for the period before Christmas through injury. A new wing, W. H. Clement, full of promise,

C. W. Jones, the Wales, Cardiff and Cambridge outside-half, scores a brilliant try against Scotland at the Cardiff Arms Park in February 1935.

had few chances and was later to serve twenty-five years as the Welsh Rugby Union secretary holding the memory of his first year as a sad one!

In 1938, C. W. Jones took over the captaincy and England were beaten in a gale at Cardiff with the Welsh backs, and especially Jones and Jenkins, playing extremely well. The Triple Crown was lost in Scotland by the award of a controversial last-minute penalty which gave the home country victory by 8–6. Prop E. Morgan left the field with fractured ribs in the first half and Wales finished with six forwards as flanker A. McCarley, scorer of the two Welsh tries, had to be withdrawn to cover an injured Wooller. Not a happy day, and Scotland went on to win their last Triple Crown and Championship under Wilson Shaw although Wales did beat Ireland at Swansea 11–5.

At the end of this season, eight Welshmen accompanied the British Lions to South Africa with V. G. J. Jenkins as vice-captain, and there were hopes in 1939 of an outright Championship. C. W. Jones had retired at the age of twenty-three and Davies and Tanner were at half-back with Wooller as captain but the promise of the Welsh back division was not fulfilled at Twickenham owing to the poor scrummaging of the pack and bad forward leadership. After the 3–0 defeat, Wales made nine changes and promoted the brilliant Lions hooker, W. Travers (a player as good as his father during the 'Golden Era') as pack leader. V. G. J. Jenkins retired after the England match and later became an outstanding writer on the game.

Six new caps were introduced against Scotland and a handsome victory resulted (11–3) at Cardiff, and then W. T. H. Davies was outstanding behind a fiery pack in Belfast when Ireland were beaten in the rain on a muddy pitch (7–0), with Davies scoring a try and a dropped goal. It marked the end of a twenty-year period between the Wars and it was seven years before the Championship was restarted.

Opposite top: Scotland v Wales at Murrayfield in 1938. The side which lost 8–6 through a last-minute penalty to miss the Triple Crown under the captaincy of C. W. Jones. *Standing:* R. A. Cornish (touch judge), V. G. J. Jenkins, F. L. Morgan, E. Watkins, W. Travers, W. Vickery, A. McCarley. *Seated:* A. M. Rees, H. Rees, E. Morgan, C. W. Jones (capt.), W. Wooller, W. H. Clement, J. I. Rees. *In front:* A. Bassett, H. Tanner.

Opposite bottom: The last international match at the Cardiff Arms Park before World War II – Wales v Scotland in February 1939. Wales won 11–3 and here outside-half W. T. H. Davies is seen taking a high pass from Haydn Tanner after a scrum in mid-field. Behind Davies is M. J. Davies, W. Wooller (capt.), and S. Williams (left-wing) and below left is right-wing E. L. Jones.

3 THE INTERNATIONAL RECORD 1940–1980

World War II did not halt rugby completely in Wales as several clubs kept playing and service units in the Principality engaged in a series of unofficial matches. Special ones were staged for leading war charities, some at international level, and as the barrier between Rugby Union and Rugby League was temporarily removed, Wales fielded a mixed side of considerable strength from the two codes.

The Welsh Rugby Union decided on 25 September to close down operations and a large number of players volunteered for the reserve forces even before War had been declared. The Union granted clubs permission to arrange fixtures in accordance with Government regulations and on 30 September the informal season was opened with several charity matches. On 14 November, it was agreed to suspend the ruling against Rugby League players, as once they had enlisted in the forces, they ceased to have any connection with the Rugby League. Only Scotland opted out and maintained the ban on league players.

At the Cardiff Arms Park, Rodney Parade, Newport, St Helen's, Swansea and Newbridge there was plenty of football and on 9 March 1940, at the Arms Park before 40,000 rugby-starved supporters, England defeated Wales 18–9 in a Red Cross International match. Cardiff maintained a strong side, even beating the Barbarians, and when most of the pre-war side went overseas, young players were recruited in J. Matthews, B. L. Williams, W. B. Cleaver and W. Darch, joined by 'golden oldies' in Edgar Jones and Hubert Johnson.

Newbridge included many miners, a very important reserved occupation, and did well, establishing itself as a first-class club when hostilities ended. Cardiff were able to resume in 1945–46 with a well-balanced side, spearheaded by some brilliant youngsters. Newport also had a ready-made side and proved this by holding the Kiwis to a draw and supplying members of the Monmouthshire side that defeated the tourists at Pontypool. At St Helen's, C. B. Jones and an active committee staged memorable charity matches where Wales once fielded a back division of R. F. Trott; S. Williams, A. Risman, B. L. Williams, A. Edwards; W. T. H. Davies and H. Tanner, against England.

From March 1942 until April 1945, the Inter-services Committee organised international rugby and did a splendid job before the four Home Unions set up in business again in September 1945. There followed a

The Kiwis XV which defeated Cardiff (3–0) on Boxing Day 1945 at the Arms Park. Both sides were unbeaten prior to this match. *Standing:* R. W. H. Scott, J. R. Sherratt, A. W. Blake, W. G. Argus, J. G. Simpson, N. J. McPhail, F. R. Allen, Col. A. H. Andrews (manager). *Seated:* S. L. Young, F. N. Haigh, J. Finlay, C. K. Saxton (capt.), P. K. Rhind, K. D. Arnold. *In front:* I. Proctor, J. B. Smith.

season of general rehabilitation and instead of a full Championship a series of matches between the countries known as the 'Victory Internationals' were staged. They were highly successful and gave the Unions and their selectors a chance to settle in again. More important, perhaps, was the visit of the Kiwis, a New Zealand Army touring side, under the captaincy of an experienced All Blacks scrum-half, Charles Saxton, and the management of Colonel A. Andrews.

They proved themselves the most popular of New Zealand sides to tour in the British Isles, especially in Wales where they were received like 'long-lost brothers' of ages past. Apart from their mixing so well, they produced exceedingly good rugby to delight spectators and revive the competitive spirit of the Welsh. They defeated Wales (11–3) at the Cardiff Arms Park and of twenty-seven matches played in the British Isles and France, they won twenty-three, drew two (Leinster and Newport) and lost two (Scotland and Monmouthshire), which was a notable achievement. Many of the battle-scarred young New Zealanders were to return home to win full All Blacks honours and some to play against the 1950 British Lions.

A total of sixteen Victory International matches were played and France rejoined the Home countries to revive the enthusiasm necessary for the return of a full Championship in 1946–47. Wales played seven Victory matches against France (2), England (2), Scotland (2) and Ireland, losing four and winning three, and actually achieving another rare victory at Twickenham. In the seven matches the Welsh selectors employed forty players and five of these, E. L. Jones, L. Manfield, H. Tanner, W. Travers and H. Thomas, had appeared before the War. Several of the others became British Lions by 1950, W. B. Cleaver, C. Davies, R. T.

Wales v France at Twickenham, February 1946. W. B. Cleaver, the Welsh outside-half in the victory international, sets off after receiving a pass from Cliff Davies.

Evans, J. Matthews, J. R. G. Stephens and B. L. Williams, while seventeen were to receive full caps in the early post-war official seasons. Highlighting the Victory International sides was the introduction of the two Pontypridd Grammar School halves, Glyn and Wynford Davies. Glyn was to captain Cambridge University and win eleven senior caps as a popular, classical, attacking player, who died tragically young as a highly successful business executive.

Expectations were high for Wales when they entered the first official Championship of 1947 and England were met at the bomb-damaged Cardiff Arms Park before a reduced crowd of 43,000 as the upper deck of the North Stand was not in use. Wales included thirteen new caps, many to become household names in the mouths of supporters and much admired in the game. Yet good players though they were to become, they lost this first match 9–6 by a converted try and a dropped goal to two tries. Bleddyn Williams played his only match at outside-half for Wales and his next twenty-one matches at centre, between 1947 and 1955.

Glyn Davies replaced him at outside-half against Scotland and did well

France v Wales in Paris, April 1946. Welsh captain, Haydn Tanner, faced by Jean Prat in the first match between Wales and France since the break of 1931. France won 12–0.

before an Army game injury forced him out and W. B. Cleaver played against France and Ireland. All three matches were won and England and Wales shared the Championship. The Welsh pack developed power under the leadership of W. E. Tamplin (surprisingly omitted from the England match which he could have won with his place-kicking), and Haydn Tanner and Cleaver controlled at half-back. Five tries were scored at Murrayfield, all by backs, and the match in Paris remains the hardest played by Wales in the post-war years. A powerful, heavy French pack was held and Tamplin kicked the winning penalty goal.

The Championship seasons of 1948 and 1949 were not happy ones. The

Welsh XV v England at the Cardiff Arms Park, January 1947. The first official Welsh side after World War II. *Standing:* J. A. Beattie (referee), G. Bevan, D. Jones, O. Williams, G. Evans, J. R. G. Stephens, G. Parsons, R. Blakemore, S. Williams, Ivor Jones (touch judge). *Seated:* H. Davies, L. Williams, J. Matthews, H. Tanner (capt.), B. L. Williams, K. J. Jones, W. B. Cleaver. (Wales lost 9–6.)

Wales v England at Cardiff, January 1947. After diving through a tackle by Nim Hall, flank-forward Gwyn Evans scores a try for Wales in the first full official match following World War II.

selectors could not get the formula right and form varied. Cardiff, enjoying outstanding seasons in club football, supplied a record number of ten players to the Welsh side for three matches in 1948, as the selectors hoped to emulate the success of the club but there was only one win, one draw and two defeats including a first victory by France in Wales. A fine win over England at Cardiff (9–3) launched 1949, followed by three disappointing defeats. Four new caps appeared in the Paris match which marked the end of Haydn Tanner's illustrious career and started those of Malcolm Thomas and R. C. C. Thomas.

The future looked unpromising since Wales had failed to make use of her resources, and coupled with the memories of the 1920s after World War I, it disturbed many. One player, J. A. Gwilliam, playing at lock, commented privately: 'With Cardiff such a fine side and so many other good young players available, Wales should rarely lose the Triple Crown. It is difficult to explain why the trophy has eluded Welshmen for over 30 years.'

England v Wales at Twickenham, January 1948. Haydn Tanner executing a perfect dive-pass watched by his back-row and referee Beattie as M. R. Steele-Bodger (England) sweeps out in defence. The match was drawn 3–3.

Welsh XV v Ireland at Belfast, 1948, when Ireland won the Triple Crown for the first time since 1899, beating Wales 6–3. *Standing:* Ivor Jones (touch judge), C. Davies, K. J. Jones, R. F. Trott, J. A. Gwilliam, E. Davies, L. Manfield, O. Williams, M. A. Allan (referee). *Seated:* L. Williams, M. James, H. Tanner (capt.), B. L. Williams, G. Evans, J. R. G. Stephens. *In front:* W. B. Cleaver, G. Davies. (Nine of the players were from the Cardiff Club.)

Unknowingly at the time, Gwilliam was to have the chance to prove his theory much sooner than anticipated, and in the three years of his new-style captaincy, Wales twice achieved the Triple Crown and the Grand Slam, although his appointment as captain was more a question of accident (or illness) rather than design. On the eve of the Twickenham match of 1950, the appointed captain Bleddyn Williams (who later was to prove a very successful leader with five wins in five matches) withdrew through illness and Gwilliam was invited to take over, sixteen hours before the match. He accepted the post with good humour and encouraged his six new caps with an unusual team talk, after the selectors had left the dressing room, some minutes before the kick-off. Another senior player, J. R. G. Stephens, had withdrawn and was replaced by E. R. John, a lineout specialist of unerring accuracy and artistry, for a first cap. Other newcomers were Lewis Jones at fullback who became a brilliant union and league player and superb goal-kicker, T. J. Brewer on the wing, W. R. Willis as a new partner for Cleaver in his first season of senior rugby and without an official trial as a result of the maxim 'play a club pair if possible', and forwards who were to become outstanding Lions in the same year, J. D. Robins and D. M. Davies, together with E. R. John.

Gwilliam appeared for the first time for Wales at number eight and during the first twenty minutes of play, slowed down proceedings with a succession of marks. Lewis Jones made a spectacular run from fullback when, by tradition, he should have kicked to touch, and launched an attack for Cliff Davies to score an unusual try that set the match and the Welsh XV alight. By the end of the season it had won both Crown and Grand Slam. Tragically, the after-match celebrations with the return from Belfast were marred when the Tudor IV aircraft crashed whilst landing in

The Grand Slam Welsh XV of 1950 was also the first to win the Triple Crown since 1911. *Standing:* Ivor Jones (touch judge), W. R. Willis, D. Hayward, E. R. John, R. T. Evans, M. C. Thomas, J. D. Robins, M. J. Dowling (referee). *Seated:* W. R. Cale, C. Davies, J. Matthews, J. A. Gwilliam (capt.), W. B. Cleaver, K. J. Jones, D. M. Davies. *In front:* G. Williams, B. L. Jones. (Twelve of this side became 1950 Lions.)

Ireland v Wales at Belfast, March 1950. Ken Jones taking a high pass in a match which Wales won 6–3 to capture the Triple Crown.

Wales v France at the Cardiff Arms Park, March 1950. K. J. Jones kicks ahead. The match was won by Wales (20–0) to clinch the Championship and Grand Slam.

the Vale of Glamorgan at Llandow. Three of the eighty-three passengers aboard survived and of the extremely fortunate ones, administrator Handel Rogers of Llanelli, was to become a president of the Welsh Rugby Union. Before the start of the French match the 'Last Post' was sounded and tribute paid to the victims of the crash. Wales won easily enough and for the first time in thirty-nine years, were at the top of the European rugby tree, happy, contented and deserving of success.

In the *Rugby Annual*, editor O. L. Owen, then the world's most experienced rugby writer commented, 'The Welsh team, little changed throughout the season, was well led and not only resilient to shocks, but able to play the kind of rugby they had set out to play, and play it both hard and skilfully, from start to finish.' Not all members of the team agreed with Gwilliam's approach as their leader. It was unusual; it contained a touch of the school master, but they accepted it in the end, realising that it had helped them to achieve long-awaited success. Gwilliam, for all the criticism at first, won over his critics and remained modest in the extreme. He enjoyed the task and would hear no criticism of his team . . . 'I am the captain and accept the responsibility of failure. The players under me win the matches and the glory is theirs. Indeed, I am just the general as the other fourteen do the real work.'

Gwilliam, Bleddyn Williams, and John Dawes have been outstanding post-war captains because they have been cool and unemotional in approach, as compared with the tremendous personal involvement of Clive Rowlands who led in fourteen consecutive matches from Wooden Spoon to Triple Crown. Of these four, and I know them well as friends and admire what they have done, I tend to favour Gwilliam for his unusual but effective approach and his comment, 'I have always asked the team not to hold anything said in the game as evidence of my personal animosity.' He admits that after ten minutes of the Twickenham match he almost lost his voice and could speak only in a whisper. As this only reached the forward next to him at the lineout, the poor chap thought his captain was blaming him for every mistake!

Yet Gwilliam was soon to find life hard as the Welsh captain, as in 1951, following a handsome victory over England at Swansea, the Welsh team was humiliated by a young and inexperienced Scottish side at Murrayfield 19–0. Let him describe the disaster:

'Ever since that fateful day the Welsh players have been bombarded with questions as to how it happened. The Scottish side had lost many matches before this one and continued to lose many after it. Innumerable theories have been propounded but most are wide of the mark. The real cause of our defeat was the remarkably good play of the Scottish team.

'It was a fine example of the tenet that the art of rugby football is to be better than the other side at any given moment. Before and, possibly, after the game, the Welsh XV were a better side but, at that moment, the Scottish were superior and their superiority lay in their liveliness. They were a more spirited side than Wales, and gained confidence as the game

Wales v England at St Helen's, Swansea, January 1951. Malcolm Thomas scores Wales' last try after a brilliant sixty yards run. On the ground is Ivor Preece (England) who chased Thomas to the posts.

The Welsh XV which lost to South Africa at the Cardiff Arms Park in December 1951. The match was billed as for Championship of the world and won by S. Africa 6–3. *Standing:* H. Lambert (referee), L. Blyth, A. Forward, E. R. John, J. R. G. Stephens, D. Hayward, D. M. Davies, Ivor Jones (touch judge). *Sitting:* M. C. Thomas, K. J. Jones, J. A. Gwilliam (capt.), B. L. Williams, B. L. Jones. *In front:* W. O. Williams, W. R. Willis, C. I. Morgan, G. Williams.

progressed, while their opponents deteriorated. This may be an unsatisfying explanation to those who feel that there was some dark unrevealed secret that caused the downfall of the Welsh team. It has been attributed by sound judges to staleness following the Lions tour and by some to over-confidence.'

Such surprising defeats, and this was one of the most surprising during the hundred years, form part of the game's attractiveness. No side can ever be sure it is going to win. Gwilliam's side could only draw 3–3 with Ireland at Cardiff in the next match and the selectors, completely confused by it all, dropped Gwilliam for the French match. Dr Jack Matthews, an able vice-captain to Gwilliam, took over the leadership but his side was beaten in Paris 8–3. The sceptics believed it was another 'flash in the pan' and that Wales would have to wait another thirty-nine years for the next Triple Crown. If such followers were wanting in faith and the selectors harassed, not so John Gwilliam and his players. He was back as captain against South Africa at Cardiff in December 1951 and although Wales lost (6–3) the effort was regarded as a mighty one encouraging the selectors to nominate the same side for the Championship.

Again, the unfortunate Bleddyn Williams had to retire through illness and Alun Thomas won his first cap in the last 'pay-as-you-enter' match between England and Wales at Twickenham. The gates had to be closed with thousands of Welshmen locked outside and 1954 saw the start of the all-ticket matches which have proved safer and easier to handle, if disap-

Wales v South Africa at Cardiff, December 1951. Bleddyn Williams scores the Welsh try as he is tackled by Chum Ochse.

Wales v France at St Helen's, Swansea, March 1952. Welsh outside-half Alun Thomas about to kick for touch as the French spread out in defence.

pointing to Welsh followers. Gwilliam led the players to victory again through a splendid team effort and despite a hamstring injury to Lewis Jones that reduced him to a limping wing but not a passenger. Although guarded on the wing by flanker Len Blyth, brought out for the purpose, Jones took part in a movement that led to the winning try, the second of the match by Ken Jones, then at the height of his long and colourful career.

Tactically, it was an interesting season, as the tour by the Third Springboks persuaded the Welsh selectors of the value of big props. Cliff Davies and John Robins of the 1950 side were intelligent, standard-sized but were replaced by a new jumbo-size pair, W. O. Williams and Don Hayward, converted from the second-row of their clubs' scrums. Either side of the clever hooker D. M. Davies, they were immediately successful against South Africa and pushed their weight triumphantly through the Championship season. However, Robins, extremely broad of shoulder, returned for a while before C. C. Meredith established himself as the complete prototype of the modern prop, big hard, strong, intelligent and quick about the field. Later he, B. V. Meredith as hooker and W. O. Williams were to form an ideal Lions front-row in South Africa in 1955.

Scotland, Ireland and France were beaten as the Welsh XV produced

Wales v New Zealand at Cardiff in December 1953. Bleddyn Williams, the Welsh captain, prevents B. Fitzpatrick from scoring for New Zealand, aided by Gerwyn Williams who tackled low. Wales won 13–8 to achieve their third and last victory over the All Blacks.

Wales v New Zealand at Cardiff, December 1953. Ken Jones, the Welsh right wing, scores the winning try against New Zealand after collecting a cross-kick from R. C. C. Thomas. Referee Peter Cooper of England (at the posts) signals a try.

some exciting rugby, even though it fell away a little in the last match, without Morgan and Willis at half-back, when beating France 9–5 at Swansea. The years that followed in the 1950s were exciting and skilful with all five countries possessing players of quality. Gwilliam made his last appearance as captain against England and as the match was lost (8–3) he was dropped and Bleddyn Williams took over the leadership. New caps who became outstanding players were Terry Davies at fullback, Gareth Griffiths at three-quarter and Sid Judd as a flanker. Scotland were beaten and Gwilliam returned for the Irish and French matches to play happily under Williams. In December 1953 they were to share in a memorable triumph over New Zealand, again at Cardiff, in an exciting match that New Zealand could have won before Wales effected a brilliant recovery. It was clean, hard, sporting and exciting before 56,000 spectators, suffering as the lead changed hands in the pattern of 1935. Wales were 8–5 down at the interval, then struggled back to 8–8 and, near the end, achieved the winning try.

Flank forward R. C. C. Thomas was covered while running down the left touch-line and near the New Zealand twenty-five yard line he checked and cross-kicked. The ball bounced in no-man's-land near mid-field for Ken Jones to race in from the right wing, gather and score at the posts. Dr Gwyn Rowlands converted and Wales succeeded (13–8) but it was the last victory in the 100 years as New Zealand won the next six matches, home and away, to establish a comfortable lead.

In 1954 Wales shared the title with France, losing one match to England (9–6) at Twickenham, where Bleddyn Williams was forced to withdraw yet again through injury and the team suffered several injuries during play, rarely having fifteen men on the field at the same time. J. R. G. Stephens led the side in the absence of Williams, and E. R. John, D. M. Davies and J. A. Gwilliam made their final appearances. One new cap was included in Glyn John, replacing Williams, and who had been reinstated

South Africa v British Isles at Ellis Park, 1955. Cliff Morgan, the Welsh outside-half and outstanding member of the Lions side, scores a brilliant try early in the second half and sets the Lions on their way to an exciting win (23–22) in the first test.

after signing on for the Rugby League Club, Leigh, before he was eighteen years old and then returning his signing-on fee of £400, to become only the third such Welsh player, following the James brothers of the 1890s.

England went on to win the Triple Crown but lost to France while Wales won their three remaining matches with K. J. Jones of Newport equalling R. M. Owen's record of thirty-five appearances and being honoured with the leadership for the occasion, in the last international match played at Swansea, against Scotland, postponed from 30 January to 10 April because of the weather. Vivian Evans of Neath played in the three matches at fullback at the age of thirty-four and contributed twenty-five points.

In 1955 Wales shared the Championship with France but missed the Triple Crown by losing at Murrayfield. The victory over France in Paris was the last appearance of W. R. Willis who was in line for the captaincy of the 1955 Lions but could not accept or make the tour, and an age limit of thirty years prevented J. R. G. Stephens and K. J. Jones from being considered. C. I. Morgan, on returning from a highly successful Lions tour, was rewarded with the captaincy in 1956 and had a new partner in the brilliant and individualistic D. O. Brace, then of Newport and Oxford University.

Morgan, an inspiring player, led Wales to the Championship, but the Triple Crown was lost in Dublin (11–3) where the forwards failed and the backs experienced a difficult match. The final match at Cardiff was notable for a winning try by flanker C. D. Williams, inches short of the French dead ball line, which they claimed as being scored extremely near to the River Taff! K. J. Jones became the most capped British player, moving ahead of G. V. Stephenson of Ireland with forty-three consecutive appearances.

South Africa v British Isles at Ellis Park, 1955. Two leading Welsh forwards and British Lions of the 1950s in action during one of the greatest test matches in 100 years. R. H. Williams (left) and B. V. Meredith (right) jumping higher than their Springbok opponents.

Morgan and Brace, though individually brilliant players, never really did themselves justice in harness and in 1957 England won 3–0 at Cardiff and went on to win the Triple Crown. K. J. Jones missed this match but appeared against Scotland for the forty-fourth and last time. Wales lost 9–6 but defeated Ireland and France although for the next four years the French dominated the Welsh.

Australia were on tour in the British Isles during the winter of 1957–58 and against them in January, Wales played two new caps at half-back as C. I. Morgan was unfit, in the Llanelli pair, Carwyn James and Wynne Evans, and won comfortably (9–3) to maintain their record against Australia. Morgan returned with Lloyd Williams, a big strong scrum-half and brother of Bleddyn, at Twickenham, and with T. J. Davies at fullback kicked superbly in a drawn match (3–3). Scotland were defeated at Cardiff (8–3), and Ireland were beaten in Dublin (9–6) before Morgan made his twenty-ninth and last appearance for Wales against France at Cardiff, who achieved their first victory at the Arms Park (16–6).

Cliff Morgan remains one of the most accomplished and colourful of post-war players, and possibly the most attractive and effervescent of all Welsh outside-halves since Percy Bush. Although Phil Bennett has equalled his number of appearances, some of these were in other positions while Morgan's were all at outside-half; a remarkable record. So talented was this player that had he appeared under the recent new laws, his perform-

D. O. Brace, who partnered Cliff Morgan in the Championship year of 1956, in action against France at Cardiff in 1960.

ances would have been even more magical and effective. South Africa regarded him as the 'General' and in his own country he achieved the apt title of 'Morgan the Mighty'. His popularity and warm personality highlight his present important sporting associations in the media and his continued genuine love of the game. Outstanding players were to follow him in David Watkins, Barry John and Phil Bennett, but even their success has not disturbed the impact of Morgan's contribution or caused the memory of his rugby manoeuvring to wane.

He was the game's spirited leader in the 1950s and it lost much through his retirement, as it was some years before brilliance returned to the outside-half position in the Welsh XV. Amazingly, Wales has always been able to produce outside-halves of outstanding ability and, since the War, they have been able to hold their places and reign for long periods with distinction. One of these, Barry John of Llanelli and Cardiff, achieved such fame as to be hailed as the 'King' in New Zealand in 1971.

There has always been a fascination for half-backs and because of the striving for perfection in the position as tacticians, stylists and individuals, as well as being devoted team men and directors of operations, Wales has produced a large number of successful pairs as well as sparkling individuals. Even in modern times with the directive hand of coaching pointing across the field of play, unseen and unheard, but still influencing the play, there is acceptance of the fact that the outside-half will 'call the attacking moves'.

In the first three-quarters of the century, outside-halves played it 'off the top of their heads', as they saw fit, and some with less success than others. When a clever, confident player appeared in the position and wanted to succeed, he made sure that his side succeeded as well as he adjusted his play to the cause, although occasionally allowing himself a

The outstanding pair of Welsh halves in the 1950s, W. R. Willis and C. I. Morgan of Cardiff. They played together fourteen times for Wales.

touch of the unexpected, and whether or not successful revealed admirable audacity. Often players were too clever, not only for their opponents but also their colleagues, and in many a year during the hundred there arose the argument, should the centres follow their outside-half or should the outside-half take his centres with him into attack and create, where possible, the half-openings?

Few former players have written as well about this as did the Welsh

captain of 1938, C. W. Jones, an elusive runner, in 1939 after he had retired. His book, *Rugby Football* contains the simple statement, 'The fly-half (outside-half) is the pivot, the spear head, the mainspring of the attack, and certainly on him rests the responsibility for the direction and nature of the attack, once the scrum-half has managed to get the ball away. Right at the start let it be remembered that a fly-half has to depend on a quick heel, and a long accurate pass before he can hope to achieve anything in the nature of an opening, and if such a heel and pass are forthcoming there are five or six different manoeuvres which he can attempt.' Individual scrum-halves and outside-halves have been successful yet, basically, 'pairs' of halves have proved much more so, and the hundred years are coloured by such combinations.

The present Welsh halves, Terry Holmes and Gareth Davies, are a club pair and enjoy the advantage of playing together regularly as have done many Welsh pairs before them. Gareth Edwards and Phil Bennett were a highly successful pair of match-winners although from rival clubs, having followed Edwards and Barry John, a club pair of singular quality. Before them were the popular Clive Rowlands and David Watkins, and they followed several pairs in which Cliff Morgan was the outside-half, but was happier with W. R. Willis than anyone else. Willis had developed with W. B. Cleaver as his outside-half, who had in turn, like Glyn Davies, blossomed behind the immaculate Haydn Tanner.

Before World War II, Haydn Tanner and W. T. H. Davies were in charge and before them, Cliff Jones and Haydn Tanner. Of the nine pairs mentioned in this forty-five year period (1935–80), five were in harness for their clubs, four of them for Cardiff, and this highlights the effectiveness of the pairs who know each other well enough to play by habit. The James brothers did so in the nineteenth century as did Lou Phillips and Llewellyn Lloyd, and then Jones and Owen, Bush and David, Bush and Vile, Trew and Owen before World War I.

The long run of success enjoyed by Wales in the 1969–79 period can be attributed to the fact that Wales was entirely happy at half-back with first the expert and sophisticated John–Edwards combination followed by the shrewd, high-scoring, tactically dominating pair of Bennett and Edwards. As their forwards supplied enough good ball, they were always able to impose their will upon the opposition. They emphasised the necessity of control and though the contribution by Wales has been considerable to other positions like fullback, centre and wing (the greatest of Welsh rugbymen, A. J. Gould, was a centre), the Principality will be remembered most, at least out of scrum, for its brilliant half-backs and especially those working in close harmony and harness. The darting individualism of Percy Bush and Cliff Morgan compares favourably with the cool, calculating, almost lazy shrewdness of Barry John, and the sudden, darting elusiveness and superb kicking of Phil Bennett. John possessed a gentle side-step and swerve that was barely discernible but as effective as the sudden electric movement of Bennett, and opponents found them equally difficult to contain!

Yet these two individualistic players who subjected their many talents to the cause of their side, were ever ready to praise the manner in which Gareth Edwards made life so much easier for them. He was an individual player, strong and decisive, and would not provide a service that left his outside-half in difficulty while he was opportunist enough to employ his own attacking skills and deceive the opposition. In scoring twenty tries for

Opposite: Composite block of leading outside-halves. *Top row:* Percy Bush, W. J. Trew, Windsor Lewis, Cliff Jones. *Middle row:* W. T. H. Davies, W. B. Cleaver, Glyn Davies, Cliff Morgan. *Bottom row:* David Watkins, Barry John, Phil Bennett, W. G. Davies.

Welsh XV v England at Cardiff in 1959. *Standing:* L. Griffin (touch judge), R. Prosser, D. Main, J. W. Faull, R. H. Williams, I. Ford, J. Leleu, J. Collins, H. J. Davies, R. C. Williams (referee). *Seated:* M. J. Price, T. J. Davies, B. V. Meredith, R. C. C. Thomas (capt.), L. Williams, C. Ashton, D. I. Bebb. (Wales won 5–0 and eight players became 1959 Lions.)

Wales in fifty-three appearances, a record for an international inside-half, Edwards revealed his awareness of the situation near to the set pieces, rucks and mauls as well as the wide open spaces. In scoring his tries against Scotland at Cardiff in 1972 and for the Barbarians against New Zealand in 1973, he was able to show his appreciation of the attacking game as a whole.

When Bennett and Edwards retired from international rugby in 1978 Welshmen believed they would not be replaced easily. However, in one season two able replacements stepped into the national XV and Wales won the Triple Crown and Championship, thus suggesting that Merlin must have waved his magic wand. If such a production line of fine players continues then Wales need not worry unduly about the next hundred years!

Continuing the story of international Championships, Wales defeated England in the mud at Cardiff in 1959 but lost away to Scotland and France although they just beat Ireland (8–6) at Cardiff. R. C. C. Thomas captained Wales and was in line for the Lions captaincy but was passed over although nine of his colleagues made the tour to New Zealand and Australia with a talented team that needed only the control and direction of a coach to have won the series it so elegantly deserved.

R. H. Williams led Wales in his last international appearance against England at Twickenham in 1960 to end a career of twenty-three caps and two Lions tours. Suffering from a heavy cold he did not play as well as expected but his seven-season career in the national side was highlighted by consistency, skill, physical hardness and a love of the game. In an age before organised coaching he did much to bring cohesion to Welsh and Lions forward play and few visiting lock forwards have been more admired and praised by discerning New Zealanders who believe they know the qualities of real forward play.

If the 1950s had produced much success for Wales and attractive players who enhanced Lions sides, the 1960s included years of disappointment, a lack of unified approach, a vision of truth, and success by the end of the decade, despite a rude awakening in a first visit to New Zealand. So much was experienced and learned in the 1960s that the 1970s were entered with dignity, power, skill and the promise of continued success, such as was thought possible by John Gwilliam as far back as 1949.

Terry Davies – brilliant fullback of the 1950s.

The ebullient French with their highly successful combined fast-moving forward play, plus skilful handling and support work behind, over-played Wales until 1962 when a Welsh pack rose to the occasion and seven of the victorious eight made the Lions team for South Africa. Yet in December 1960, Wales played a match against South Africa, more remembered for the weather than the result. It had rained in 1912 and 1931 when the Springboks challenge was faced but, in 1960, the ground was ankle deep in water at Cardiff and the night after the game saw the River Taff overflow and flood the Arms Park with three feet of water.

Playing into the wind and rain in the first half and changing ends only three points in arrears through a penalty goal by Keith Oxlee, Wales appeared to have the winning of the match, and a first victory over South Africa, well in hand. Unfortunately, the first half had taken its toll of the Welsh pack and the Springboks, suitably inspired by number eight forward, D. J. Hopwood, just held out.

The twenty-one match career of the tall, handsome Llanelli fullback, T. J. Davies, ended with the French match of 1961 and few players, before or after in his position, combined all the qualities of defensive play better and more efficiently. During the 1960–61 tour his crushing tackle on Springboks centre, François Roux, at Stradey Park, remains one of the great ones, even more 'curtailing' than that of Haydn Mainwaring's dramatic charge upon Springboks captain, Avril Malan, in the Barbarians match at Cardiff. Mainwaring's bull-like charge, worthy of the hottest Corridor, saved a try but Davies's perfectly legal tackle on Roux stopped him in concertina fashion and appeared to repay many of the fierce tackles made upon British players by the fiery little Springbok!

The Welshmen forming the hard core of the 1962 Lions pack were deserving of a better fate in South Africa, and not to be awarded their well conceived 'push-over' try was the greatest injustice committed against a British team abroad, even more so than the disallowed last-minute try by W. R. Evans in Dunedin in 1959 in the controversial 18–17 match. Both incidents remain as scars on the hearts of Welshmen even before the days of instant TV recording. Many may have forgotten that it was an outbreak of smallpox in the Rhondda Valley that postponed the Ireland v Wales match of March 1962 until November, and such was the game's ordinary quality that it has been remembered as the 'hang-over' match that mercifully ended in a 3–3 draw.

B. V. Meredith, the world's outstanding hooker of 1955–62, played with distinction for Newport, Wales, Barbarians and British Isles.

This match also marked the end of another outstanding player's remarkable career as B. V. Meredith stepped down after thirty-four appearances and three Lions tours; a quick-striking, accurate and legal hooker, who was as busy about the field as any scrum-half. A fine handler of the ball and support player and a guardian of the blindside at lineout, maul and ruck. A most able performer of quality with a modesty that matched his rare skills and gentle humour. No player who knew him, travelled with him or played with or against him, ever uttered a criticism of him. Newport can feel proud of a player who served them as skilfully and faithfully as Arthur Gould, Ken Jones and the other great ones of Rodney Parade.

The year 1963 launched new men and new tactics, and the next three seasons of mixed fortunes were dominated by a swash-buckling, pirate-like figure at scrum-half in D. C. T. Rowlands, then of Pontypool but previously of Llanelli and later of Swansea. Surprising even the most radical of critics, the selectors gambled heavily by making Rowlands captain against England in his first match, as partner to another new cap, David Watkins of Newport. They played fourteen times together in successive matches and ended with the Triple Crown although their first season together provided only one victory, and that over Scotland received scant praise. The other three matches were lost but Rowlands created enough controversy in his first international season to set him along the road of seventeen years of service to Welsh rugby and the Welsh Rugby Union.

David Watkins, the brilliant Newport, Wales and British Lions outside-half who enjoyed an equally successful career with the Rugby League.

The first match was lost to England on a frozen surface at Cardiff (13–6) and while Wales staggered along, England won their last Championship before suffering a decline over a long and tiresome period that was not good for British rugby. In 1963 Welshmen were equally despondent although the kicking of Rowlands, who was probably the best of the tactical punters under the old laws in the scrum-half position, brought the first victory at Murrayfield in ten years. He hugged the touch-line like a bow-legged grizzly bear and 111 lineouts were the result. Some called him a genius; others, including many Scots, said his tactics would bring an early demise to the game, and Rowlands, who removed his dentures to play, merely smiled, 'We had to win. We played to win!'

At outside-half, as if cocooned by the kicking of Rowlands, was a colourful and potential attacker of exciting quality in David Watkins and while New Zealand won again in December 1963 at Cardiff (6–0) by a dropped goal and a penalty to nil, it was a special occasion, at least for the visitors. It was their first official international match victory at the Arms Park and well-deserved as the Welsh forwards were no match for them, even if the back play of New Zealand disappointed and would have received no praise from those heroes of the past, Dave Gallaher and Mark Nicholls. The 1963–64 All Blacks, under their admirable and efficient captain and prop Wilson Whineray, lost only one match during their tour, to Newport at Rodney Parade, by a dropped goal to nil. They accepted this

The Welsh XV which lost 6–0 to New Zealand at Cardiff in December 1963. *Standing:* R. C. Williams (referee), L. J. Cunningham, B. E. Thomas, B. E. V. Price, A. I. E. Pask, K. D. Jones, N. R. Gale, S. Harris (touch judge). *Seated:* J. Uzzell, A. Thomas, D. C. T. Rowlands (capt.), D. J. Hayward, D. K. Jones. *In front:* D. I. E. Bebb, D. Watkins, D. R. R. Morgan, G. T. R. Hodgson.

defeat in good spirit, as modestly as the victory over Wales, and their behaviour on and off the field was a tribute to careful management and wise, understanding captaincy.

Wales drew at Twickenham 6–6 through two excellent tries by D. I. Bebb, a wing who quickly assumed the mantle of K. J. Jones in effectiveness and sportsmanship and defeated Scotland and Ireland, mainly through the attacking brilliance of David Watkins before sharing a draw at Cardiff with France 11–11. An unbeaten season; the first since 1952 and the smile of Rowlands grew larger bringing forth the comment, 'Wait until next season!' Yet before that next winter there was to be a summer of vital importance for the game in Wales, its players, its image, and its ability to match the glories of the past. It all happened at King's Park, in the heat of the Durban sun, where the least sporting members of the crowd made amusing remarks about the whiteness of Rowlands' legs as he kicked to touch.

Saturday, 23 May 1964 was a vital milestone in the hundred years of rugby endeavour as Wales suffered a humiliating defeat in Durban (24–3) after being level (3–3) at the interval. The International Board had amended the laws of the game at their March meeting concerning the scrummage, touch, off-side, penalty kick and conversion, and all were intended to make play more open and attractive. The main item was the new offside-line ten yards from the line of touch at a lineout but, after free scoring experimental matches in Wales, the Welsh team did not exploit them while on tour and kicked away much good possession, especially in

The first Welsh touring team to visit South Africa in May/June 1964. *Back standing:* D. K. Jones, D. J. Hayward, N. R. Gale, L. J. Cunningham, J. Isaacs, K. Bradshaw, H. J. Davies, S. J. Dawes. *Middle standing:* R. Waldron, S. J. Watkins, A. I. E. Pask, B. E. V. Price, B. E. Thomas, D. Williams, J. Mantle, G. Prothero, H. J. Morgan. *Seated:* D. I. Bebb, A. Lewis, M. Young, D. C. T. Rowlands (capt.), D. J. Phillips (manager), A. G. Thomas (assistant manager), D. Watkins, P. M. Rees, G. T. R. Hodgson.

the test match. One severe critic in South Africa declared that much of the play of the Welsh was not a good advertisement for British rugby. Four matches were played on tour with two wins and two defeats.

The test defeat impressed upon the minds of the management, David Phillips and Alun Thomas, as well as captain D. C. T. Rowlands, that under the new laws, Wales had been playing in 'blinkers' and the need for a thorough examination of the Welsh approach was necessary. Coaching at club and national level with something of a standardised pattern in the basic approach was required. An advisory committee sat for some time and produced a blueprint and although it was several years before this could be implemented it was the forerunner of the success enjoyed in the 1970s.

The 1965 season brought the Triple Crown back to Wales again after an interval of thirteen years following a spectacular match against Fiji at Cardiff in September 1964, notable for superb handling, brilliant running and three tries by Fijian prop, Walisoliso, as the tourists almost overtook the Welsh with a whirlwind finish. A total of thirteen tries were scored; seven by Wales and six by Fiji who played with fourteen men after ten minutes, in a match excellently refereed by Frenchman Bernard Marie before 50,000 spectators. Caps were not awarded and there were only two new players when Wales met England at Cardiff in January 1965 and soundly beat an England side whose basis was a combination of Oxford and Cambridge University players. The Welsh pack was in determined mood and controlled play through the Triple Crown triumph, employing the 'double banking' system most effectively at the lineout.

B. E. Thomas was replaced after the England match at lock and his successor W. J. Morris after the Scottish match so that K. A. Rowlands could play against Ireland and France. The Irish match at Cardiff was hard and fullback T. G. Price, in his first season, emerged as a match winner with eighteen points in the three matches before a brilliant French team demolished Wales. Trailing at one stage by 22–0, Wales fought back to 22–13 for a respectable final score and the match marked the end of Rowlands as an international captain and player, although he was to continue to make an important contribution to Welsh rugby and share in the success of the 1970s as a coach.

A. I. E. Pask, a tall rangy, loose-forward from Abertillery and a rugby back-row twin with H. J. Morgan, took over the captaincy in 1966 and although one match was lost as in 1965, this time to Ireland, the Championship was retained. England and Scotland were beaten but an over-confident Welsh side was defeated 9–6 in Dublin as the Irish rose to the occasion with traditional fire, disrupting the Welsh and taking swift advantage of mistakes. France was defeated at Cardiff (9–8) through a remarkable try scored by Newport wing, S. J. Watkins, ten minutes from the end, who ran seventy-five yards to score. The selectors nominated ten

Alun Pask scores a brilliant try against Fiji at the Cardiff Arms Park in September 1964. Wales won 28–22, but the Fijian tour heralded regular visits by developing countries to Wales.

forwards for this match and only named their pack some hours before the kick-off. After trailing 8–0 Wales fought back to win against a strong wind after the interval. The 1966 Lions side to Australia and New Zealand included eleven of the Welsh players appearing in the Championship and one uncapped player, W. D. Thomas of Llanelli. Pask was originally recommended for the captaincy, but the four Home Unions full Committee reversed the recommendation and brought M. J. Campbell-Lamerton into the party as leader.

At long last, after fifty-eight years of trying, Australia defeated Wales in November 1966 at Cardiff (14–11). The victory was deserved and notable for a splendid display at half-back by Phillip Hawthorne and Kenneth Catchpole, as well as for the last of twenty-seven appearances by H. J. Morgan, a superb flanker, and the first by three players who were to make an important contribution to Welsh rugby in the years ahead, T. G. R. Davies, B. John and W. D. Thomas, all three from West Wales. Thomas was already a Lion and the other two were to be honoured in 1968 and 1971.

In the 1967 Championship the first three matches, against Scotland, Ireland and France, were lost and depressingly so. T. G. Price made his last appearance, against France, before turning professional. David Watkins was the captain in this match in Paris and had a nineteen-year-old student with him at scrum-half, Gareth Owen Edwards of Cardiff College of Education, making the first of fifty-three consecutive appearances to launch a career and enjoy even greater success than that of Owen and Tanner.

Keith Jarrett of Newport and Monmouth School being carried from the field at the Cardiff Arms Park after his memorable debut against England in April 1967. He scored nineteen points playing at fullback to equal the individual Welsh record created in 1910 by Jack Bancroft.

It had been agreed by both countries to play the England match at Cardiff in April, and in good conditions a spectacular affair was provided with eight tries. Wales won 34–21 to provide a taste of what was to come in the years ahead and a schoolboy, the eighteen-year-old Keith Jarrett, captured the headlines by equalling the existing individual points-scoring record with nineteen. It remains 'Jarrett's match' and his first appearance at fullback, as he was a three-quarter by habit and later played in that position for Wales and the Lions.

In November 1967 New Zealand were met again at the Cardiff Arms Park and, in difficult weather conditions, Wales made it easy for the tourists through a series of unforced errors and the victory (13–6) enabled New Zealand to draw level with their great rivals at three matches apiece. Against the wind Wales were trailing 8–0 at the interval and never looked like winning. The side was not chosen particularly wisely and several changes were made before a drawn match at Twickenham (11–11). Only Scotland were defeated in the season (5–0) at Cardiff as Wales lost to Ireland and France, and the French celebrated at Cardiff by achieving the Grand Slam for the first time, thanks to the unusual match-winning ability of the Camberabero brothers who provided a lesson in shrewd half-back play that was not lost upon Barry John and Gareth Edwards, playing together for the fifth time. It was the last time for the Camberabero brothers to appear for France and in the years that followed John and Edwards took over the role of half-back leaders in Europe. The season had not proved a successful one but it was special in the hundred years in that it launched a coach for the national XV. Former forward, David Nash of

The Welsh XV against Scotland at the Cardiff Arms Park in February 1968. Wales won 5–0 and in this match Gareth Edwards became the youngest player ever to lead Wales at twenty years of age. *Standing:* S. J. Watkins, R. Jones, W. D. Thomas, W. D. Morris, A. Gray, M. Wiltshire, G. C. Lamb (referee). *Seated:* K. Jarrett, T. G. R. Davies, G. O. Edwards (capt.), D. J. Lloyd, B. John. *In front:* K. Jones, J. O'Shea, J. Young, D. Rees.

Ray Williams became the first WRU coach organiser in 1967 before he was appointed Centenary Officer in 1979. On the right he is seen demonstrating mini-rugby.

Ebbw Vale, was the man entrusted with the task and the first man outside the Union to be appointed a selector.

During the season, Gareth Edwards became the youngest man to lead Wales (against Scotland at Cardiff at the age of twenty years) while he dropped a goal against Ireland in Dublin that was allowed although it appeared to pass outside one of the uprights. Fortunately, one credited to C. M. H. Gibson was allowed after being touched in flight. In this match S. J. Dawes led Wales for the first time leaving Edwards to assume command again against France!

Prior to the Irish match, the General Committee of the Union held its famous meeting in the Royal Hibernian Hotel, Dublin to select the management of the Welsh side to visit Argentina in September 1968, and neither of the two officials nominated was a coach; an indication that the decision to use a national team coach had been reversed. The matter became a controversy and at the Union's Annual General Meeting strong words were spoken. Fortunately, D. C. T. Rowlands was elected to the executive as a vice-president and immediately appointed as coach to the touring team! Never again was there any controversy concerning this matter of team coach as long as he was a duly elected member of the executive. During the season Ray Williams was appointed coaching organiser to make it something of a special one, for although not successful in itself, this season saw the laying of a few important foundation stones for future success.

The team in Argentina was led by S. J. Dawes who, like Rowlands before him, was to enjoy a long career in the side, eventually becoming its captain and the leader of the 1971 Lions, and then succeeding Rowlands as national team coach and selector. Wales had to tour without eleven of its leading players who had spent the summer with the Lions in South Africa, and the final tally for the six-match tour was three won, one lost and two drawn. The unofficial test series produced a defeat (9–5) and a draw (9–9) and among the touring party were two young players destined to play a vital part in the success of the 1970s, J. P. R. Williams and Phil Bennett. The coach, D. C. T. Rowlands, forced to acquire the art the hard way, learned much and was able to face 1969 with an experienced side and an enthusiastic approach. All proved well and Wales remained unbeaten, taking the Triple Crown and the Championship and only missing the Grand Slam through a drawn match in Paris. The forwards were a forceful, intelligent unit and the backs try-scorers, providing enjoyment and great hopes for the future.

The *Playfair Rugby Annual* paid elegant tribute to Wales with its headline on the report of the 1969 Championship: 'Wales all the Way,' and the *Welsh Brewers Rugby Annual*, launched in 1970, carried the heading: 'Wonderful Wales'. Scotland were beaten at Murrayfield (17–3) and Ireland at Cardiff (24–11) in a match before the Prince of Wales. Like his great-uncle before him, the Duke of Windsor, who enjoyed his rugby visits to Wales when Prince, the young Prince Charles enjoys the relish of a hard, sporting encounter, and the Irish match was a mixture of stern forward play and swift-moving back play. At one stage following some provocation, the Welsh captain, experienced lock Brian Price, took a

Wales v Ireland at Cardiff, March 1969. A royal occasion with the Prince of Wales greeting both teams before the kick-off. Behind the Prince is Brian Price, the Welsh captain, who introduced the royal visitor to the WRU members.

Gwynne Walters who, at twenty-one years of age, became one of the youngest referees during the Century to have charge of first-class matches.

swing which connected with Noel Murphy's chin and after a moment's hesitation, Murphy went down. Referee McMahon of Scotland called Price to the touch-line and all wondered whether the captain was to receive his marching orders. It was, in fact, a warning and many have asked since, 'Was it due to the presence of the Prince or did the referee see the provocation?' He will not say and is not obliged to say but his warning cooled proceedings and the Prince proved a worthy talisman for his people, at least his rugby subjects!

The match in France provided an exciting draw in the hundredth post-war international match played by Wales. Gareth Edwards and Maurice Richards scored tries; Keith Jarrett converted one and just failed with a penalty attempt that would have achieved the Grand Slam. England were met again in April at Cardiff and Wales gave a superb display. This was easily their most convincing victory over England (30–3) since the first 'Golden Era' and was memorable for the four tries scored by Maurice Richards to equal the record held jointly by W. Llewellyn (1899) and R. A. Gibbs (1908). Llewellyn's tries were against England and like Richards, he was a son of the Rhondda Valley. Jarrett had his best season for Wales with a total of thirty-one points in the four Championship matches, a new record for an individual, later to be beaten by international rugby's most prolific points-scorer Phil Bennett.

At the end of the 1968–69 season, a notable referee, Gwynne Walters, retired from first-class rugby after officiating at twenty-one full international matches (a record he shares with Kevin Kelleher of Ireland) and seven inter-varsity matches. He was regarded as one of the best produced by Wales or indeed any country, and a friend of the players who sought to enjoy himself as much as they did. Since his retirement he has helped the game in the lower grades and as a Welsh Rugby Union assessor of referees.

After the success of the 1969 Championship, Wales flew out to New Zealand, confident they would do well despite the highly-demanding nature of an ill-chosen short tour. The European champions were to fall quickly and heavily, suffering their two biggest consecutive defeats, and continuing the harrowing saga of failure on tour, after 1964 and 1968. New Zealand, through a superb pack of forwards (probably the best of the post-war years) plus some lax refereeing and the outstanding goal-kicking of fullback W. F. McCormick, won the two tests easily (19–0 and 33–12). The Welsh returned downcast and unhappy and it would appear that since that tour, relationships between the two rival countries have not improved.

Handel Rogers was manager, Clive Rowlands coach and Brian Price the captain, and of the touring party, sixteen players were either British Lions or to become British Lions. Nine were to return to New Zealand in 1971 and share in the notable Lions triumph. On their way home from New Zealand, Wales played a first match in Australia, winning it at Sydney narrowly 19–16 and a first in Fiji, winning comfortably 31–11.

Despite the disappointment of the tour, Wales entered 1970 full of confidence. Scotland were defeated at Cardiff (18–9) and England at Twickenham (17–13) with Edwards as captain. Then came an upset in Dublin when the Irish went mad and outplayed and harassed the Welsh to defeat them 14–0. A selection error, playing a new cap out of position on the wing, contributed to the defeat but in the main it was due to the Welsh forwards being outplayed and the halves harassed. Edwards lost the captaincy; it went to Dawes for the French match at Cardiff that was won 11–6 for Wales to share the Championship with their Gallic rivals.

Before the start of the 1970 Championship season the last South African side to visit the British Isles, the Sixth Springboks, bravely carried out a tour under extreme duress like true sportsmen, on and off the field. Other sides would have returned home long before the end as a result of political demonstrations, smoke bombs, flares and other disturbing activities but their captain, Dawie de Villiers, the present South African Ambassador in London, refused to surrender and despite the turmoil, mainly off the field

Gareth Edwards, the Welsh captain, racing back in delight after scoring the equalising try against South Africa at Cardiff in January 1970. It was a draw (6–6) and the first occasion Wales avoided defeat by South Africa.

Carwyn James, coach to Llanelli and the British Lions teams which both defeated the All Blacks. He is now a TV commentator.

but sometimes on through non-participants, they engaged in some interesting and exciting matches.

That against Wales was played at Cardiff in January in the mud and it was the first occasion Wales avoided defeat by a Springboks side, as they shared a draw (6–6), scoring the equalising try in the very last minute of play through Gareth Edwards. Wales fielded three new caps and wondered when they would ever overcome the sturdy Springboks or indeed have the chance to play against them again, and it appeared almost inevitable that in Wales conditions would be rarely other than muddy and wet!

Of the later seasons in the Century, one believes that the 1971 Championship was enjoyed more than any other. Wales won the Grand Slam with four fine victories and scored seventy-three points against thirty-eight. It was the best season since 1952 and S. J. Dawes moved nearer to the image of J. A. Gwilliam as a successful captain. He was honoured with the captaincy of the 1971 Lions in New Zealand and led them to a first victory in a test series with the support of twelve of his Welsh team colleagues. Even if the 1974 side under W. J. McBride of Ireland was to achieve a slightly better record than that of 1971, by remaining unbeaten and also winning the test series, there is no doubt that these two teams were the greatest of Lions sides, providing an image of British rugby to the world that was admired and respected. The sides were truly representative of the British Isles but the strength, skill and application of their Welsh members proved decisive. The first half of the 1970s will be remembered as the Years of the Lions while the success of Wales continued until the end of the decade as the second 'Golden Era'.

England were beaten at Cardiff in 1971 (22–6), Scotland were defeated in a desperately exciting match at Murrayfield (19–18) due to a magnificent late conversion of a T. G. R. Davies try by John Taylor (classed by a saddened Scot as the greatest conversion since that of St Paul!), Ireland were beaten at Cardiff (23–9) and France only narrowly defeated in a tremendous match in Paris (9–5). It was the French victory that clinched the Championship and the Grand Slam, and the first win in Paris since 1957.

The Welsh side was J. P. R. Williams; T. G. R. Davies, S. J. Dawes (capt.), A. J. Lewis, J. C. Bevan; B. John, G. O. Edwards; D. Williams, J. Young, D. B. Llewellyn, M. G. Roberts, W. D. Thomas, W. D. Morris, T. M. Davies and J. Taylor. Denzil Williams became the most-capped forward during the season with thirty-six appearances, later overtaken by T. M. Davies with thirty-eight before he was forced to retire through illness in 1976. When the members of this side decided to retire, and M. G. Roberts was recalled for the England match in 1979, they had made 417 appearances between them.

It was this season more than any other that finally convinced the other Championship countries of the basic need of the squad system in the preparation of national teams and while Clive Rowlands did a noble job with the Welsh team, Carwyn James was equally successful with the Lions side in New Zealand. Their methods were strongly contrasted for, whereas the wise former warrior of good times and bad, Rowlands, with his shrewd knowledge of Championship rugby, appealed successfully to the hearts of players and pride in their country, James was more sophisticated in his approach and appealed to the minds of his players. They both enjoyed remarkable success and set the pattern for modern team coaching; suggesting that any one able to combine the two approaches would be a super coach!

The Welsh Union and its clubs rejected James when he attempted to win a seat on the executive while Rowlands continued to coach the Welsh squad successfully before handing over to S. J. Dawes, who had developed under both coaches at home and abroad. James eventually turned to the media and then to coaching in Italy while Rowlands stood down as a selector at the end of the 1979 season, after sixteen years of genuine effort with Welsh teams who dubbed him 'Top Cat' for his emotional and talkative approach.

John Lloyd, the successful captain of Wales in 1972, leads his team out at Twickenham and on to victory over England (12–3). Now the coach to the national team, he appeared twenty-three times for Wales and captained Bridgend in six seasons as an outstanding prop.

The 1972 season was not wholly satisfactory, since Scotland and Wales did not play Ireland, and Wales playing three and winning them under the leadership of John Lloyd, the sturdy Bridgend prop, headed the Championship. Ireland played two matches without defeat and although Wales were unofficial champions, Ireland believed they could have won the Triple Crown and Grand Slam after beating France and England away from home. It could well have happened and the meeting of Ireland and Wales in Dublin for the Crown would have proved a tremendous affair. The decision not to visit Dublin was taken by Scotland and Wales because of the difficulties in Northern Ireland.

England were beaten at Twickenham (12–3), Scotland at Cardiff (35–12) and France at Cardiff (20–6). S. J. Dawes had retired from international rugby at the end of the Lions tour with twenty-two caps to his credit and Barry John followed him at the end of 1972 with many records to his credit in twenty-five appearances. An astute, leisurely player, his pace and guile were deceptive and his kicking, whether punting, placing or dropping, was immaculately accurate and without fuss. His approach always appeared to be in the minor key yet he was able to dominate tactically and lead his backs and forwards alike in the manner of an unobtrusive master conductor.

Many thought he would be easy to mark; but New Zealand found how difficult it was. He always enjoyed playing for club or country. To him rugby was a game and while it may have laid the foundation of a successful second career upon retirement, he never once besmirched the game he loved. By May 1972 he had scored ninety points for Wales to take the lead from Jack Bancroft. In 1972 he scored thirty-five points in the three matches to create a new individual record as was the case of his eight dropped goals, although many of his records were overtaken later by Phil Bennett. Edwards and John were in harness on twenty-three occasions.

The brilliant pair, Gareth Edwards and Barry John (10), in action against France in Paris in 1971 with their captain, John Dawes, moving up in support.

This remained a record until Edwards and Bennett just moved ahead in 1978 while the half-back control of the 1971 Lions was assumed by John and Edwards, in 1974 Bennett and Edwards were able to match it. John rightfully takes his place as one of the six leading Welsh outside-halves of the 100 years. Edwards in 1972 scored his best try for Wales, against Scotland at Cardiff.

Following a run of eight matches without defeat, Wales found the 1972–73 season a comparatively unhappy one and their disappointment was highlighted by an unsatisfactory defeat by a New Zealand touring side that fell well short of its country's finest traditions. Wales believed themselves to be a better side, and not unreasonably so, in losing narrowly (19–16). The All Blacks approach on and off the field would have sent a shudder down the broad back of Dave Gallaher and even a fine victory by Llanelli and an even better one by the Barbarians did not erase completely the Welsh disappointment. Llanelli enjoyed a special season, defeating New Zealand 9–3 and winning the Welsh Rugby Union Cup while the Barbarians match against New Zealand was the outstanding occasion of the season and, possibly, the decade. The quality of the play from both sides was of the highest order and the excitement often breathtaking, and when the Barbarians left the field as winners (23–11), everyone present and the millions watching on TV must have felt that rugby football, in all its natural glory, had carried the day.

Wales defeated England at Cardiff (25–9), lost narrowly but deservedly at Murrayfield (10–9), defeated Ireland at Cardiff (16–12) and then lost to France in Paris (12–3) without a try being scored. Disappointing, yet a timely reminder that any side, however great, is only as good as its last match and that players of world class face a constant challenge. At the end of the season, a lineout expert, W. D. Thomas of Llanelli in the mould of Brian Price, Roy John and the like, retired after twenty-four appearances and three Lions tours, and another splendid team-man, centre Arthur Lewis of Ebbw Vale, stood down after eleven appearances. Wales faced 1974 uncertainly and the doubts were realised as there was one victory, one defeat and two drawn matches.

It was as if the well-oiled machine required recharging to prepare itself for the years ahead. Both players and selectors were having a breather before launching themselves into 1975 and eventually the unprecedented run of four successive Triple Crowns between 1976–79. Such a feat was not thought possible at the start of the 1975 season but it happened and the selectors opened a fresh page to ensure that the 100 years ended on a high note. Only Scotland was beaten in 1974 but England won again after eleven years of waiting.

In January 1975 Wales set off for Paris with six new caps, not expecting to achieve a convincing victory (25–10) but rather to put on a good performance after sadly losing an unofficial match (12–3) against New Zealand in November at Cardiff. Wales played poorly and New Zealand, without being brilliant, well deserved their victory. Bennett failed with five attempts out of six and it was again the strong play of the New Zealand pack that carried the day. The disappointment of this display brought forth the six new caps against France and several of them, R. Gravell, S. P. Fenwick, A. G. Faulkner and G. Price, were to share in the triumphs of the years ahead.

Bennett was replaced by J. D. Bevan at outside-half and in the next match England were comfortably defeated at Cardiff (20–4) only for

The Welsh touring team to Japan in September 1975. *Back row:* A. G. Faulkner, G. Price, R. Blyth, D. L. Quinnell, A. J. Martin, B. Clegg, G. A. D. Wheel, R. W. R. Gravell, R. Thomas. *Middle row:* P. Bennett, C. Rees, S. P. Fenwick, T. P. Evans, D. B. Llewellyn, G. Jenkins, R. T. Bergiers, T. J. Cobner, J. Bevan, R. C. Shell. *In front:* R. W. Windsor, J. J. Williams, G. O. Edwards, L. M. Spence (manager), T. M. Davies (capt.), S. J. Dawes (coach), T. G. R. Davies, J. P. R. Williams, G. Lewis (physiotherapist).

Princess Chichibu, patron of the Japanese Rugby Union, being introduced to Phil Bennett (who scored 34 points in the match) by the Welsh captain Mervyn Davies before the start of the 1975 Second Test at Tokyo. Standing between them is Ray Gravell, the Welsh centre.

Opposite:
Phil Bennett, the brilliant Llanelli, Wales, Barbarians and British Lions outside-half who made twenty-nine appearances for Wales, led his country in 1977 and 1978 and the British Lions in 1977 as well as Llanelli in six seasons. He is seen here bursting away against France in Paris, 1977.

Wales to come unstuck, partly through injuries behind, at Murrayfield to lose (12–10) and miss the Crown. Ireland were beaten handsomely at Cardiff (32–4) with Wales playing extremely well, and it was this side with a change here and there that set its hands upon the Crown in the next four years. It was the first occasion during the twentieth century and certainly since the advent of specialisation at forward, for a club front row to play for Wales in Faulkner, Windsor and Price of Pontypool. They appeared together on seventeen occasions before injury in 1979 took out Faulkner and Windsor against England.

Mervyn Davies, now at his best as a mature number eight, immensely talented and efficient, directed operations as captain with G. O. Edwards and Phil Bennett (returned to the outside-half position) revealing the complete understanding developed in South Africa during the invincible 1974 Lions tour. A short and enjoyable goodwill tour of Japan in the autumn, admirably led and producing sparkling play, set up the Welsh side for a year of triumph in 1976 when the Triple Crown and Grand Slam were confidently won in a record-breaking Championship. For the first time since 1908–9, five matches were won in a season as the touring Australian side lost at Cardiff (28–3) in an enjoyable pipe-opener for the Championship during which the support from followers reached a new high in enthusiasm.

England were defeated at Twickenham (21–0), Scotland at Cardiff (28–6), Ireland in Dublin (34–9) and France at Cardiff (19–13), and it was

the Irish victory that highlighted this remarkable side and sadly, near the end of the season, after the Grand Slam victory had been celebrated, the much-admired leader, Mervyn Davies, suffered a serious illness while playing for his club, Swansea, in a Welsh Rugby Union Cup semi-final at the Arms Park that ended a magnificent career in the game, and almost his young life. From a tall, spindly and almost inexperienced number eight, having recently joined the London Welsh Club in 1968, he developed at such a pace as to become the world's number one player in his position within a few years and one of the best in the position by 1974. He appeared to play by instinct, with a sense of position that was uncanny, and his long easy, effortless stride belied a swiftness that always got him to the ball and the breakdown. In his very last match, against France, in a tremendously exciting Championship decider, he played through it with an incapacitating leg injury that revealed the courage in his heart and hardness in his frame. Welshmen, ever given to nicknames for their sporting heroes, christened him 'Merv the Swerve' and his shock of dark curly hair, wide white headband and generous moustache were the trade marks of rugby greatness.

With him in the successful Welsh side were many outstanding players. Phil Bennett, as his able lieutenant, called the moves while Gareth Edwards adjusted his approach to the state of each match, racing towards a record number of caps. J. P. R. Williams, as strong as ever at fullback, indulged in his crashing forays up-field, and the darting deftness of Gerald Davies and J. J. Williams on the wings saw to it that none of the trojan work of the ball-winning forwards and strong running centres was wasted. Records were created as Bennett overhauled Barry John's ninety points individual record with thirty-eight in the season and 117 for his career in twenty-one matches. Edwards became the top try-scorer with eighteen, passing R. A. Gibbs, K. J. Jones, and J. L. Williams, and Mervyn Davies became the most-capped forward, a record he still retains, and likewise J. P. R. Williams passed the seventy-five-year-old record of the illustrious W. J. Bancroft. For the side itself, the 102 points registered became the highest in a full Championship season; a far cry from the dark days of the 1920s!

Welshmen could hardly have expected anything better than that achieved in 1976 and they were grateful when the national team retained the Triple Crown after conceding the Grand Slam to France under the leadership of Phil Bennett in 1977. Yet before the Championship season started Wales had been frightened by the touring Argentinian side, although a victory was gained (20–19) in the final minutes of play with a penalty by Bennett after a head-high tackle on J. P. R. Williams. It was an exceedingly close-run thing and Wales was more than fortunate to survive, as on the day the Argentinians looked an extremely good side. It was only the domestic troubles on their return home which robbed them of a potential that was considerable.

It was an unusual season in that Bennett succeeded to the captaincy after

The Welsh XV of 1976 which won the Grand Slam led by Mervyn Davies. *Standing:* G. Price, T. P. Evans, A. J. Martin, G. A. D. Wheel, A. G. Faulkner, T. J. Cobner, S. P. Fenwick. *Seated:* J. J. Williams, J. P. R. Williams, P. Bennett, T. M. Davies (capt.), G. O. Edwards, T. G. R. Davies, R. W. Windsor, R. W. Gravell.

being an able lieutenant to Mervyn Davies and he did the job well. Geoffrey Wheel and Willie Duggan became the first players in the history of the Championship to be sent from the field, by referee Norman Sanson of Scotland; France defeated Wales in Paris 16–9 and Wheel's absence was one of the reasons. At this stage in the Century, each of the two major countries in the Championship, France and Wales, appeared to win the Grand Slam on the occasions they were at home against the other.

Ireland were beaten 25–9 at Cardiff and poor refereeing in the first twenty-five minutes allowed the lineout play to deteriorate and produce the first sendings-off in Championship history. Though deserved at the time, they could have been avoided. After the defeat in Paris, Wheel returned and England were beaten at Cardiff in an exciting match (14–9) before the best match of the season at Murrayfield saw Wales gain an exciting late victory (18–9). A final Bennett try started by Fenwick and carried on by Gerald Davies and D. H. Burcher after J. P. R. Williams had fed back from a ruck in the Welsh twenty-five highlighted the season and the vast crowd at Murrayfield stood to cheer this effort. Wales left the field having won the Triple Crown in successive years for the first time since 1908–9.

At the end of the season, Bennett was chosen as the captain of the Lions side to tour New Zealand and had seventeen Welshmen with him, including three replacements, J. Squire, A. G. Faulkner and A. Lewis. Six matches were lost including three of the four tests in a dismal, wet and unhappy winter. Six leading British players were not available and their

The Welsh XV of 1978 which won the Grand Slam led by Phil Bennett. *Standing:* M. Watkins (R), J. R. West (referee), G. Price, J. Squire, D. L. Quinnell, A. J. Martin, G. A. D. Wheel, A. G. Faulkner, T. J. Cobner, J. Richardson (R), D. B. Williams (R), A. Bevan (touch judge). *Seated:* G. Evans (R), R. W. Gravell, T. G. R. Davies, J. P. R. Williams, P. Bennett (capt.), G. O. Edwards, R. W. Windsor, J. J. Williams, S. P. Fenwick.

absence tipped the balance in favour of New Zealand.

On to the 1978 Championship season with the firm suggestion that after a Lions tour, in which almost all the team was engaged, Wales would not do well in the Championship. Once again the Welsh proved that their resilience was quite remarkable with another Grand Slam and a third consecutive Triple Crown to create further records. Only sixteen players were employed and it would have been the same XV throughout the Championship except that T. G. R. Davies was forced to withdraw from the last match, the decider against France. S. J. Dawes as coach, much criticised after the Lions tour of 1977, regained his status in this season and Bennett silenced his critics by excellent leadership and a superb display in the final match.

England were only narrowly beaten at Twickenham (9–6) through the marginally superior place-kicking of Bennett with three penalties to two by Hignell of England. Scotland were beaten at Cardiff (22–14) in the coldest day of the season which ended in a blizzard blanketing South Wales and pinning down the Welsh XV at their Cardiff hotel for the weekend. Ireland were overcome (20–16) in a hard and often bitter match but only in the closing stages, before France were defeated (16–7) in the final match at Cardiff.

It was a difficult season for Wales but the tenacity, team spirit and character plus experience, as characterised England in the early 1920s, saw the side through to the end. England wasted chances; Ireland took it all too seriously and appeared over-motivated while France failed with ample opportunities to kick goals and stay in the hunt. Many criticised Wales in this season but as the results revealed, they won their matches and took the chances that came to hands and feet. Bennett, with twenty-five points, took his personal tally for Wales to 166 and with his Lions test match points added to this total, claimed the world's leadership with 212, five points ahead of New Zealand's powerful fullback and place-kicker, D. B. Clarke.

For Bennett in particular, and all other fifteen Welsh players, it was a happy season as the second 'Golden Era' was firmly established and one sensed that even the most fanatical of supporters was satisfied. At the time it was believed that such good fortune and fine play could not continue and that the amazing run of success at Cardiff must surely end!

Before the 1978–79 season started rumour suggested that the big names would stand down and retire from the alleged 'pressures' of Triple Crown competition. Gareth Edwards left first, after completing his life story in book form, followed by Gerald Davies, also to write a book, and they were followed by Phil Bennett and Terry Cobner who while not writing books, remained eligible to play and lead their respective clubs, Llanelli and Pontypool. The Newport utility three-quarter, G. L. Evans, was prevented from playing through injury and so Wales set off without five of the sixteen who had proved so successful in 1978.

Hopes were not high when J. P. R. Williams took over the leadership with D. L. Quinnell as pack-leader, hoping to surprise a New Zealand side, whose record on tour flattered. Against Wales they won in the closing minutes by a 'con trick' that left most Welshmen disgusted when able to

Gareth Edwards scoring one of his 'special' tries against Scotland at Cardiff in 1978. Edwards scored twenty tries in fifty-three matches for Wales, a record shared with T. G. R. Davies.

The Welsh XV which won a fourth successive Triple Crown in 1979 under the leadership of J. P. R. Williams. *Standing:* S. Lane (R), P. Morgan (R), G. Price, J. Richardson, J. Squire, A. J. Martin, M. G. Roberts, A. Phillips, D. Richards, W. James (R), J. Dixon (R). *Seated:* P. Ringer, E. H. Rees, J. J. Williams, J. P. R. Williams (capt.), D. L. Quinnell, S. P. Fenwick, T. D. Holmes, W. G. Davies. *In front:* D. B. Williams (R), C. Griffiths (R).

appreciate its full significance after watching the replay on TV. Two New Zealand players 'fell out' of a lineout and referee Quittenton of England awarded a penalty against Wales for barging by Wheel, for McKechnie to kick the winning goal at 13–12. Never did a match against a touring side have such a controversial and unsatisfactory ending and New Zealand left the country as a team far less popular in Wales than when it arrived. It was tragic for both countries, especially as New Zealand had been invited as the guest of honour for the Welsh Centenary season of 1980–81.

Despite the unfortunate and unpleasant defeat, the Welsh selectors kept faith with their new-look side and moved into the Championship season, hoping that the impossible would be achieved. The loss of the great players had to be made good quickly or there would follow a period of possible decline and, fortunately, Cardiff produced out of the hat, two halves, one east and one west, in Terry Holmes and Gareth Davies. By the end of the season they had made good, unbelievably so, the loss of Edwards and Bennett. It surprised their followers as much as it did their opponents and the purpose and spirit of the Welsh team in retaining the Triple Crown for a record-breaking fourth successive time, was due more to the tour of Australia in the summer of 1978 than anything else.

Invited to tour Australia to help fill the depleted coffers of the Australian Rugby Union, the Welsh touring team was subjected to exceedingly poor refereeing and undisciplined play that disturbed them and their rhythm while losing the two test matches. Injuries were so numerous that in the Second Test, fullback J. P. R. Williams was forced to play as a flank forward and Gerald Davies was honoured with the captaincy in his last and forty-sixth international match. Australia, hiding their own blemishes and unhappy approach, blasted the Welsh who returned home disillusioned but equally determined. Young players had been blooded and G. Davies and T. Holmes emerged, despite the presence of D. B. Williams at scrum-half, as the natural successors to Edwards and Bennett, two outstanding halves who had broken so many records together.

Scotland were beaten at Murrayfield (19–13) but it was a close call until a decisive try scored by Terry Holmes in the wake of his forwards late in the match. Ireland were beaten at Cardiff (24–21) and this was an even closer call, and when Wales were beaten in Paris by France (14–13), few believed that the Triple Crown would be retained after England had beaten France at Twickenham. Yet the Welsh team, following several stern encounters which had burnished their steel in cauldron-like fashion, had reserved their best for the final encounter against England at Cardiff.

Before the match J. P. R. Williams was involved in a controversial episode that threatened his amateur status until the Welsh Rugby Union cleared him after writing a book for which he was not to receive the royalties. Again he was to suffer a nasty leg injury and leave the field twenty minutes from the end of his last international appearance. At that stage Wales led by 7–3 and then ran riot with four more tries to win 27–3, retain the Championship and Triple Crown, and set foot into the 1980s full of spirit.

Wales acclaimed Terry Holmes as player of the year and J. P. R. Williams was given a remarkable and emotional send-off at the Arms Park when he appeared to acknowledge the chant of the crowd. The great names had departed the scene after adorning it in splendour and with success. J. P. R. Williams, T. G. R. Davies, P. Bennett, G. O. Edwards, and T. J. Cobner had gone, revered and remembered, for the new men to take over readily and confidently and prepare for the Centenary Year and the next decade.

Terry Holmes, a natural successor to Gareth Edwards at inside-half, in the Welsh XV, seen here against England at Cardiff in 1979.

4 THE PLAYERS

PART 1: 1880–1914

An English friend, A. A. Thomson, once told me that he did not know which quality he admired most in Welsh players, their 'hwyl' or their guile, and he described 'hwyl' as a light that 'shines inside a Welshman, a power that works outward from his bones', and many other Englishmen believe this 'hwyl' to be based on a kind of national fervour that manifests itself in spiritual exaltation. It is something unique in rugby and special only to Welshmen. To combat it a New Zealand coach can tell his team before it takes the field at the Arms Park, as its members sit nervously in the dressing room trying to shut their ears to the noise of the traditional hymn-singing in the minor key, that it is like a New Zealand Army Division cut off by the Germans in Italy in World War II, pleading with the light of battle in his eyes, 'We must fight our way out!'

The Scots cannot call upon the spirit of Bannockburn when they play Wales because they are brother Celts 'once persecuted by the English', while the Irish with all their fire and brimstone believe the Welsh suffered as much at the hands of Cromwell as they did. The English have everyone against them and can encourage their players at the Arms Park by saying, 'We always used to beat the Welsh at everything, why not today?' Nothing can subdue 'hwyl' in its many forms!

Some Welsh players have been blessed with more 'hwyl' than guile and this was true of many a hard-working forward, while some players had more guile than 'hwyl' but those who possessed the qualities in equal measures were the great ones, whether they revealed the sang-froid of Trew and Gwilliam, the dapper confidence of Bancroft, the super competitiveness of J. P. R. Williams, the worried look of Phil Bennett or the smile of Gareth Edwards. Welsh football has capped almost 800 players and of these nearly sixty have made twenty or more appearances. Thus while the post-war years have staged many more matches per year than the period prior to World War I, the more modern of players have had the opportunity to achieve a greater number of caps and points. Yet there have been many outstanding players who made less than twenty appearances, for various reasons, and some who fell foul, unconsciously, of uncertain selectors!

Those best remembered had something special about them in skill,

The great man, A. J. Gould, and his Newport team of the 1890s. *Standing back:* J. Bowley, T. Newcombe, T. Pook, W. Groves, T. C. Graham. *Standing middle:* T. England, H. T. Day, W. G. James, C. J. Thomas, W. H. Watts, F. C. Parfitt. *Seated:* F. H. Dauncey, A. W. Boucher, A. J. Gould (capt.), J. Hannan, H. Packer. *In front:* M. Hannan, H. P. Phillips. (Eleven of these players won Welsh caps.)

charm, robustness, confidence, aggression; or the charisma of true greatness. It was much harder for the earlier players to impress their personalities upon the sporting public as a whole – there was no radio or TV to constantly remind the memory through ears and eyes. In the early days players had to be seen in the flesh to be believed! This was why small boys used to touch the jerseys of the great players as they took the field in club and representative matches. Nowadays, the great ones can look into the living rooms of followers and say 'Hello!' They are part of normal Welsh family life and everyone feels he knows them and even refers to them by their Christian names.

In the early days, to refer to a player by his Christian name was a sporting accolade beyond compare, and even more so if a 'nickname' was used like 'Monkey', 'Billy', 'Rusty', 'The Dancing Dicks', and so on. It was some years before the personality cult developed but it did so as players became more successful, more prominent and more revered by their clubs. In the formative days, Cardiff produced F. E. Hancock and Newport A. J. Gould, and they became legends in the game. One was an Englishman who saw the possibilities of a four three-quarter system and attempted to break down tradition and, the other, a Welshman of many talents from a gifted sporting family, who, though not amused by it at first, eventually saw the system become part of Welsh rugby heritage.

Hancock was one of many brothers who learned the game in their garden in Wiveliscombe, Somerset and developed his prowess with Cardiff. An outsider for some time, he became the first Englishman to lead the pre-eminent major Welsh club and an excellent job he made of it. His family of brewers were readily adopted as Welshmen, as their name accompanied many a glass of cheer down through the years!

Arthur 'Monkey' Gould is truly the King Arthur of Welsh rugby; the first of the great ones, and there have been none greater. Never having seen the great man play, one is at some disadvantage, and it has to be from his deeds and not his words that we recall him, but those who did see him, who knew him and admired him, make an assessment of greatness. To him must go the accolade as the most outstanding of all Welsh players.

In my lifetime, Gareth Edwards has proved himself the most complete all-round player but, through the hundred years, no man did more than Gould to shape the destiny of Wales in the game. All research lends itself to this salient belief that he was truly the 'King' and the player who sought and found the Holy Grail in the game. As the years passed by, great Knights joined him by deservedly winning a coveted place at the Round Table of honour and distinction. One believes that whatever Welsh XV was chosen, from all eras, one would be loth to omit the name of A. J. Gould, player extraordinary, captain, coach, referee, selector, administrator and International Board member. Such was his fame and standing that a reward for his achievements in the form of the deeds of a house subscribed by many admirers halted the game at international level!

There were splendid leaders to come and outstanding players but he led Wales more times than any other player and like Arthur, out of the darkness of defeat into the Camelot of victory and the Triple Crown. He was the first of the truly great ones; the boy who acquired his nickname because of his ability to climb trees and whose first match for Newport was at fullback, from where he set the pattern for modern attacking fullbacks by scoring two tries after running through the opposition of Weston. He played three seasons at fullback and won his first cap there for Wales. Gould could drop goals and place-kick but he was left-footed and when his opponents spotted this and covered him, he developed his right foot and soon kicked as well with either foot.

Townsend Collins (Dromio).

Townsend Collins of Newport, a writer of repute who knew Gould well, comments, 'Never did a rugby player work harder to improve his natural gifts and perfect his technical equipment'. One could say the same of Gareth Edwards who started for Wales with a comparatively poor pass and ended his fifty-three cap career with his long torpedo passes as the main weapon in his armoury. Gould changed himself from the individualist he had to be when he began his career in order to meet the needs of the game at the time, into a splendid combined player in the four three-quarter system later in his career. A handsome man, much loved, he played from 1882 until 1898 in first-class rugby, and his reputation never wavered. It was written of him in 1892: 'Gould is entirely devoid of objectional swagger.' How nice a compliment.

Gould played for several clubs because his profession as a public works contractor took him across the length and breadth of England, and while he entertained and gave the game a new dimension, his admiring sister, who I believe played hockey for Wales, kept a complete record of his career as he wore in turn the jerseys of Southampton Trojans, London Welsh, Richmond, Hampshire and Middlesex. He ran at a pace just short of even-time, and could play almost any game with ease. He never approached any match without assessing the strength of the opposition and the ability of his own side to counter it. The grace, versatility and physical prowess of the man, so much admired in print by Collins, made him the greatest of all; the man for all seasons, the man of the 100 years. When he died, an Arthur Gould Memorial Bed was endowed in the Royal Gwent Hospital at Newport and the brass plaque above it reads: 'To the memory of Arthur Gould, the greatest of rugby football players . . . this bed is dedicated by admirers in five continents.'

Horace S. Lyne (Newport).

In contrast, W. J. 'Billy' Bancroft was a dapper little man, confident and cheeky, with a brain as sharp as a knife, a rugby sense that was uncanny and ability beyond all that could be expected from a man of his size. He comes near to Gould as a folklore hero in Welsh rugby. Although there have been many outstanding players in the fullback position since his time there has never been one as spectacular as Bancroft, even allowing for the Lewis Jones counter-attack at Twickenham in 1950 and the many charges of J. P. R. Williams.

In a Welsh career embracing twelve seasons he was never out of the side. In the same number of seasons, Edwards won fifty-three caps, and so it is right to suggest that in modern times, Bancroft would have won fifty caps. Likewise, in the days of Bancroft, Edwards would have made thirty-three consecutive appearances. Bancroft did not have the chance to play against France or make any tours or, indeed, play against a touring side as none visited Wales during his career. From the time rugby was first played at St Helen's until his death in his eighties he was at the ground, first as a ball-boy, and grew into an institution. Bancroft became the greatest rugby player to wear the 'lilywhite' jersey of the Swansea club and first of the world's leading fullbacks.

R. T. Gabe paid remarkable tribute to Bancroft when he said:

'He seldom kicked immediately he caught the ball unless he was sorely pressed. Being very fast, he would run towards one touch-line with opposing forwards chasing him hotly. Then he would turn quickly and speed across to the other side before kicking to touch. He was 'hated' on the field by his opponents – and this was to his credit as well as a compliment to his technique – because his own side were having a welcome rest, while his pursuers were wasting their energies! When I played for Llanelli against him, I confess that I never caught him, for he was

Gwyn Nicholls (Cardiff).

always artful enough to kick at the critical moment, and a tackle became unnecessary.'

Bancroft was not a giant of a man, like Marsburg, Gamlin, Jenkins, Davies or Williams but a dapper little man, immaculately dressed and groomed; a Beau Brummell of rugby, as his trim moustache and well-brushed hair gave him the appearance of a dandy. Many an opponent, on sighting him for the first time, expected him to be 'easy' and were encouraged to have a 'go' at him but how wrong they were, for the first of the game's outstanding players in the fullback position had amazing speed, ability to dodge, sense of position, cradle-like hands and a long, accurate kick with either foot.

Bancroft was incredible and the lesson he left for all to digest was his unique ability to destroy an opposing pack of forwards. He was caught only once, by the famous pair of Irish forward brothers, the Ryans, at Cardiff when they threw him into the crowd after a 'sandwich' tackle that cracked a Bancroft rib, but he was back again in the next season, tormenting the very same brothers! The secret of his success was simple, 'I practised and practised; never less than a couple of hours a day. Place-kicking was essential as I was given all the kicks for Swansea and Wales. I just had to be accurate as there were fewer chances in my day for penalty goals than in modern times. In practice I would start kicking from one touch-line and move across slowly, kicking all the time, to the other touch-line and finish by kicking at goal from the corner flag.' He was never short of young ball boys to help him, as he wore a Welsh jersey with the name W. J. Bancroft on the back of it. He was the eldest of eleven children and his brother Jack received his first cap eight years after W. J. retired!

The next in the honours list should be either a pair of centres, maybe the best produced by Wales, or a full three-quarter line, also one of the best in the scarlet jersey. The centres, Erith Gwyn Nicholls and Rhys Thomas Gabe, and the two wings, William Llewellyn and Edward Morgan, have remained legendary heroes although their supreme moment of triumph was as far back as 1905. Better known as Gwyn Nicholls, Rusty Gabe, Willie Llewellyn and Dr Teddy Morgan, they were the ultimate in the four three-quarter system and Nicholls, having been taught by Arthur Gould, saw to it that these players enjoyed the game as much as he did in the achievement of technical perfection.

R. T. Gabe (Llanelli and Cardiff).

Nicholls was an Englishman, born at Westbury-on-Severn, who came to Wales as a young boy and became a successful Cardiff business man. Gabe was the son of a Llangennech publican who became a school master and taught mathematics, Llewellyn from Llwynypia in the Rhondda Valley became a chemist, and Teddy Morgan from Brecon became a medical practitioner. Gabe said of his fellow centre, 'Nicholls was my hero when I first played for Llanelli at the age of seventeen, and a few years later I was to join him in the Cardiff side. He told me then, "The opposition know me well and will be watching me, so take full advantage of it", and as I became more experienced we were both well marked! Yet he had one outstanding maxim, the importance of timely and accurate passing, and he was an absolute expert in this art, believing that a pass not accepted was purely the fault of the giver. I never saw Nicholls give a bad pass.'

If Gould was the W. G. Grace of Welsh rugby, then Nicholls was the J. B. Hobbs, and he was not called the 'Prince of Centres' by the rest of the world for nothing. Long will be the discussion as to who was the best centre or who formed the best pair for Wales; the Gould brothers, Nicholls and Gabe, Spiller and Dyke, Davey and Wooller, Matthews and Williams, or Dawes and Lewis. It is difficult to place them in order. Gould was the man who did most for Welsh rugby in its formative years while Nicholls may have been the purest of stylists and technicians in his position; possibly the most unobtrusive of them all, and yet a man who inspired through his sincerity, strict sense of fair play and sportsmanship, as well as his belief in team spirit and combined play rather than individualism. Nicholls was completely unselfish – the ideal team man.

Even if Nicholls had not been a truly great player he would have been remembered for his address to the Welsh team before the 1905 match against New Zealand. It did not have the passion of Clive Rowlands, the wit of Watcyn Thomas, the school speech day inclination of John Gwilliam or the appeal to the family of Delme Thomas for Llanelli against the 1972 All Blacks, but it contained the secret of success: 'We have already discussed tactics, so it remains only for me to appeal to you to be resolute in your tackling. You all know what they (All Blacks) are like if given any latitude. They throw the ball about and their system of intensive backing-up makes them very dangerous, so there must be no hair-combing, and every man with the ball must be put down, ball and all. You forwards already know what to do to get the loose head. Come on, let's get out, and show everyone we can win!'

Nicholls was right; it was the tackling that made victory certain for Wales after scoring their special try. Nicholls did a great deal of tackling himself and his friend and protégé, Rhys Gabe, made the all-important tackle on Deans. Yet Nicholls, for all the disappointment of the 1906 defeat by South Africa when he made his last appearance for Wales, much against his will, shared in the memorable triumph by Cardiff over the Springboks on New Year's Day 1907. The victory was important (17–0) and still one of the best achieved by the club over a touring team and both he and Gabe scored fine tries in the mud.

For Cardiff he scored 111 tries in thirteen seasons and on retirement enjoyed an off-the-field career of service to the game as did Gould. He refereed for a period then became a Cardiff committee man and a member of the Welsh Rugby Union from 1925 to 1931, often serving as a national selector. He died in 1939, much mourned by rugby men everywhere. The final accolade could not be awarded to his memory until after World War II when it was fitting that his co-centre and friend of so many years, Rhys Gabe, should open the Nicholls Memorial Gates at the Cardiff Arms Park. Every time a Welsh follower passes through the gates for any big match, his thoughts turn to the gentle genius, Erith Gwyn Nicholls, the Englishman who helped to make Wales great in the game.

Rhys Gabe played six seasons for Cardiff and, like Nicholls, twenty-four times for Wales. He was a close friend of Percy Bush and was better able to relate stories of the 'Golden Era' than any other player of the period. As one of my senior tutors in the game, he taught me much yet preferred always to talk of others in preference to himself. Strong, fast, with a powerful hand-off and an all-embracing tackle, he ran with his knees lifting high and was a most difficult player to stop. The lesson of how to pass the ball accurately, acquired from Nicholls, was never forgotten by Gabe, and while he was an intense competitor and believed that one played to win within the laws, he enjoyed relating the antics and tricks employed by Dickie Owen and Percy Bush, and often spoke of the tremendous rivalry between East and West in Welsh rugby. None better than he to feel and understand this, as he was born in the West and played most of his rugby in the East, launching one of the notable trends in Welsh rugby; the great trek of promising young players from the West to the Cardiff Club. This has not eased in modern times for Gareth Edwards, Barry John, Gareth Davies, T. G. R. Davies, D. K. Jones and C. H. Davies are some of the brilliant backs who learned the basic arts in the West and developed them in the East. Gabe was a capped player when he came to Cardiff and soon became an automatic choice for Wales, bursting through like a powerful cruiser cresting an Atlantic wave and, with Bush, Vile, Llewellyn and Morgan, achieved noble deeds with the 1904 Lions in Australia and New Zealand.

Teddy Morgan scored the try for Wales in 1905 against New Zealand playing outside Gabe on the left-wing, and Llewellyn was on the right-wing outside Nicholls. Morgan played sixteen times and after his playing days suffered a shooting accident and lost the sight of an eye but remained immensely popular, almost a folk hero, because of his try. In all he scored fourteen tries in sixteen matches and Llewellyn seventeen in twenty matches and these figures are indicative of the success of the four three-quarter system in the 'Golden Era', and how the purpose of the tactical play was to win the ball, work it as quickly and accurately as possible to the wings, providing them with enough room to get round their opposing wing and beat the fullback. Ken Jones in the late forties and fifties scored seventeen tries in forty-four matches and in the late 1960s and 1970s, T. G. R. Davies collected twenty in forty-six appearances. Did the later wings have fewer chances or had the field become more crowded with speedier defensive coverers?

The James brothers were a remarkable pair of half-backs who enjoyed an unusual career while playing for Swansea and other clubs as well as Wales with distinction. A contemporary writer said, 'The smart inter-passing and the complete understanding that existed between David and Evan James enabled them to do practically as they liked against all halves they met'. By 1890 they were outstanding and in 1891 they appeared for

The James brothers – Evan and David (Swansea).

Wales for the first time and the Revd F. P. Marshall recorded:

'They played in conjunction at half-back for the first time in an international match and are undoubtedly the finest pair of halves in Wales that play regularly together. Considering their size, they are recklessly daring in defensive tactics, tackling with great resolution and effect. David generally works the scrum, picking up smartly with low and rapid transfers to Evan, who handles brilliantly. Both dodge and feint cleverly. David, particularly, being very clever near the line. They are remarkably difficult to stop when clear of the forwards. They are skilful dribblers but rarely resort to kicking.'

Thus they were the originators of the inside and outside-half specialisation as, previously, halves generally fed the scrum in turn. Even Townsend Collins regarded them, David (5 ft 6 in.; 10 st) and Evan (5 ft 7 in.; 9 st 10 lb) as 'geniuses as individuals and geniuses in combination' but also argued 'they were not so much interested in what they enabled the team to do but what they did themselves'. Opponents used to say of them, 'Go for the brother who hasn't got the ball, because when you arrive he will have it!'

They were suspended in 1892, suspected of playing for payment with Broughton Rangers and returned after an absence of four years to be reinstated by the Welsh Rugby Union and eventually to play against England at Swansea in 1899, helping Wales to a comfortable 26–3 victory. They did not play again, for England protested bitterly and the two brothers returned to the North taking their families with them, where they earned their money legally with the Northern Union. Their performances

G. Llewellyn Lloyd (Newport).

for Swansea remain legendary and they had more stories related about them than many more famous pairs, yet they did not have the classical durability of Owen and Jones or Owen and Trew. The latter pair were brilliant although it was Llewellyn Lloyd of Newport who standardised outside-half play before the turn of the century.

Even in 1948, Townsend Collins was adamant that George Llewellyn Lloyd was the greatest he had seen and, obviously, he was an accomplished player who developed and thrived in the heyday of Newport rugby. A splendid all-round sportsman he did most things well, and thought a great deal about his play while ensuring that everything he did was for his side. He was a link rather than an individualist but a talented link and when deciding to 'go alone', did it successfully. He first appeared for Wales in 1896 and made twelve appearances by 1903 when R. 'Dick' Jones of Swansea partnered the diminutive genius R. M. 'Dickie' Owen. Lloyd's partner for several years was Lou Phillips, his Newport clubmate, and from the days of the James brothers it was proved that club pairs usually were best for the national side and the maxim has held good through the years. Much of this, of course, may well have been the result of the intense rivalry between the clubs as halves from different clubs were often incompatible.

Jones and Owen were happy together with Jones playing second fiddle to Owen, the controller and originator, while Trew and Owen could blend their genius as did Tanner and Jones in the 1930s and as have John and Edwards and Bennett and Edwards during the last decade of the 100 years. This has not always been possible but the pairs mentioned rank very high in world rugby both as individuals and pairs.

Owen and Trew were the very heart and brain of Swansea rugby during the first decade of the present century with Owen as the most effective small scrum-half, possibly, of all time and Trew one of the leading utility players in the hundred years. They were 'survivors' and had a tremendous influence upon the rugby of their time at club and international level. To suggest that they were heroes is an understatement but they were West Walians when the rivalry was at its highest and such was their fame, power and charisma that they could decide for themselves when and where they would play for Wales. Indifferent selection found them withdrawing occasionally from the national XV, preferring to play for their club. Today the Welsh Rugby Union would regard this as an unacceptable rebuff but the tough, sinewy, mighty atom that was Owen was a law unto himself. When he played for Swansea and Wales, they played his way, and it *was* his idea that produced the winning try against New Zealand in 1905!

R. M. 'Dickie' Owen (Swansea).

Because he was 'greedy' for the ball and wanted to dictate events he did not like playing with Bush who, with a slightly different approach, wanted to control from outside-half. Owen was not a great captain but he knew every trick in the book and believed in leading the forwards himself! He was the originator of the ploy of holding the ball in the back-row of the scrum to catch opponents off-side and what D. O. Brace did in the 1950s with a dummy pass from the scrum to catch opponents off-side, Owen employed against England at Blackheath in 1902, and when he was tackled in possession running from the scrum without the ball, Wales were awarded a penalty and Strand Jones kicked the goal for Wales to win 9–8.

W. J. 'Billy' Trew (Swansea).

Trew was vastly different in style, temperament and approach from Owen and that is why they formed such an able partnership. The lean, leathery-looking Trew was a superb tactician, a thinker and an immaculate performer with an approach that gave his fellows courage and confidence in the manner of a natural leader. He looked so out of place; such a delicate man on a rugby field, where physical prowess often reigns supreme but once he had the ball in his possession, the transformation was as magical as if Merlin had waved his wand. Trew ran elusively and was as good a wing or centre as he was an outside-half. He appeared first for Wales in 1900 when twenty years of age and made his last and twenty-ninth appearance at the age of thirty-three in 1913 when leading against France in Paris.

He did not enjoy good health and his death at the age of forty-six in 1926 was sad and it is believed that the many injuries he received on the field hastened the end for a man who had the right to claim he was the most marked player of the 'Golden Era'. Yet his genius as a tactician was never better revealed than when leading Swansea against South Africa in 1912 in the mud at St Helen's. In order to ensure that Swansea held their winning lead (3–0) in the second half, he cast aside possession and played six forwards and nine backs, and ended the match with five forwards and ten backs. Brilliant, imaginative, and revolutionary, it was the plan of a genius, and it has never been employed since in any match of representative status. William John Trew, named by Rhys Gabe as the greatest all-round player of the century, will never be forgotten!

Thomas H. Vile (Newport) and Percy F. Bush (Cardiff) were the half-back 'kings of the East' while Owen and Trew ruled the West. Vile had few chances with Owen so dominant (like D. B. Williams waiting for Gareth Edwards to retire) and Bush was a character and sometimes a 'wayward rugby genius', so much so that he often alarmed the selectors with his antics and overpowered them with his personality! Bush and Vile won only eight caps apiece because Owen would not play with Bush if he could help it, and would not give his place away to Vile unless injured and even now one wonders how Owen tolerated Bush (earning his first cap) in the match against New Zealand in 1905! The rivalry may well have been caused by the fact that most of the Cardiff backs were professional men and the Swansea players artisans. Rugby in Wales today is for the people and played by the people with no class distinction whatsoever, but in the 'Golden Era' there was an atmosphere akin to that of cricket's original 'gentlemen and players', or professional men and working men. Some of the great players were sensitive about it, others did not worry and Bush was as 'wicked' off the field as was Owen on it! No Cardiff captain before or since Bush, and he led the club in three seasons, escorted his fiancée across the playing pitch just before the kick-off at every home match from the north-west corner of the then club ground to the front row of seats in the old stand (South side) before returning to lead the team on to the field! No captain ever led his committee a merrier dance; no captain except Wilfred Wooller won more matches on his own for Cardiff, and no other captain ever led his side on to the field against Australia (1908) brandishing a sword and shield! In 1904 he became the first Lion to score 100 points on tour. Bush was an amazing rugby character by any standards.

His players worshipped him; never has a player revealed such confidence in such masterly fashion. He made fools of opponents with a smile that highlighted audacity. Cardiff missed an invincible season (in 1905–06) because Bush failed to kick the ball dead over his own goal-line and New Zealand scored. It was a decisive error as New Zealand won 10–8 and Bush had to live with the mistake for the rest of his colourful career. Like all erratic geniuses, when he made the occasional mistake it was a big one.

His puckish sense of humour; his love of the practical joke, especially at the expense of administrators, and the fact that he played the game for fun, however cleverly, produced much criticism of his play, but he was a great one, even if he was the 'wickedest' and most confident of them all.

P. F. Bush (Cardiff) and T. H. Vile (Newport).

Vile, though playing in the shadow of Owen throughout his career, did much for the game. He won his first cap in 1908 in the fog match against England at Bristol and his last in 1921 when thirty-five years of age, against Scotland in the 'crowd invasion' match at Swansea. For Newport he was a creative genius in a club career from 1902 to 1921; nineteen years of devoted service. He was a rugby thinker, a tactician, who took it all seriously and learned from others. A tough little man, rugby was his life, and when he retired he became one of the best referees of the 1920s at representative level and then joined the executive of the Welsh Rugby Union, became a member of the International Board and, finally, president of the Union. He was a visiting coach to Cambridge University and respected as an authority on the technique and administration of the game throughout his career, forming with Horace Lyne and Arthur Gould the great Newport and Wales triumvirate who did all things well and helped give the Principality its true international image on and off the field.

The forwards of the early days of the 100 years were hard-working but less glamorous than the backs. They had to scrummage and wrestle for the ball while the backs did the clever stuff, and it was a case of the chiefs behind and the braves in front but, occasionally, the braves rose above their colleagues for their unusual qualities. C. B. 'Boomer' Nicholl of Cambridge University and Llanelli was such a character. At 14 st 8 lb and 6 ft 2 in., he was a mighty man in those early days, expert in the scrum and lineout, and was the outstanding Welsh forward of the 1890s and a first Triple Crown team member. His fifteen consecutive appearances plus four inter-varsity match appearances (1890–93) must earn him the title of the best and most consistent Welsh forward of the nineteenth century.

One suggests this honour in face of fierce competition from the four Newport 'tigers', T. C. Graham, W. Watts, J. Hannan and the powerful A. W. Boucher, together with F. Mills of Swansea and the Cardiff 'giant' A. F. Hill who later adorned so many club team pictures as a committee man with his immaculate bowler hat while another rival, Harry Packer of Newport, climbed the ladder of administrative fame, especially as a selector, and was the British team manager in South Africa in 1924. Yet it was 'Boomer' Nicholls who takes the 'Gold' as the first of the really big and successful men at forward for Wales.

Dick Hellings of Llwynypia, one of a family of thirteen children, was a powerful man; a typical migrant into Wales from Devon when his family answered the call of the industrial revolution. He achieved his fame in Wales after being born in England as a strong young man working at the coke ovens at Coed-Ely and playing with Llwynypia, one of the leading clubs at the turn of the century. Hellings was first capped in 1897 and helped to launch the 'Rhondda' type of hard-working forward. To celebrate his cap he carried an iron girder from Coed-Ely to Tonyrefail and back, and became a legend in his own time. Many fine forwards followed him from the Rhondda Valley and in the first 'Golden Era' the miners and iron workers featured regularly in the Welsh pack.

J. J. Hodges (Newport).

Two unique forwards were George Boots and Jehodia Hodges, both from Newport, who played superbly well in the period when specialisation began to take hold of the forward game. Boots was primarily a loose-forward; one could mark him as the first of the genuine Welsh loose-forwards, a prototype of many to come and an originator of loose-forward tactics later brilliantly developed by Ivor Morgan of Swansea. Hodges was an expert tight-forward and scrummager but also an excellent all-round footballer, able to deputise for anyone injured in a specialised position, in or out of the scrum.

Boots, who played sixteen matches for Wales between 1898 and 1904, helped his club develop a form of back-row cover-defence that became the symbol of England dominance before and after World War I and in a modernised form was still in force in 1939. It became known as 'corner-flagging' and when employed by a weakened Newport against the strong Harlequins at Twickenham, it impressed that keen student Adrian Stoop, and was later employed in masterly fashion by the English back-row in the early 1920s. A year after Boots was capped Hodges was selected for Wales and won twenty-three caps by 1906. Only George Travers with twenty-five caps earned more as a forward until after World War II and Hodges is best remembered for his quite remarkable performance in scoring three tries against England at Swansea when brought out of the pack to the wing to replace Tommy Pearson who had been forced to retire with cracked ribs. Hodges was a big match player, much as was Alun Pask of the 1960s; the greater the occasion, the better he played. He loved a challenge and playing for Wales against the leading players of other countries provided the necessary motivation.

J. Webb (Abertillery).

Another powerful Valley forward was Jim Webb of Abertillery; yet another Welsh international born in England, he won twenty caps in the 'Golden Era' before turning professional as a protest against the social status distinction between backs and forwards that existed at the time. He signed for £80 (while in 1979 Clive Griffiths, a young Llanelli fullback, after only twenty minutes on the field against England signed for St Helen's for a fee near to £30,000). Actually, the Webb signing-on form was the first sighted by the author. In those times to turn professional was to become an outcast, but by then Webb had toured with the 1910 Lions in South Africa. A proud and outspoken man, he was born and died in the Forest of Dean, and one of many born in England who played for Wales.

Like Dick Hellings before him, Webb's family migrated to Wales where work was more readily available than in the agricultural areas of the West Country. He was just over 6 ft tall and weighed over 14 stones and was called a 'big man' at the turn of the century. Other Welsh internationals born outside Wales were T. J. S. Clapp (Somerset), Frank Hancock (Somerset), Charles Allen (had a holiday home in Beaumaris!), John Bevan (first Welsh captain, born in Australia), Gwyn Nicholls (Gloucestershire), Harry Packer (Devon), Wallace Watts (England), M. J. Davies (South Africa), Dr Gwyn Rowlands (Herts.) and John

J. Webb's contract on joining Rugby League.

An Agreement

made this 21st day of October One thousand nine hundred and twelve Between Arthur Rudd of St Anns Road St Helens (Chairman), and Harry Mercer of Prescot Road St Helens (Secretary) being Two Members of the Committee of the St Helens Football Club, on behalf of themselves and all other members of the said Club (hereinafter called the "employers" of the one part, and Alfred Webb, of York Street Aberavon Glamorgan (hereinafter called the "player" of the other part, WITNESSETH, that in consideration of the stipulations and agreements on the part of the employers hereinafter contained, THE player hereby agrees with the employers that he will during the { ~~next playing~~ season of the Northern Rugby Football Union [remainder of the present] } well and faithfully and to the best of his ability and skill play the game of Northern Rugby Union Football for the said St Helens Football Club as and when and where he may from time to time be called upon by the said Club so to do.

AND the player further agrees to abide by and observe all the Rules of the said Club, and also to obey, observe, and perform all directions of the Committee thereof, and of the Captain of the Team to be from time to time selected by the said Club; and also to abide by and observe all Rules and directions, or alterations or additional Rules (if any) which may from time to time be made by the said Football Club or by the Northern Rugby Football Union.

AND the employers, in consideration of such good and faithful services as aforesaid, and of his observing and performing the several stipulations and agreements herein contained hereby agree that they will during the { ~~next playing~~ season of the said Union [remainder of the present] } pay the player the salary of One pound per match when playing with the 1st team with a Bonus of seven shillings for each match won and two thirds of these amounts when playing with the A team as remuneration for such services over and above travelling expenses actually paid.

AND IT IS HEREBY MUTUALLY AGREED between the parties as follows:—

IN CASE the player shall from sickness or injury be unfit or unable to play when called upon, the said salary shall cease during such unfitness or inability; but should such unfitness or inability be caused by an accident whilst playing for the said Club, then the player shall be entitled to the benefit of the insurance next hereinafter provided for.

THE employers shall, at their own expense, cause an insurance policy against accidents at Football, to be issued in respect of the player to secure payment of One pound per week in case of accident, and the player shall be entitled to the moneys to become payable thereunder in lieu of his salary.

AND IT IS FURTHER AGREED that during the said term the player shall not, without the express written permission of the said St Helens Football Club previously obtained, play either in practice or in matches, whether ordinary fixtures or not, the game of Football with or for any Club or Team other than that of the said St Helens Football Club.

AND IT IS HEREBY EXPRESSLY AGREED between the parties that if at any time during the said term the player fails to punctually attend and play in any match or practice arranged by the said Club, and in which he shall have been called upon to play, or shall be guilty of disobedience or misconduct of any kind on the field, or at practice, or shall make breach in the observance or performance of any agreement or stipulation herein contained, he shall be liable to instant dismissal or suspension, and to forfeit any salary which may be due to him whenever the same shall happen, unless such course shall be disapproved by the Committee of the said Union, under Rule 3 of the Professional Laws of the Union.

Printed and Sold by J. Allan Hanson, 1, Bottom o'th' Moor, Mumps, Oldham.

Arthur Rudd

Reggie Gibbs (Cardiff).

Taylor (Herts.). Clapp was the first regular forward in the Welsh side, making twelve appearances in the 1880s and then doing noble work as captain of Newport after coming down the valley from Nantyglo. Charles Allen, who became the proprietor of the *Manchester Guardian*, qualified for Wales by spending a few weeks holiday each year in the Principality having learned the game at school and Oxford University.

Cardiff were the first club to supply all four three-quarters to the Welsh side, and against Ireland in 1910 they created another notable first in the 100 years. Wales scored eight tries in a 1911 win over Scotland (32–10) with R. A. Gibbs (3), W. Spiller (2) and J. L. Williams (1); L. M. Dyke being the odd man out. Gibbs and Williams were the wings and Spiller and Dyke the centres, although Gibbs also appeared in other positions. The quartet appeared in three matches of the 1911 Triple Crown year playing behind Trew and Owen at half-back and scored eleven tries between them.

The first of the master hookers and of several outstanding specialists in the 100 years was George Travers of Pill Harriers and Newport who was the first of three remarkable experts who wore the Newport colours and added skill and all-round ability to the performances of club and country. George Travers, father of a large and united family that played with enthusiasm after him, was first capped in 1903 as a general-purpose forward and retired at the end of the 1909 season as the first specialist hooker, only to be recalled again in 1911 to help Wales win her last Triple Crown for thirty-nine years. Gabe says of him, 'He had long legs, could twist his feet, and was expert for the job of raking the ball in the scrum'.

George Travers (Pill Harriers and Newport).

Bill Travers, his most famous son and Welsh hooker between 1937 and 1949, says of his father, 'He became a hooker because he was so much fitter than the other forwards and he was always first to the break down and in the "first up, first down" system of scrummaging at the time, the other seven forwards gathered round him'. It is recorded that George had tears in his eyes when he heard of the passing of R. G. 'Bob' Deans, although his last words that he had scored against Wales brought forth a comment from Travers senior through his tears, 'That's a lie!' He began with Pill Harriers, a docks area club that supplied so many able players for Newport. His son Bill, a British Lions of 1938, was regarded by South Africans as a superb all-round forward as well as a master hooker, a reputation he maintained until it was shared by Bryn Meredith during the 1955 and 1962 Lions tours. Bill was extremely hard and lively in the loose while he did more than enough at the lineout ('I had to do so; there were very few forwards in the Welsh pack taller than me'). He had a spell of ten years between his eighth and ninth cap and in the 1949 season played international rugby with an injured neck. He was amusing, quick-witted, speedy over the ground like his father before him, and an excellent dribbler – an art long since departed from the game.

Will Joseph of Swansea, a member of the 1905 pack, played sixteen times for Wales and, with Travers and Hodges formed the heart of the scrum while A. F. 'Boxer' Harding was an all-round forward specialising in the loose play. His twenty caps suggested a high standard of fitness before he emigrated to the Antipodes after leading a British team on tour there in 1908. Good flank forwards were few and far between and after Harding, Scrines and Hayward, came the first of the real masters of the art of loose play and one who has never received the full credit for his intelligent work. Indeed, who but the Welsh selectors would play their fastest forward and surest handler in the centre of the pack, on his first experience in the side and on the occasion of the first international match at Twickenham in 1910? Ivor Morgan of Swansea suffered such a fate, even though considered at the time to be slightly superior to England's specialist, Charles Pillman of Blackheath.

Ivor Morgan (Swansea).

The England backs enjoyed just enough latitude to win this important match with Morgan hemmed in and contained. He was a rare opportunist as well as a strong bodyguard for the diminutive Dickie Owen, and the two of them engineered many a try. His thirteenth cap was an unlucky one as he played brilliantly against Scotland in 1912 only to lose his place against Ireland although this could have been influenced by Owen and Trew not wanting to play and Morgan being cast out as a result.

The 'terrible' eight of 1914, a powerful and unchanged pack of forwards led by the Revd Alban Davies of Llanelli who died in his late eighties in California, started gathering in the 1912 season and the other seven were D. Watts (Maesteg), J. Bedwellty Jones (Abertillery) – what a magnificent name for a Welsh forward – T. C. Lloyd (Neath), Percy Jones (Pontypool) – also a fine boxer – Harry Uzzell (Newport), Tom Williams and Edgar Morgan (Swansea). In their photograph with Welsh secretary Walter Rees they appear as if attending a Men's Fellowship with their pastor leader but, on the field, they were hard men who survived the roughest of Ireland v Wales matches, at Belfast in 1914. Indeed, they would have expressed more than mere surprise had they seen Noel Murphy collapse at Cardiff in 1969, wondering what had happened to Irish forward play since the days of Collopy and Tyrrell!

Behind this vigorous pack of forwards was Jack Bancroft, younger brother of W. J., who became a pace-setter for future prolific points scorers for Wales, creating records in the first 'Golden Era' that were not overtaken until the second. His personal tally of eighty-eight points in eighteen appearances up to 1914 was not overtaken until the 1970s by Barry John and later by Phil Bennett and Steve Fenwick.

Several of the 1914 side survived World War I to appear again for Wales and none were more impressive than two Newport experts, forward Harry Uzzell and utility back Jack Wetter. The fast-moving Uzzell held the quarter and half mile Welsh track titles and was acclaimed the outstanding forward in the British Isles in 1914, and carried on after the War, playing from 1903 to 1920 for his club, and received the first of his fifteen caps at the age of twenty-nine years. A splendid sportsman and much revered by colleagues and respected by opponents, in his last season with Wales in

Jack Bancroft (Swansea).

The Wetter brothers – all six played for the Newport Club.

1920 he was thirty-seven years of age, and this feat must cheer another 'veteran' A. G. Faulkner of Pontypool who was first capped at thirty-three years of age.

Jack Wetter came from a large Newport family, similar to the Travers, and was one of six brothers, four of whom played for Newport 1st XV. Two of the family were rugby internationals and five played baseball for Wales. A Great Western Railways employee, Jack played before and after World War I at centre, outside and inside-half, although it was in the last-named position that he achieved fame for Newport, as captain during the invincible year of 1920–21. Townsend Collins believed he kicked too much at scrum-half and preferred him at outside, although in many ways, Wetter, who also served his club for many years as an administrator and referee, was not far behind Vile as a tactician.

Uzzell, Vile, Wetter, Glyn Stephens, Walter Martin, J. P. Jones and Clem Lewis played for Wales before and after World War I and Vile, recalled after an eight-year absence to lead Wales against Scotland in the 'crowd disaster' match of 1921, was said to have cried in the hotel at Swansea before the match at the responsibility of having to lead the side upon his recall, believing he was the 'forgotten' man. Sadly, the match went sour because spectators invaded the field and gave Scotland time to recover as did the 'long count' for heavyweight boxer Gene Tunney in the championship fight against Jack Dempsey.

In the first 'Golden Era', as in the second, consistency was the hallmark of the leading players, at forward and behind, and a typical example was Billy Neill of Cardiff who played eleven times for Wales and 204 times for Cardiff between 1898 and 1909, and just as Travers became the first specialist hooker, Neill became the first lineout expert. There was no high leaping as in the era of Roy John in the 1950s but much less spoiling than exists at present. Neill, a sure catcher and deliverer with a quick eye aided by good timing, could snatch the ball out of the air at the lineout without the magnificent leaping of Roy John, because comparatively few jumped as contemporary pictures reveal.

Billy Neill (Cardiff).

Before leaving the first period of Welsh rugby, it is fitting to record the sustained brilliance of the top men of the 1880–1914 period in appearances. There are eleven of them among the top fifty in the century of Welsh honours but they enjoyed fewer opportunities to win caps, with France not entering the scene until 1908, long intervals between touring teams visiting Britain, and no Welsh teams travelling abroad. Again, one could argue that such fine players, exemplary in skill and approach, would grace the game today with equal success and charm, once they had adjusted to modern methods, to the atmosphere of the ever-increasing media coverage and the considerable increase in the number of laws and penalty awards, plus the highly demanding squad coaching and training sessions. The eleven are R. M. Owen, W. J. Bancroft, W. J. Trew, A. J. Gould, G. Travers, R. T. Gabe, E. G. Nicholls, J. J. Hodges, A. F. Harding, W. Llewellyn and J. Webb, each of whom made more than twenty appearances.

The cream of the nation's manhood died in 1914–18, mainly in northern France and Belgium and left Britain a poorer place suffering from a lost generation. This affected every walk of life and rugby union football in Wales was one of the pursuits that lost players and administrators. Little did their successors realise how long it would take to recapture the golden days of 1900 to 1914, and re-establish the honoured place held by Wales in the rugby world.

PART 2: 1919–1939

The break caused by World War I, as explained in an earlier chapter, found Wales bereft of outstanding players and, although a few carried over, the 1920s did not sparkle with the same lustre as the first 'Golden Era'. The times were bad and sad, the mood of the people depressed, and although players employed the vigour of the past, they lacked the rare skills, elusiveness and pace. Few players remain indelibly in the memory and the most-capped during the decade of the 1920s was the powerful and consistent Cross Keys forward, Steve Morris, with nineteen appearances. Others spanning the 1920s and 1930s made more appearances, like the indestructible W. C. 'Wick' Powell, policemen E. M. 'Ned' Jenkins and Archie Skym. The 1920s are remembered as the era dominated by policemen and a record of six appeared in the Welsh pack against England in 1926!

They were Tom Lewis and S. Hinam (Cardiff), J. H. John (Swansea), R. C. Herrera (Cross Keys), D. M. Jenkins (Treorchy) and Bryn Phillips (Aberavon) who led the pack. Rowe Harding, who won seventeen caps, captained the side and W. J. Delahay, who won eighteen, was the scrum-half who scored what would have been the winning try only to have it disallowed. In the 1920s unemployment was high and the Glamorgan Constabulary was an outstanding force. All its members were at least six feet tall and able to play rugby because the Chief Constable, an unusual character, Colonel Lionel Lindsay, would examine all entrants before they were admitted and would test their upper arm muscles and fetlocks! Consequently, the Glamorgan police could field the best club pack of forwards in Wales during the 1920s but Lindsay's men were on the 'receiving end' of many a punch-up because he did not encourage retaliation when the 'locals' attempted to take advantage of the powerful, well-drilled and able constabulary 'out of uniform'. Occasionally, he would take the field and abandon a particularly rough match!

Tom Webster, an outstanding sporting cartoonist between the Wars often drew delightful sketches of the Welsh police at work in the scrum and maul. They were strong and they could wrestle but they played in an unhappy period of Welsh rugby. Best remembered from the 1920s was Llanelli's amazing Albert Jenkins, a powerful centre and expert kicker and his club proved an outstanding combination during the decade.

Albert Jenkins (Llanelli).

Many stories are told about Albert and most of them apocryphal, like the one suggesting he always enjoyed four or five pints of ale before taking the field. Totally untrue, although he was an extremely shy and quiet man off the field and liked to escape to his local after the match. On the field he dominated but had his off-days and although they were rare some of them were for Wales. He was an individualist but his clubmates at Llanelli knew him well, idolised him and played to him, an approach that enabled him to win many matches. For Wales, in an era when selection behind the scrum was poor and rarely blended individuals, Jenkins in his fourteen appearances was often less successful.

It is said that the only time he was knocked out in a tackle was by a young Cardiff fullback then unknown, Jim Sullivan. Jenkins remains the most loved of Stradey Park heroes by the older generation of followers for whom his feats have become legends, even if the younger generation think of Phil Bennett as the 'great one'. Jenkins led Llanelli in three seasons and in more stable times of back play one feels he would have attained greater heights, internationally. Of his colleagues, Ivor Jones remains the foremost and as flank forward he captained Llanelli a record number of eight times first in 1925–26 and last in 1936–37 while playing for the club from 1922 to 1939. He made sixteen appearances for Wales and was outstanding with the 1930 British Lions in the Antipodes. He became an administrator and was a regular touch judge at internationals, once lighting-up a cigarette at half-time at Twickenham, and then became president of the Welsh Rugby Union in 1968–69. An amazingly accurate place-kicker and active flank forward, Jones was the brains of the Llanelli pack for many years.

Ivor Jones (Llanelli).

Archie Skym who made nineteen consecutive appearances for Wales between 1928 and 1933 and one more in 1935, played in each row of the scrum which is a national record. He excelled as a prop for Wales and shared his club career between Llanelli and Cardiff, while another powerful Llanelli forward, Watcyn Thomas, shared his career with Llanelli, Swansea and Waterloo, winning fourteen caps as well as being captain at Twickenham in 1933. A humourist who was not averse to telling selectors what he really thought of them, he once played through an international match with a broken collar-bone because there were no replacements in 1931, and on retirement became a well-known and much loved schoolboy coach in the Midlands, coaching the England Schools XV. He gave them pep talks before their matches against Wales and then 'held court' afterwards in the corner of an hotel bar in Cardiff. 'I did it all for the love of rugby. That is what counts most of all.' His fellow Welsh players always speak highly of him, and his 'fire dance' act after international matches made a bold impression upon the new caps while his pre-match talks were an inspiration. Thomas once removed a policeman's hat, kicked it down the street to his hotel chased by the irate officer, then found out the policeman was a rugby man, and they made their peace over a couple of pints. Most rugby men remember him as the 'slayer' of the Twickenham bogey but he was much more: a character, a wit, a player of strength and high technical skill.

Aberavon supplied E. M. 'Ned' Jenkins in the same era as Thomas and he was a strong lock who used to swing his arms when running and, if you were too close behind him, you would receive a 'Ned's where are you', a nasty knock on the chin, unintentional, of course! In France in 1930, he moved up to prop with Tom Arthur, his fellow policeman, from lock and the proceedings quietened down considerably. Later, while serving as a sergeant in the Glamorgan force he stopped a runaway horse at full gallop in the main street, bringing it down with a neck tackle. The judge commended his strength and bravery.

Watcyn Thomas (Swansea and Llanelli).

Jenkins made twenty-one appearances, most of them with Tom Arthur, a giant lock who once crossed the French goal-line for a try carrying a handicap of three opponents. He caught the ball from a Welsh kick-off and most of his colleagues were still on the half-way line when he scored! Arthur never stood for any nonsense in club or representative rugby and he and Jenkins were hard men in a hard era of forward play. Dr Craven regards the Welsh pack of 1931 as the hardest he played against.

Tom Parker of Swansea was a steelworker and from a large family, many of whom played rugby for Swansea. He made fifteen appearances for Wales and in a period of 'battering-ram' forwards was a most intelligent player, revealing an awareness of the other fourteen players in the team. Forwards often used to 'die' with the ball but Parker liked to make full use of it. The best hooker of the era was F. A. 'Lonzo' Bowdler of Cross Keys who made fifteen appearances and is famed for working a night shift underground at the local colliery, then travelling down to Cardiff to play for Wales and returning home after the match to work the Saturday night shift. Such an achievement called for exceptional enthusiasm and stamina even though Bowdler could ill afford to lose a shift during the days of the economic depression.

Behind the scrum there was Rowe Harding of Swansea on the wing and he has been quoted in an earlier chapter, providing shrewd observations on the era. A truly classical wing with seventeen appearances he suffered from constant changes in mid-field and also a reluctance on the part of Wales to employ the changed tactics of the era.

The utility player of the decade was W. J. 'Billy' Delahay of Bridgend and Cardiff who played fifteen matches at inside-half, one at outside-half and two at centre. He recalls that the expenses in those far-off days were two shillings for tea and eleven pence for a packet of twenty cigarettes. Delahay was a tough, durable character who gave of his best, often in poor sides, and remained a survivor when selectors chopped and changed, often without good reason for doing so. The end of Delahay's career overlapped the start of the leading scrum-half of the 1920–30 era, W. C. 'Wick' Powell of the London Welsh, the biggest scrum-half to play for Wales.

W. C. Powell (London Welsh).

Powell came from the valleys of Gwent and was bought out of the Welsh Guards by Captain Geoffrey Crawshay, a colourful patron of Welsh rugby during the era who founded the Crawshays Welsh Rugby Football Club. Trying his hand at several positions, Powell was first capped on the wing against Scotland in 1926, before settling for the scrum-half position which he held for six seasons before missing 1934 and then being recalled in 1935 for a final season. Soon afterwards he emigrated to South Africa but his career for the London Welsh and Wales was extremely colourful. Big, strong, hard and audacious, nothing deterred him and he was as ready to 'belt' his own forwards as he was the opposition. One of few players who had a better reverse pass than a normal one, he always ate a large meal before an international: a large steak with two eggs topping it!

Immensely strong, many an attempt was made to put him off the field but he survived. Powell had big hands, powerful arms and a large posterior. He played best with A. R. Ralph of Newport although Windsor Lewis and Harry Bowcott were happy with him. As he was the biggest scrum-half to play for Wales, he set a pattern which was followed by Haydn Tanner, Rex Willis, Lloyd Williams and others with the latest player in the position, Terry Holmes, every bit as big and strong as Powell. Only two scrum-halves have played more times for Wales.

Two fullbacks were prominent in the 1920s, Joe Rees of Swansea with twelve caps and B. O. 'Ossie' Male of Cross Keys and Cardiff with eleven. Both players led their country, both tackled and kicked extremely well. Rees was a school attendance officer or 'Boardie' as they were known, and Male a schoolmaster who was withdrawn from the 1924 Welsh side bound for Paris because he played inside the seven day rule before an international.

B. O. Male (Cross Keys and Cardiff).

This pair were followed by an outstanding fullback in J. A. 'Jack' Bassett of Penarth who played from 1929 to 1932 in fifteen matches, leading Wales in his last eight appearances. His forte was tackling and accurate touch-finding and although he did not kick an unusual length, he certainly 'arrested' every opponent he tackled, as befitted an able police sergeant. Once tackled by Bassett, one did not seek further confrontation. His place-kicking was steady and New Zealand regarded him the equal of George Nepia when a Lion in 1930, and that was praise indeed.

Guy Morgan of Brecon and Cambridge, a nephew of Dr Teddy Morgan, was a dapper and elusive centre who played eight times and led Wales four times but, after retirement and while a housemaster at Radley School, he suffered severely from arthritis. A fellow mid-field back for Cambridge and Wales was Harry Bowcott, a fine 1930 Lions centre who also won eight caps and kicked immaculately from outside-half with either foot. Later he served as an administrator for London Welsh, as a national selector, Welsh team manager and president of the Welsh Rugby Union.

One of the best looking and smoothest of mid-field players in the late 1920s and early 1930s was Frank Williams of Cardiff with fourteen caps, while the rumbustious Claude Davey of Swansea started as a flank forward at school but played first for Wales at centre in 1930 and had made twenty-three appearances in the position by 1938. He was captain on eight occasions, including the New Zealand match of 1935. Gentle and unassuming off the field as an efficient electrical engineering executive, he was a tackler in the Albert Jenkins and Jack Bassett mould, and later emulated by Dr Jack Matthews.

Davey, like Matthews, was often accused of not having safe hands but it was an unkind criticism for both scored many a try for club and country. Davey played for Wales with several co-centres but was best with Wilfred Wooller, his club partner at Sale. As a leader he was popular and argues that his introduction to the Welsh side was in the roughest match of his career, the last in Paris for seventeen years, and the next one was equally tough for his successors! The early 1930s produced an ideal wing pair, fit

Claude Davey (Swansea).

R. W. Boon (Cardiff).

to be bracketed with Morgan and Llewellyn before them, and T. G. R. Davies and J. J. Williams after them, since R. W. Boon and J. C. Morley were audacious try-getters. Boon from Cardiff was the most confident of players and team mates used to chant as he entered the dressing room, 'Have no fear, Boon is here!'

Morley was a quiet fellow who turned professional at the height of his career after fourteen appearances for Wales. He was a qualified dentist. Much loved at Rodney Parade, he possessed a unique skill in being able to turn inside sharply without losing pace. Boon was a strong, speedy runner with a clever change of pace, and enjoyed success on the track as well as being a Glamorgan county cricketer, and is now a county councillor and lawn bowls player; truly a man for all seasons!

A. R. Ralph also turned professional after consecutive appearances which suggested a career of outstanding quality. Sure hands, elusive pace and a keen tactical sense hallmarked Ralph as one of the leading outside-halves of the 100 years. Tough flank forward Arthur Lemon was engaged in many a friendly feud during his thirteen-match career. He was a hard man, every bit as hard as Jamie Clinch of Ireland, and their 'engagements' persisted for eighty minutes with no punches pulled and no complaints made.

Vivian Jenkins (London Welsh) and his close friend in the game, Arthur Rees of the same club.

Cliff Jones (Cardiff).

The second half of the thirties produced a host of outstanding backs. Vivian Jenkins, converted from an Oxford University centre, became the best fullback in the British Isles between 1933–39 because he was strong, technically correct, observant and remarkably cool for a Welshman. One of several Llandovery College products in his generation, he had the safe hands of a county cricketer (a double blue) and was the best torpedo punter seen in the position as well as a safe place-kicker. Jenkins enjoyed tackling and his casual air was deceiving in defence, trapping many an unwary wing.

Vice-captain of the 1938 British Lions, he was a member of the Welsh back divisions that first won at Twickenham, defeated New Zealand and achieved an unbeaten Championship in 1935–36. Idwal Rees, Cliff Jones and Wilfred Wooller were at Cambridge: Rees was a shrewd intelligent utility back, completely unobtrusive but effective, Jones played rugby like an everlasting firework and stakes a major claim to be one of the best attacking outside-halves of the 100 years, and Wooller, the biggest of Welsh centres, was an individual match-winner who worked in close harmony with Jones. Certainly the most effective centre of the 1930s if not between the two wars.

Wilfred Wooller of Cardiff, rugby and cricket hero then and now.

The pair set alight the Cardiff and Welsh backs with flashing brilliance before World War II ended their careers. Wooller came back to lead Glamorgan cricket with distinction and, like Vivian Jenkins, writes shrewdly about the game while Jones moved into administration and will be the Union's president in Centenary year, an honour fully deserved. Personalities, both on and off the field, they helped to illuminate the 100 years as truly great ones.

Arthur Rees, a busy flanker and pack leader, was one of the few Cambridge University forwards to play for Wales, while Tommy Rees of Newport, was the heaviest Welsh forward as an 18 st prop. Donald Tarr was the hooker who broke his neck yet survived, while Les Manfield played before and after World War II at number eight. Rugby between the wars was hard and often a survival course. Wilfred Wooller with eighteen caps by 1939 was the most capped member of the last side to play, against Ireland in Belfast, before World War II, and he had no matches against France and only one against a touring team. Yet this was to change after the War and from 1947 until 1980 it was non-stop rugby and new appearance records were created with forty-six players achieving the target.

Gareth Edwards is the record holder at the end of the Century with fifty-three appearances, followed by J. P. R. Williams with fifty-one, T. G. R. Davies with forty-six and K. J. Jones with forty-four. It was Jones who first overtook R. M. Owen, a record that survived for forty-four years, and he was an Olympic sprinter who remained naturally fit, needed no special training for rugby and always ate a hearty meal before each match. Yet he was a fine, long-legged, fast-moving wing, a hero at Newport and the scorer of many a match-winning Welsh try. A son of Blaenavon, he did not receive his first cap until he was twenty-five years old, after serving in India during the War, and then toured with the 1950 Lions before playing his last match in 1957 at the age of thirty-five. A schoolmaster and freelance rugby writer, Jones was only a few years younger than the 'master' scrum-half of the era, Haydn Tanner who made thirteen appearances before the War while with Swansea and thirteen after the War with Cardiff. A superb long passer of the ball; a strong and sudden breaker from the scrum, an accurate kicker with either foot and fine tackler and covering defender. Despite his keen sense of humour he did not suffer fools easily, on or off the field; he set his own high standards and was unhappy if his play fell below them.

Ken Jones (Newport), double international.

Dr J. Matthews (Cardiff).

Bleddyn Williams (Cardiff).

W. B. Cleaver (Cardiff).

Clifton Davies (Cardiff)

PART 3: 1946–1980

In the years immediately following World War II there were some splendid players, many of whom would have been outstanding had not the War intervened. Some of the leading players were at school when the War started and this was the case of the three Cardiff mid-field players, Jack Matthews, Bleddyn Williams and Billy Cleaver, who when joined by the masterly Haydn Tanner in 1947 formed the best mid-field quartet in British club rugby. Before Tanner arrived, Matthews led Cardiff with distinction. He was strong, tough and inspiring, with a devastating burst. Extremely popular; he was an ideal leader who coined the phrase, at least in rugby, 'all the best', and played with more bandage and strapping protecting injured muscles, broken and bruised bones, than any player before or since. His fierce tackling and short sharp bursts complimented the devastating side-step of the clever runner and beautiful handler, Bleddyn Williams. They were an ideal pair as Williams scored from many a sharp Matthews burst and once in open field, he was strong and fast enough to clear the opposition. They provided attractive, match-winning centre play for Cardiff for many years, and although individually successful for Wales did not play all that number of times together as centres. Matthews, as the elder, retired before Williams. Matthews was an under-19 schools cap and Williams an under-15 cap before the War and they matured in the wartime Cardiff side. Williams scored 185 tries for Cardiff, which remains a club record, Matthews scored fifty-four, and each played in a Welsh Championship and Triple Crown side. The third member of the trio, Billy Cleaver, has never received the full credit due to him, and is remembered only for his kicking which was superb. Yet he was the outside-half, the pivot in attack, in the brilliant Cardiff 1947–48 side which scored 803 points (when a try counted as three points and 182 of them were scored in the season!). Cleaver must have been much more than an accurate kicker; he could play anywhere and was an intelligent effective pivot in the Grand Slam side of 1950. He was a mining engineer and manager during his playing days and wore one pair of boots through his six-season career. He sang tenor beautifully and was an able utility Lion in 1950 with Williams, Matthews, Willis and Clifton Davies of Cardiff. The three were the brains and the show case of a remarkable club team.

The last of the pre-war style, short, stocky, powerful props to excel after the War was a notable son of Kenfig Hill, Clifton Davies, who though no more than 5 ft 9 in. tall and several pounds under 14 st, scrummaged as well as anyone, arguing, 'You have got to get under your man!' He played sixteen times between 1947–51 and was a happy 1950 Lion, charming New Zealanders with his delightful lilting Welsh accent, sweet singing and choir leading, his ability at cribbage and his eighteen inch neck, since rarely could he find shirts or collars to fit him. After the formal proceedings at any function he would remove his collar for 'singing comfort'. A delightful character; a player with an even temperament and a heart of gold who once took a 'little nip' of a French prop's ear, in an attempt to cool down the fiery gentleman in the heat of a France v Wales match at Stade Colombes. Although different in style and approach, he can be classed with Ray Prosser of Pontypool as two of the most popular of post-war tight-forwards. Unfortunately Davies, who worked hard as a miner for most of his life, died at an early age and was deeply mourned, he was indeed a happy man who loved the game he played so well. Many a Saturday on missing the last bus he would walk home from Cardiff to Kenfig Hill, singing as he went!

Bill Tamplin (Cardiff).

With him for Cardiff and Wales was a big, strong, rugged police officer, William Ewart Tamplin, and another prematurely bald police officer, Gwyn Evans, and these three internationals, with a 'veteran' hooker, Maldwyn James, were expert ball-winners. Tamplin was a match-winning place-kicker and pack-leader and if an opponent had to be 'discouraged' from over-vigour and unlawful activity, then the Gwent-born 'bobby', who performed so well at lock, took him into custody unobtrusively. No-one was any the wiser except the wrongdoer who thought twice about repeating his action. Gwyn Evans was a non-stop tearaway flanker who made twelve consecutive appearances and loved every one of them, smiling his way through the hard work. He was another happy, honest forward who often had to smuggle his boots from the police station to play, as his Chief Constable in those years did not approve of his force engaging in rugby. Later, he served under a Chief who helped him revive the old spirit of the Glamorgan County force in the South Wales Constabulary.

Gwyn Evans (Cardiff).

In the Welsh pack at the time was a young forward, Rees Stephens, son of a leading pre-World War I forward, Glyn Stephens. Rees won thirty-two caps as a forceful, galloping lock who shone in the powerful 1952 Championship, after starting in 1947, and later captained Wales on six occasions with five victories. Many wanted him to play at number eight but lock was his best position as he was an all-round worker who preferred the tight physical play to the clever work in the open. At Neath he formed an able partnership with the prince of lineout jumpers, the best of the post-war years, Roy John, who possessed the grace of a ballet dancer, the timing of a high-wire man, the sure hands of a cricketer and enough pace to make him effective in the loose. These attributes plus a shrewd rugby brain earned him nineteen consecutive appearances, two Grand Slams, and inclusion in the select list of the top ten forwards of the 100 years.

J. R. G. 'Rees' Stephens (Neath).

A clever hooker, and by that one really means 'clever', was David Maldwyn Davies, a Somerset police officer born at Penygraig, who did not play a great deal of first-class rugby outside the Welsh XV and the British Lions but had long legs, a quick rugby brain and a bundle of tricks that enabled him to survive as the Lions hooker in 1950. An imaginative village 'bobby' in the heart of Somerset, he was a close friend of railway fireman Don Hayward of Newbridge, who played lock in the 1950 side and prop in the 1952 side, and was the prototype, with W. O. Williams of Swansea, originally a lock, of the new-look big front-row.

W. O. Williams (Swansea).

Don Hayward (Newbridge).

Hayward had large beefy hands, as befits a footplate man firing a Great Western Railways express through the Severn Tunnel in the days of steam, and once put out a carriage fire when travelling with the Welsh team to Paris on the 'Golden Arrow' out of Calais. He emigrated to New Zealand and literally cried every time he met a visiting Lions side, while Williams made the 1955 Lions tour to South Africa. Hayward travelled to New Zealand in 1950 and played in eleven of the first twelve matches including the first two tests – a remarkable feat of endurance! Williams propped with Hayward in the 1951 Springboks match and the five matches of 1951–52 season produced a superb Welsh pack with these two supporting hooker Davies. Williams went on to win twenty-two caps before retiring in 1956.

There emerged in 1951 a mercurial, traditionally Welsh outside-half, destined for rugby glory as a schoolboy; a man of the Rhondda, gifted in many ways, yet essentially Welsh in enthusiasm, sparkle and love of rugby. For him it was something to be enjoyed and although he is now head of BBC TV outside broadcasting and a world traveller, he still has a genuine love for rugby football and a loyalty to his country and the game in Wales. Cliff Morgan remains one of the best loved of post-war Welsh and British Lion players and in his first match, against Ireland at Cardiff, faced the man of the moment in J. W. Kyle, in his second against France in Paris, celebrated his twenty-first birthday with a large key of the door presented by the Union and team members, and in his third match against the Springboks was criticised for not kicking accurately to which he replied, 'They didn't teach me to kick at school!'

He bubbled with enthusiasm and efficiency in the 1952 Grand Slam side and went on to make a record twenty-nine appearances at outside-half to secure a firm place in the top six of the Century. His performances with the 1955 Lions in South Africa won him acclaim and the accolade of the best outside-half to visit that country. Morgan had the lot although he rarely attempted to drop for goal, and his pace off the mark, sure hands, a body swerve that resembled the leaning tower of Pisa and an ability to dodge that was matched by a surviving resilience, highlighted a successful career where the marking of the outside-half, as in the times of Cliff Jones, was all-important. His cover-tackling and rapidly developed touch-finding completed his armoury, while his happy, infectious enthusiasm for life and fun, mimicry and piano entertaining, made him the ideal tourist. He was the radio-active particle around which the whole social side of the 1955 tour revolved. The coloured folk called him the 'General'; they loved him, and in his personality there was manifested the real 'hwyl' that is so much a part of Welsh rugby.

Cliff Morgan (Cardiff).

A great deal has already been said of John Gwilliam, and he admired Morgan greatly, as he did Rex Willis, faithful partner of Morgan for Cardiff, Wales, the Barbarians, and almost for the Lions, for Willis refused the captaincy of the 1955 touring team, having completed his international career. As a strong scrum-half with an accurate, long dive-pass and ability to survive, Willis had few superiors, while his defensive work was always heroic. Knocked out while playing for the Lions in New Zealand in 1950, he suffered concussion and kept asking how his original club, Llandaff, were doing and what was the score! Dr Jack Matthews, the 'iron man' in the centre for the Lions, kept telling him all was well, and because there were no substitutes in those days, Willis had to complete the match. Later, when playing against Scotland at Cardiff in 1952, his jaw was broken but again he completed the match. Little wonder the decision to employ substitutes eventually eased the lot of the badly injured players even though Willis was not one of them. He walked straight into the Welsh team without a trial after leaving Llandaff to join Cardiff in September 1949 and appeared at Twickenham in January 1950. A character, a fast car driver, and a generous rugby patron.

Alun Thomas, player and manager (Swansea).

Ray Cale of Newbridge and Pontypool was one of rugby's unluckiest players. An outstanding flanker in 1949 and 1950, he was not selected for the 1950 Lions because he was thought to be too vigorous. Almost the same fate befell Dr Jack Matthews, but after the team had played a few matches in New Zealand and met a certain flanker in the tests who specialised in unseating scrum-halves, all wished the selectors had sent Ray Cale, Des O'Brien and company! Cale, terribly disappointed, turned professional and he was a tragic loss to the Union code. Fortunately, such unrealistic days are far behind the four Home Unions selection committee.

Malcolm Thomas (Newport) and Alun Thomas (Swansea) were fine utility players and British Lions. Malcolm Campbell Thomas started in 1949 at the age of nineteen and finished in 1959 making two Lions tours, 1950 and 1959, nine years apart, which is something of a record. He played twenty-seven times for Wales and was always immaculately turned out, on and off the field. Alun Gruffydd Thomas played thirteen times for Wales as a utility player and was chosen as a fullback for the 1955 Lions tour but through illness and injury appeared in only six matches. He returned in 1974 to manage the most successful Lions side of all time, truly adequate compensation for his earlier misfortune.

Lewis Jones of Llanelli was a remarkable player in the Union and League codes and his scoring achievements justify him a place among the great ones who played for enjoyment. First capped at the age of nineteen he joined the Lions as a replacement in the same year, scoring sixty-three points in seven matches, and after ten matches for Wales turned to rugby league where his amazing scoring feats as a professional indicate the loss suffered by rugby union through his departure. Amusing, outspoken, he was never afraid to tell the selectors what he thought of their decisions.

Another outstanding Llanelli fullback and one of the ten best of the Century was T. J. 'Terry' Davies, who began his career with Swansea, did national service in the Royal Navy, damaged a shoulder and had it wired by the Welsh Rugby Union's present honorary surgeon Gordon Rowley, and then played with distinction for Llanelli. After starting with Wales as a twenty-year-old in 1953, he missed three seasons and returned in 1957 to

Lewis Jones (Llanelli).

Terry Davies (Swansea and Llanelli).

R. C. C. 'Clem' Thomas (Swansea).

C. C. Meredith (Neath).

Russell Robins (Pontypridd).

retire after being captain in 1961. A handsome, broad-shouldered fellow, Davies would have been outstanding in any era and is remembered for his happy temperament, his bone-crushing tackling, controlled accurate torpedo punting and sure place-kicking. He was a popular favourite, a happy Lion of 1959 admired by New Zealanders and is now a successful business man at Bynea.

Gareth Griffiths was a fine wing who always wanted to play in the centre. A Rhondda lad and Schools international, he started in the centre and while there helped Wales beat New Zealand in 1953, although he had to leave the field for ten minutes to have a dislocated shoulder replaced, and became an outstanding Lions wing in 1955 after being flown out as replacement. Now a company director, he is still intensely keen about the game.

Gerwyn Williams was another artistic fullback who caught and kicked beautifully. Always happy in his play, he is now a splendid coach of schoolboys and was in the same Welsh side on many occasions as R. C. C. 'Clem' Thomas, now one of the many former Welsh internationals to be seen in the press box. Actually, a recent count revealed twelve of them in action, with some as full-time journalists and others making a little pocket-money on Saturdays.

Thomas began in 1949 when it was thought every one of the five selectors nominated a new cap to give the Welsh side a 'shake-up'. It was Haydn Tanner's last match and Thomas recalls that the five new players were almost afraid of the player who was then 'God' in Welsh rugby. Thomas had to wait three years for his next cap but then held his place to finish with twenty-six and made a Lions tour as well as leading Wales. Tall, rangy and always in the thick of the hard play, he was said to be one of only two wing-forwards who could put the 'Indian sign' on Cliff Morgan when their clubs were opposed, yet they worked in harmony for their country!

Much has already been said of the modest, immaculate Bryn Meredith and one of his props, W. O. Williams. The other prop was Courtenay Meredith, one of the most handsome of players in his position and a man of steel. He made fourteen appearances and 'cracked' a few opponents with his strong scrummaging yet never complained when injuries befell him, as when he split his tongue open while packing against the Springboks for the Lions in 1955. He must have been in intense pain but shared in the after-match proceedings and had his tongue restitched three times. He remains, with Ray Prosser, one of my favourite prop characters of modern times.

Packing behind this trio either at lock or number eight was one of the most intelligent forwards of the era, Russell Robins of Pontypridd, who earned praise in South Africa in 1955 at number eight for his skill, pace, adaptability, sense of humour and charm. A close friend of R. H. Williams, they possessed an uncanny skill of 'reading the crystal ball' on the morning of match days and forecasting the result. Robins turned professional, which was a considerable loss to Wales, and a decision one believes he much regretted later.

The two outstanding lock forwards and lineout specialists of the 1950s were Roy John of Neath and Rhys Williams of Llanelli. Intelligent, controlled players with considerable technical knowledge and an appreciation of the game's requirements. Roy John remains the most effective and graceful lineout specialist of any country since World War II and his success even brought about a change in the laws! He was a superb two-handed jumper and while he could be shielded by colleagues at the lineout in his era, his timing and catching was perfect. He was the Nijinsky of the lineout and an excellent forward in the loose and tight play. His build was ideal, tall and rangy with sure hands and a remarkable calm, while he never put a foot wrong on the field in nineteen appearances.

Roy John (Neath).

His first was made against England in 1950 when his Neath clubmate and close friend, Rees Stephens, withdrew through injury. John remained in the side for the Grand Slam season and Stephens was not recalled until the following season. John shared in the second Grand Slam season of 1952 with Stephens and both were British Lions of 1950. In 1954 the lineout laws were amended and no longer was 'shielding' allowed. In fact the lineout was completely changed, for the worst unfortunately, and it has never recovered, however much the International Board had tried.

R. H. Williams (Llanelli).

Rhys Williams, who took over at lock from John, proved a fine lineout specialist and an even better tight man than John but what a magnificent pair they would have made had their careers run in parallel! As did John for the 1950 Lions, so did Williams for the 1955 and 1959 Lions, to win the admiration of critics in both countries. He made twenty-three appearances for Wales ending his career as captain in 1960. During his career Welsh fortunes fluctuated but his consistency was as remarkable as was his fitness, in victory and defeat. He was a master of basic rugby and not fond of over-complication, as he believes a side can only be at its best if everyone is giving one hundred per cent plus. Popular with a splendid sense of humour, Williams had the skill and temperament for success and is now a Welsh Rugby Union member and selector.

C. D. Williams (Cardiff and Neath).

Another player, Sid Judd played at number eight and on the flank and possessed the same natural gifts as Robins, although entirely different in approach. Unfortunately, his career was cut short by a terminal illness but not before he had scored identical tries for Cardiff and Wales against New Zealand on the very same spot at the Arms Park in 1953. Another flanker, from Cardiff and Neath, C. D. Williams, was a shrewd player who deserved his cap but was said to have achieved it only because his passport was in order for France when receiving a late call to the colours. He also refutes strongly the statement that his try against France later was scored in the River Taff, answering with a handsome smile, 'I slid over the deadball line after I had touched down and didn't get wet!'

Two scrum-halves, one large, one small, were strong rivals with quite different approaches to the game. David Onllwyn Brace of Gowerton

Ray Prosser (Pontypool).

Grammar School, a rugby nursery that produced Haydn Tanner and many others, was an inventive live-wire behind the scrum who revitalised rugby at Oxford University and found the critics strongly divided over his attractive unorthodoxy.

The bigger fellow was Lloyd Williams of Cardiff, younger brother of Bleddyn, who became known as a 'ninth' forward, rather unfairly since he was an expert youth player at outside or inside-half. He played more often at scrum-half and eventually joined Cliff Morgan in the Cardiff side. Brace played five times with Morgan for Wales and Williams seven. Both had fine qualities and Welsh followers were strongly divided in their support of these two young men in a manner strongly reminiscent of the old East–West rivalry.

Haydn Morgan (Abertillery).

Carwyn James, best remembered for his powers as a coach, won two caps in 1958 before there emerged a group of powerful young forwards who worked hard for the 1959 Lions. The names are familiar still, Ray Prosser, W. R. 'Roddy' Evans, John Faull and Haydn Morgan, all of whom travelled to New Zealand with Bryn Meredith and R. H. Williams. This tour was memorable for the pyrotechnics of some brilliant play on the field, and a laugh a minute off it. Prosser was at once a homesick and yet happy tourist as his ready wit amused all and won him life-long friendships. Having toured with many, I cannot think of anyone more loved than Ray Prosser and players of his ilk like the mercurial Cliff Morgan, the practical joker Gareth Edwards and Barry John the 'King', who give no substance to the suggestion that Welshmen are not good tourists. When the Irish and Welsh combine in quality and numbers then the Lions are strong, successful and happy. Faull was a splendid hard-working number eight in New Zealand and Haydn Morgan a most effective flanker, a colourful tourist and the best 'tipster' in the business although not claiming to be a judge of horse flesh. Auburn-haired, agile and active, he played twenty-seven times for Wales and only David Morris achieved more appearances. Morgan's party trick was a magnificent back somersault off any piano that was handy, as befitted an ex-parachutist.

It was Prosser who reported after one match in New Zealand that Marques had been roughed-up, while lying half out of a ruck, by a big Maori forward. When the match was over, Marques shook hands with the 'assailant'. 'What the hell did you do that for?' asked Prosser. 'I thought I'd make him feel a cad!' replied the smiling Marques.

Dewi Bebb (Swansea).

Dewi Bebb burst on to the scene as a young North Wales student from a well-known literary Welsh family, to help beat England at Cardiff in his first match. During his career he made thirty-four appearances and two Lions tours by 1967. A fine runner-in and a gentle person, much in the mould of another Swansea captain, Rowe Harding, he scored some match-winning tries and loved every moment on the field of play. Ken Richards was a points-scoring outside-half who suffered an untimely early death in a motor accident, and of the 1962 Lions, David Nash a splendid, big, foraging forward, suffered a severe illness in South Africa when destined to become one of the truly great ones. Glyn Davidge was one of the best and bravest defensive number eights of the 100 years, and the rounded, smiling Len Cunningham a worthy prop, unlucky not to make the Lions trip. Kingsley Jones was a strong prop in a powerful pack and Ken Jones, a delightful attacking centre, handsome and dapper, who always treated rugby as a game to be enjoyed. Big Keith Rowlands suffered unlucky leg injuries that curtailed his Welsh career but in 1962 he was the 'big lock' of the Lions side, like R. H. Williams before him, and now both are Welsh selectors.

Keith Rowlands (Cardiff).

Two long-serving forwards, lock Brian Price with thirty-two caps and Alun Pask at number eight with twenty-six caps, were masters of their craft and both successful leaders for club and country and able Lions. Price was the master of the lineout leap with sure hands and a strong forward at the scrummage. With battling Brian Thomas (twenty-one caps) they formed a strong, hard core of the Welsh pack for several seasons, deserving their Triple Crown success of 1965 and 1969. Thomas was the best mauler and 'ripper-out' of the ball in his era and Geoffrey Wheel has followed his example in the 1970s. He was a big man who, it is claimed, 'terrorised' the Oxford pack with his strength when an undergraduate at the rival University!

Price and Thomas were an ideal, effective pair and Wales has been fortunate to have had Allan Martin and Geoffrey Wheel succeed them and maintain a strong core, since good scrummaging is the very basis of a successful side. Price is often remembered for the knockout punch on his Lion friend, Noel Murphy of Ireland, at the Arms Park but there was a fair amount of unseen provocation, while Price has been lost to the game as an admirable coach and administrator for a statement made in a newspaper article. The Centenary Year would be an opportune time to fully reinstate a worthy captain of Wales.

Lucky with the quality and effectiveness of their locks, Wales has been equally fortunate with number eights. After John Faull came Alun Pask, a player in the classical mould with height, pace and sureness of hand to match his natural ability. A man for the big occasion, as was his successor Mervyn Davies, Pask was a quiet personality and worked extremely well with the ebullient Haydn Morgan for Abertillery and Wales. His appearances were consecutive and highlighted his consistency and some of his tries at Twickenham, Cardiff and Cape Town are recorded in spectacular pictures (see overleaf).

Tribute has been paid to the half-back pairing of Clive Rowlands and David Watkins who appeared together in fourteen consecutive matches. Watkins played twenty-one times before handing over to Barry John, and all three, Watkins, John and Bennett, were outstanding yet amazingly modest, and endeared themselves to their followers as well as being admired throughout the rugby world.

In the era of Rowlands and Watkins were Grahame Hodgson and Terry Price at fullback, Norman Gale the third most-capped hooker, Denzil

Alun Pask (Abertillery) scoring a marvellous try for the Lions in South Africa, 1962.

Stuart Watkins (Newport) scoring a try for Wales at Cardiff.

Williams the most-capped prop and flanker Gary Prothero. They all shared in the 1965 Triple Crown. Stuart Watkins was a long-serving wing who ran 'into history' with his memorable 1966 try against France at Cardiff and was a much better player than many believed. Maurice Richards, in a short but happy career on the wing, collected a record-equalling four tries against England in 1969. He turned professional but could have collected a much larger fee because he really had that something special – class. In Australia he was penalised after the referee had awarded a try to the opposition as, quite out of character, he roundly criticised the official for a doubtful decision.

A centre who started in 1964 and finished in 1971, he was said to be too slow at first although he had sure hands and he proved his critics wrong (including the author) by becoming the smoothest player in the position since Bleddyn Williams and ending his playing career at the top of the tree – as a successful Lions captain in New Zealand. He led Wales six times with five victories, he was outspoken to critics and others but loyal to his team, he played for enjoyment always and went on to select and coach Wales and coach the British Lions. Now Sidney John Dawes finds himself the coaching-organiser to the Welsh Rugby Union in Centenary Year. He still does not suffer fools gladly but loves his rugby and remains very much a Welshman despite having spent most of his rugby career living in England as a London Welsh player, captain and coach.

A stalwart forward was prop John Lloyd, Welsh captain in 1972, an extremely popular player with a tremendous appetite, who played twenty-four times and led Bridgend with distinction. Strong and straight-forward as a prop yet lively in the loose, reminding one very much of the New Zealand captain, Wilson Whineray, he has now succeeded Dawes as team coach. London Welshman John Taylor, born in England, was selected for Wales before he was ready but learned quickly while in the side and eventually finished with twenty-six caps and two Lions tours. Sharp about the field with sure hands and a keen sense of position, he was a creative back-row forward who fitted in well with Mervyn Davies and David Morris.

Much loved by Welsh followers was Morris, the tough as teak flank forward, who earned the title of the 'Shadow' because of his outstanding support play. Taylor was known as 'Basil Brush' because of his beard and

John Taylor (London Welsh).

W. D. 'Dai' Morris (Neath), the ever-present, did not require a white stick (actually it is a touch flag).

with Morris and Davies formed the effective back-row of the 1971 side. Morris was unlucky never to make a Lions tour but his thirty-four appearances, twenty of them consecutive, highlight his tireless consistency. As quiet as Taylor was ebullient, Morris was the perfect pattern of the real valley forward; a man of the coal who, unobtrusively, served Wales faithfully as a man of few words but always a ready smile for friend and foe! In his own special and admirable way, 'Dai' carried high the banner of the Welsh mine worker, as a colliery welder, thus preserving a tradition of Welsh forward play that began in the last century.

Keith Jarrett moved into the international scene as a schoolboy, like a meteor, achieving all the honours and then turning to Rugby League for a short period before illness cut short his career. In his day he was a match-winner with considerable natural ability, while Ian Hall was a brave centre whose career was interrupted twice by double fractures of leg bones. As befits a young police officer he would never give up and was an 'ever ready'. He now coaches the national youth side.

Jeff Young was a hooker in the regal line as Wales has always found the right player for the position and retained him for a long period. George Travers, Fred Bowdler, Bill Travers, D. M. Davies, Bryn Meredith, Norman Gale, Jeff Young and Bobby Windsor were all long-serving 'strikers' as well as good forwards out of the scrum but the strain on the neck and shoulders is considerable for a hooker and forced Jeff Young out of serious rugby after twenty-three appearances. Hookers are at the very heart of matters and modern experts have to be extremely accomplished and resilient to survive.

There remains now in the gallery of outstanding players over the hundred years, the immediate moderns, the heroes of the final year of the last decade who have brought fresh and lasting glory to the cause of Welsh rugby. They were men of unique ability and dedication with a love of rugby who devoted so much of their time to the cause, in the glare of the powerful media which, at times, exerted undue pressure upon them. They were men of a new age, tempted by all forms of financial gain and in considerable demand by their followers and, occasionally, those who attempted to exploit them.

The whole rugby world changed completely between 1969 and 1979 and the rugby stars replaced the pop stars for the greater part in Wales. It was a return to the first 'Golden Era' but with a more pressurised professional approach and never before has a team been automatically selected so regularly, with injury often being the only reason for disturbing a winning combination. The Welsh launching of the squad system with an honorary coach developed the national team as a club side. They spent so much time practising and talking together that a bond of close friendship developed among them, and their continued success became the envy of many countries; an envy that occasionally materialised on the field of play.

Rowlands and Dawes, as coaches, with their fellow selectors and able captains in Price, Dawes, Lloyd, Edwards, Davies, Bennett and

Three Welsh captains – Mervyn Davies, Phil Bennett and Terry Cobner.

Mervyn Davies (left) and W. Delme Thomas in action in Paris.

T. G. R. Davies (Cardiff), super wing.

The 'King', Barry John (Llanelli and Cardiff).

Williams, helped create the 'Club' and when younger men came in to replace those established heroes who retired, the system still worked and the Club held together. It is fitting therefore to end this section by looking at the giants of the last decade who have set Wales up for the second century.

At fullback with fifty-two caps, the indestructible J. P. R. Williams, a member of the six elite of the Century and, if not the best, one of the outstanding world players in his position; strong fearless, and ideally suited to the attacking game. Wings Gerald Davies (46), J. J. Williams (30) and John Bevan (10) were all different in approach but equally effective as match-winners. Davies with twenty tries, a record he shares with Edwards, was elusive and fast off the mark, Williams a track champion, slim and swift, almost ethereal in his running, and Bevan, the powerful charger who would run through a brick wall to score for Wales and the Lions. At centre, Dawes (22) himself, smooth and accurate, a good reader of the game; Arthur Lewis, strong in attack and defence, famous for his turning inside to run across the defence; Steve Fenwick, an all-purpose player and accurate place-kicker, chasing after new points records, Ray Gravell, the emotional Welshman and a one-man power house, extremely self-critical of his own play, and Roy Bergiers, superbly built for the position and well-balanced but plagued by injuries.

Two outside-halves of world-class and both record-breakers: Barry John, the smooth, casual yet extremely alert all-round controller and Phil Bennett, the fast moving, dapper, dodger and self-effacing record-breaker and inspirer, much under-rated. The one scrum-half whose career spanned almost the decade, the incomparable Edwards, who had the lot and, like Gould in the early days of the hundred years dominated the closing years, truly a 'Lord of the Fields'.

At forward, the Pontypool front row of A. G. 'Charlie' Faulkner, R. W. 'Bobby' Windsor and Graham Price; the first club front-row (the Viet Gwent trio) to play for Wales. They created new records and were held in

J. P. R. Williams (Bridgend), spanning the decade 1969–79.

Graham Price (Pontypool) (left) and Derek Quinnell (Llanelli) (in possession) of the 1975–79 era.

awe by other front-rows. Faulkner, a senior forward who turned from judo to rugby in his mid-twenties, Windsor who played for Newport Saracens, Cross Keys and Cardiff before becoming an international with Pontypool, and the silent Graham Price, destined to become a world-class prop when still a schoolboy.

The second-row locks, Geoffrey Wheel of Swansea, who played soccer for Swansea City in the Welsh League before turning to rugby and winning a cap in his third season. Allan Martin known as the 'Panther' was an all-round athlete as a schoolboy, and at 6 ft 5 in. destined to become a lineout expert; one of the few top-class men in the decade or at least the quadruple Triple Crown period.

In the back-row, Terry Cobner, nine consecutive seasons as captain of Pontypool and a tremendous driver of forwards; Mervyn Davies, a giant in height and ability who was succeeded by Derek Quinnell playing at number eight or flank, as did flanker Jeff Squire, a Newport number eight who moved to Pontypool. There were others, too, like props Clive Williams and Glyn Shaw for odd matches, and flankers Clive Burgess, Tom David and Trevor Evans. All served their country well and set Wales racing into the next century. There have been many names in the 100 years; players who are still honoured by their clubs and almost worshipped by the followers. If as many great ones are produced in the next hundred years, then Welshmen need not worry unduly about the future of the game in the Principality.

5 CHARACTERS AND AMUSING INCIDENTS

Sport is full of characters, some wholesome, some wayward and some exceedingly amusing. Rugby football is no exception and in the century of the Welsh Rugby Union there have been many characters on and off the field, most of them completely dedicated to the cause of the game. Some have been advanced in years, some young, and much that has happened to them cannot be repeated, at least not in print, although such stories are frequently recalled verbally in club rooms late on Saturday nights. It is then that the meatier stories which form the folklore of the game are repeated.

The Welsh have a passion for nicknames and they shorten the names of as many public figures as possible, even to the use of initials only, a ploy in which the Welsh engaged long before their American cousins. Providing the background to the humour in the game are characters who are funny by design, habit and accident. Rivalries between clubs, as well as players and personalities, have also produced much humour, for even in the heat of battle on the field, players have been able to laugh at their misfortunes.

Happenings and amusing experiences live on to haunt the characters involved; no personality is allowed to forget them, while followers love to recall them before the person involved as if revealing a long-kept secret, in the manner in which they go up to Cardiff committee man and former Welsh flank forward, C. D. Williams, and say, 'I remember you scoring against France in the River Taff!' all because the player touched down for a try before sliding over the deadball line at the River End at the Arms Park. The referee was thirty yards away and the French disputed the try but Williams *did* score a vital and winning try and has perhaps the satisfaction of having to live with it.

C. D. Williams – did he score in the River Taff?

One believes the greatest character of all in the Welsh Rugby Union's hundred years to have been Captain Walter E. Rees, the longest-serving secretary of any national union, starting in 1896 and retiring in 1948; a remarkable span of duty in a career as colourful as any enjoyed by a European diplomat in the first forty years of the present century. He lives on in the stories which are legion and a remarkable tribute to a quite remarkable rugby figure. The first recalled is an occasion towards the end of his career.

After the 1947 Welsh victory at Stade Colombes in Paris, feeling ran high among French followers that they should have won the match and

The five WRU secretaries in the 100 years. *Top row:* R. Mullock, W. H. Gwynn, Walter Rees. *Bottom row:* Eric Evans and W. H. Clement.

with it the championship. As a result, the riot squad of the gendarmerie stood shoulder to shoulder to form a safe path for the Welsh party from the dressing-rooms to the coaches. Captain Rees and myself were the last to leave and the venerable secretary, apart from having been a recruiting officer in World War I was ever a public figure in Welsh life, thrilled with pride at the sight of such a show of strength and whispered to me, 'Thomas, it must be a guard of honour on my behalf!'

On a journey back from Scotland by train from Edinburgh on the Sunday after a Welsh defeat in the 1930s, the Welsh players got a little out of hand and in those days there was no close relationship between players and the Union's executive committee. Wanting to give vent to their anti-committee feelings, they decided to pack the secretary, Captain Rees, into one of the skip baskets containing the playing kit, parked in the corridor. Then they proceeded to throw all the cutlery and china plus table cloths out of the dining-car windows. There was pandemonium by the time the train reached Crewe and half the team forgot to get off there to catch the train to South Wales. In fact they travelled on to Euston and had to pay their own fare from London to Cardiff, so it was Captain Rees who had the last laugh.

He was the centre of many a controversy and humorous story during his long career and was particularly keen concerning the expenses paid to players and settled claims as if giving away his own money. The smaller the claim, the harder he appeared to be, demanding even a penny change from half-a-crown. Yet he was extremely kind and understanding towards undergraduates from Oxford and Cambridge. Two of them once travelled by train from Cambridge to Edinburgh and then took a taxi from the station below the North British Hotel which was the team's headquarters and drove round to the front entrance. One student popped into the foyer to collect from Captain Rees the taxi fare for the two from Cambridge to Edinburgh amounting to £13 simply to pay the taxi driver a couple of shillings! Modern players did not originate the system of 'generous' expenses!

Captain Rees used to hold a 'levee' on international match mornings, dispensing tickets to those paying homage with an accent on the 'Captain'. Often when these matches were over he would find several stand tickets left over in the pocket of his immaculately tailored melton overcoat. He issued tickets to clubs without committee reference and some clubs did better than others, as did some committee men. All details of ticket allocations were kept in Walter's little black book; one that held a thousand and one secrets and would have been a best-seller in twenty languages.

Always an autocrat, Captain Rees, with Horace Lyne (president for forty-one years) ran the Welsh Rugby Union from 1906 to 1947. Rees had served ten years as secretary before Lyne became president, well into the first 'Golden Era'. They were able administrators, JPs and public figures, and in Welsh rugby their word was law, the committee generally playing a passive role.

When the Welsh team played away from home, Captain Rees had two special coaches attached to the train for the official party and one of these was a saloon coach, known as 'Walter's Saloon', in which many a devious plot was devised. Every committee man had to pay homage to Walter, or else he could be suitably rewarded with a cut in his ticket allocation.

Occasionally, on an away trip, a member of the committee would over-imbibe the free spirits and wine and make rude remarks to Walter about his 'dictatorship'. Immediately, a few of his sycophants would rally to his aid. On one occasion in the foyer of the Palais D'Orsay Hotel in Paris, a committee man was justly reprimanded by Walter for 'playing up' to a respectable female guest. The committee man turned on Walter as if to strike him and his days on the Welsh Rugby Union were quickly numbered. His next misdemeanour saw him retired from the Union without the slightest reference to it in the official minutes.

I had to visit Walter at his Neath home once a month, after the Union's general committee meetings to ascertain what was happening on the 'inside'. He was a generous host and after coffee he would refer to the items discussed but often added, 'That's not for publication!' Referring to two piles of correspondence on his desk, he would say confidentially, 'The small one contains the letters I read to the committee; the large one those I deal with myself, as there is no need for them to give an opinion on the required replies!'

Captain Rees had the best-known face in Welsh rugby and his autograph was eagerly sought at functions by young and old. I recall him signing busily at the Tumble Club's Jubilee dinner and heard a comment, 'Why do you want my signature? You can see it on international match tickets!' Back came the prompt reply, 'But we haven't any tickets, sir!' Walter dug into his inside coat pocket and produced a few for the autograph hunters.

Welsh prop Clifton Davies of Kenfig Hill and Cardiff was a fine penillion singer (impromptu speaking in rhyme and song) and while waiting for the coach to arrive at the Paris Hotel, en route to the Gare du Nord to catch the 'Flèche D'Or' to Calais (headed by the magnificent SNCF pacific locomotive hauling superb wagon-lits coaches) Davies started to sing about Walter. His lovely voice filled the foyer and awakened those who had had little or no sleep during the night, 'And there's Walter Rees,

Walter Rees (centre) seen here with Sir David Rocyn Jones, the WRU president, and his successor as secretary, Eric Evans (right) after the veteran secretary had retired.

printing tickets in Neath, and selling them at the Gnoll!' Everyone laughed, of course, and even Walter enjoyed the joke as Davies offended no-one in his short but happy life.

Yet Walter made one vital error towards the end of his career as senior committee members became restive and wished for a new secretary. He outshone the president at Twickenham, and that was unforgivable, setting in motion his retirement. England were playing Wales in 1948 and by tradition the Welsh party used to travel from their hotel to Twickenham in two coaches having lunch on the way. On this occasion the party stayed at the King's Cross Hotel and arrived in good time at Rugby Football Union headquarters with the president, Sir David Rocyn Jones, and the committee in the leading coach and the players and reserves in the second, headed by Haydn Tanner. I recall standing outside the Committee Room entrance with Sir David chatting about the prospects of the afternoon when into the ground roared a large, black Rolls-Royce saloon, preceded by two police outriders on motor cycles with sirens blazing. 'It must be royalty!' remarked a surprised Sir David, but no, out stepped Walter Rees and while Sir David's comment is unprintable, the gist of it was, 'He will have to go!'

Clifton Davies – the 'Singing Prop'.

Because Rees had been secretary for fifty-two years, his resignation at the age of eighty-two still came as a shock to most rugby followers. One day in the summer of 1948 I was summoned to the Queen's Hotel in Cardiff by Sir David Rocyn Jones, a famous orthopaedic surgeon and public figure whose son Nathan played for Wales and followed his father in becoming the Union's honorary surgeon and president. He was short and dapper yet imposing and powerful, and when I arrived at the dining-room for lunch I found a third man, Captain Rees. After an austerity lunch of plaice and french fried potatoes (remember there was food rationing at the time), Sir David turned to Walter and said, 'Now Rees, tell Thomas all about it!' The illustrious secretary hunched his shoulders and with tears in his eyes, whispered, 'I am going to resign!' I could hardly contain myself, so eager was I to race next door and tell Editor David Prosser the news, since it was an obvious page one story. Before departing from the historic lunch, Sir David requested me to attend at the same place, at the same time, two weeks later when a successor would be appointed.

I duly arrived at the dining-room of the Queen's Hotel two weeks later and lunched with Sir David and Eric Evans, a friend of many years, and after the coffee, Sir David turned to Eric and said, 'Now Evans, tell Thomas the news!' and Eric the politest of officials, replied, 'I am the new secretary of the Welsh Rugby Union!' It was another page one story. Sadly, Eric Evans died in 1955 while the Lions were on tour in South Africa and one Welsh Rugby Union member sent me a cable enquiring if I was interested in the post. I thought about it for a few days before deciding against it because the lure of touring was too great. Not that I would have achieved the post; in the end it went by one vote to Bill Clement, a friend of twenty-five years, who just pipped another international, Rees Stephens.

G. V. Wynne-Jones.

When Centenary Year ends Bill Clement will retire and thus only five secretaries will have served the Union in 100 years.

It was always unwise to upstage the all-powerful Welsh Rugby Union presidents. Once a month I used to visit Sir David's house at Llantarnam to discuss Union matters and he would sit at one end of the table, with Lady Rocyn Jones at the other, and myself somewhere in the middle. Sir David would don his small scarlet blazer, presented during the 1936 Championship Year, and make shrewd and often cutting comments about Welsh rugby, the Union, its members and leading players.

When my friend G. V. Wynne-Jones dared to suggest in print that certain clubs were paying their players generous expenses by 'putting the money in the boot', it created a controversy that rocked the corridors of Welsh rugby power. Sir David rode through it all like a knight in shining armour, defender of the faith and the cause of amateurism. Wynne-Jones wrote a book *Sports Commentary* in 1951 but the publishers wanted it to contain some revelations to boost sales. He contributed an additional chapter which included references to illegal payments. The *Western Mail* reviewed the book and made play of the allegations because there was strong suspicion at the time that such things happened, but no proof. Soon the telephone rang and Sir David summoned me to Llantarnam. Accompanied by colleague Dewi Lewis, a splendid news man and rapid shorthand writer, we set off in his old Ford Prefect. Sir David, complete with night-cap, was sitting up in his night-shirt in a great four-poster bed when we entered the bedchamber, and he was soon pounding the bed with his hand and threatening poor Wynne-Jones. 'Scandalous', he said, 'we'll ban him!' Dewi Lewis and myself suggested a lesser punishment, but Sir David persisted and we realised that the budding author was in for a rough ride. He *was* banned from broadcasting on Welsh Rugby Union matches and asked for proof to substantiate his allegations. In fairness to Wynne-Jones, there was no way in which he could produce the proof in writing and the Union would not accept the evidence of a Rugby League player.

Wynne-Jones could not be proved wrong, either, and immediately followers began recalling 'incidents' but it is one thing to suggest illegality and another thing to prove it in Welsh rugby. Sir David retired as president in 1953 and Wynne-Jones eventually was reprieved and continued his commentaries. The bedside interview with Sir David, with myself asking the questions and Dewi Lewis taking down the answers, filled the back page of our paper and was one which Lewis and I still discuss whenever we meet.

Politics within the Welsh Rugby Union was a feature of its daily machinations thirty years ago, but now it does not break surface so often although there are occasional eruptions which recall the comment of that great parliamentarian, Aneurin Bevan. His brother attempted several times to become a member of the Welsh Rugby Union executive but failed, and after complaining to the Member of Parliament one day at the Tredegar home, Nye replied, 'I can hold my own in Parliament even with

Winston Churchill, but I doubt if I could do so in the Welsh Rugby Union where you have to be a super politician to survive!'

The hardest thing is to get elected to the Union and once there, a member attains considerable local stature. In the old days, being a member of the 'Big Five' was something akin to being one of the twelve disciples. Many would-be aspirants for Welsh Rugby Union executive membership spent many pounds helping to kit out clubs and entertain officials but it was the opportunist rugby politician who generally carried the day. Nowadays there have been democratic changes but deep down, as in most ways of Welsh life, canvassing is necessary and the clubs in a member's district have to be visited regularly, with a great deal of hand-shaking. Personally, I have no complaints about the Union set-up. I have been treated with the greatest courtesy at all times by members and officials since 1935, so I can write freely in praise or criticism, and continue to enjoy the friendship of many.

Les Spence, WRU president of 1973–74.

After the memorable 1950 victory over Ireland in Belfast (the last time Wales played there) the Welsh party and supporters drank the cross-channel ferry boat dry even before it cast off. Obviously, the chief steward aboard did not expect Wales to win! In one cabin belonging to a noted Cardiff player who was eventually to become a president of the Welsh Rugby Union, Leslie Spence, a party developed with the aid of a giant pork pie and dozens of bottles of Guinness purchased beforehand. After cutting the pie into slices a former Welsh international and character sent the knife sailing through the cabin port-hole. This heralded a session of 'throwing overboard' and by the time the Cardiff player, who had gone to try and settle a quarrel between two senior Union members in another part of the ship, returned he found his cabin bare. Not a thing remained; even the mattress had gone through the port-hole. In my wildest days in the Royal Navy during the war I could not remember such a clear-out – even on a sinking ship!

When the ship docked at Heysham, no-one was allowed ashore until two detectives had interviewed suspects and officials; and eventually no-one went ashore until Welsh Rugby Union secretary, Eric Evans, had presented a cheque for £80 to cover the loss of the cabin equipment. To this day Les Spence has no concrete proof as to which of his many friends started the clear-out!

However, in his day Les caused a little damage and almost all of it unintentionally. He was travelling with the Welsh Press in France on one occasion, representing the *Fur and Feathered World*, and went to visit a sick member of the press party who was suffering from eating a bad oyster. Les attempted to sit on a valuable chair at the foot of the sick man's bed but, alas, it collapsed into a dozen pieces, and on Sunday morning, the recovering patient had to pay heavily for the broken chair. So much so that he was about to pay for his taxi to the Gare du Nord with his gold watch before Wilfred Wooller spotted the act and rushed to deal with the taxi driver, employing his fluent French (Welsh style).

Eric Evans was a 'down the middle', no-nonsense secretary and during the Irish match of 1952 in Dublin, the ball was kicked into touch among a group of merry Welsh supporters and not returned. The game was held up while another ball was produced but Mr Evans was determined to regain the stolen ball. Through the Welsh press he announced that if the ball was returned no action would be taken, and soon after the return from Dublin he received an anonymous letter from Tredegar, asking that Mrs Evans, a fanatical rugby enthusiast and hard worker for the cause, meet the 'villain' with a shopping basket near to the Evans home at Rumney Hill, Cardiff. The ball was duly placed in the basket at the nominated spot, and the image of Welsh rugby restored when Mr Evans posted the deflated football to Lansdowne Road, Dublin.

In Evans' first season as secretary, Wales met England at Cardiff and for the first time in the 100 years played in white shorts, which he distributed after the match practice. In those days, players did not wear the 'hot pants' of modern times but rather longer ones and these new white ones were akin to the knee breeches of 1880. It was too much for Welsh captain Haydn Tanner, who enquired as to how his side would run in them. Mr Evans suggested that the players' wives or mothers could shorten them. Tanner, something akin to a rugby God at the time and in the last season of a long and magnificent career, threw them back on to the dressing-room table suggesting in no uncertain terms that it was the Union's task to provide suitable gear, and that this was not 1880!

I do not know who shortened the shorts, it could have been Mrs Evans, but the team turned out in immaculate style for the match and won it! Since then they have always played in white shorts except when TV has requested them to play in dark shorts for the aid of viewers with black and white sets. Today, much is done for the benefit of TV, rightly since the BBC pays large sums of money to the Four Home Unions for live television rights.

Pontypool's former prop and club coach Ray Prosser remains one of the original wits of Welsh rugby and a fine, happy, effective Lion of 1959. He once played for Wales with a young lock behind him not renowned for his solid scrummaging. After receiving very little 'weight' behind him during a match Prosser, when asked by master hooker Bryn Meredith what was wrong with the young player, smiled and said, 'When the opposing shove came on he snapped like a stick of celery!'

It was Prosser who said of a rather mean Welsh Rugby Union member, 'He has short arms and deep pockets', and about the 1959 Lions, a rather educated group, he commented 'We Blues must stick together', particularly when addressing David Marques. The much-loved Prosser has the real Gwent dialect and says of many players, 'They'm dull 'uns!' and often refers to sparkling backs as 'Them prima donnas!' Behind his bustling façade and fruity language, Prosser is a deeply sensitive and kindly man, and to be greeted by him with a traditional bear hug is an accolade. In Pontypool he is still the king of rugby.

Haydn Tanner (capt.) with his Welsh XV wearing their new white shorts against England in January 1949.

Fred Phillips, a local builder from the West Wales village of Pontardulais was a good and emotional speaker in Welsh and the firebrand leader of the West Wales Rugby League of the 1940s. In the 1930s he was a notable referee and had charge of the Swansea v New Zealand match of 1935, won so well by Swansea. Mr Phillips spoke to the Swansea team in Welsh and warned the All Blacks in English!

When he became president of the Welsh Rugby Union in 1958 he gave the English language a new meaning and as fair a working over as did Eliza in 'My Fair Lady'! He told Cliff Morgan, who had just joined the *Sunday Times* after retiring from the field he had adorned so well, that the sales of his paper were tumultous. Then referring to new houses being constructed with Government aid in his area, he confirmed that they were built by 'subsidence'. At one dinner where he was guest speaker, he turned towards Swansea's Ron Griffiths and myself and announced with a wicked smile, 'All pressmen should be boiled in oil', the words rolling from his tongue like utterances of an Eastern potentate of the Genghis Khan vintage.

Fred Phillips, WRU president of 1958–59.

Tommy Vile, an outstanding player, referee, administrator, International Board member, Welsh Rugby Union president and public figure, had a reputation for being careful with his pennies, and suffered one black weekend in Paris. First he lost his black melton overcoat but found it again minus a gold cigarette case presented to him by the Newport Club on the occasion of the victory over the Springboks in 1912. He also bought a bottle of quality brandy and hugged it carefully throughout the long journey home, brandy being a rarity in the immediate post-war years. He carried it by boat, train and taxi to his Newport home only to drop it while getting out of the taxi in front of his own gate, where he could only watch,

Referee Tommy Vile at Twickenham in 1928 meeting King George V.

tears in his eyes, as the golden liquid scuttled down the gutter to cause many a local dog weakness in the legs and indigestion!

Another unique president was Enoch Rees of Maesteg, successor to Glyn Stephens, who, when he handed over the chain of office to Rees at the Annual General Meeting of the Union at the Reardon Smith Lecture Theatre in Cardiff, announced, 'Gentlemen, I give you Mr Henoch Haitch Rees!' Mr Rees knew more about sport than most people, having promoted professional boxing and Powderhall racing (professional sprinting) in the Maesteg area. He was a well-known local businessman and a member of the 'Forty thieves', a group of characters who ran the town. While he was a member of the International Board and attending a meeting in New Zealand (the first ever held outside the British Isles – indeed the first outside London and Edinburgh), Vivian Jenkins and myself took him to a shop that sold only protective clothing. He commented, 'It reminds me of the crusades, no wonder the New Zealand Union won't vote for substitutes!' Dickie Jeeps, the Lions scrum-half of the 1959 tour, repeatedly suffered weals on his body from the All Blacks protective clothing, but it was some years before the Board had such accoutrements banned.

Enoch H. Rees, WRU president of 1957–58.

Lt Col Percy Howells of Tenby was a colourful and generous president of the Welsh Rugby Union who once fell asleep after lunch on a Friday in Edinburgh only to be awakened in the evening and told that the match between Scotland and Wales was over. 'Who won?' he asked, and was told, 'Scotland!' to which he replied, 'I told you the selectors should have played the Possibles XV!' At the time, Col Howells was the chairman of the Match Committee that used to select the Possibles XV for Welsh trial matches after the five selectors had chosen the Probables. There was great rivalry between the two committees and, sad to say, many a nomination for a place in the Possibles XV was a district vote-catcher. Col Howells, on being told it was Friday, enjoyed the joke at his own expense and then had the last laugh when Wales lost the following day.

Captain David Hopkin Thomas of Llanelli was a most dignified selector, Welsh Rugby Union president and Board member who delighted in the pomp and ceremony of the upper echelon in the game. His greatest comment was made during a presidential address at the Union's Annual General Meeting when referring to club workers, saying, 'There must be hewers of wood and carriers of water'. A brave World War I soldier, he was known affectionately as 'Dai Hop'. I recall the occasion when he was invited to propose the toast to the Llanelli Wanderers at a dinner to celebrate their becoming members of the Welsh Rugby Union. I was sitting next to him and he suggested that I should give his coat a tug after he had been on his feet for fifteen minutes so that he could wind up his speech. When I duly tugged his coat he turned round and looked down at me with some surprise, and amid roars of laughter said in a loud aside, 'I've only just started!' whereupon a wit shouted, 'Carry on, it will shorten the winter!'

Danny Davies, the Cardiff Club historian, was a cheerful president, and known as the singing president as he invariably led the assembled guests at the end of a big match dinner in the classic, 'Are you from Dixie?' As assistant manager of the 1955 Lions tour he was much loved and created a new team song, 'I was sailing round the Cape, when I had a narrow escape!' Incidentally, he was called Massa Dan, a title still employed with affection by his many friends, because at one stage of the 1955 tour he had almost arranged to bring home with him a native houseboy! As a youngster

D. E. 'Danny' Davies, WRU president of 1963–64.

who had spent his life in Cardiff Docks before World War I, he had a wonderful rapport with the blacks. He has always been an extremely kind man and now, at eighty-two years of age, is as keen as ever about rugby football and its traditions.

Harry Rees, the Cardiff lock or prop of the 1930s, was a worthy police sergeant and something of a character and while often initiating trouble on the field was rarely on the receiving end as can be seen in the story of a friendly match with Aberavon, following a break in fixtures between the two clubs. The wheel always turns full circle in rugby and in 1938 at Murrayfield when he was playing at prop against Scotland, he was caught at the bottom of a pile-up and penalised by Cyril Gadney for not playing the ball. The successful kick at goal decided the match. Gadney commented, 'It was a horrible thing to do at that time of the game. To me it was almost as bad as taking a man's life.' Harry Rees, some time after the end of play said, 'I was lying on the ground with the ball partly under my ribs and with Haydn Tanner, unconscious, lying under me. I could not have played the ball however much I tried.'

Harry Rees – dreaming of aeroplanes.

Another Welsh player explained that Rees was suffering from concussion at the time and kept chattering about aeroplanes – and one did not see many of them forty years ago! The day proved a chapter of accidents for Wales under the leadership of Cliff Jones, with prop Eddie Morgan off the field injured and Wilfred Wooller hurt and almost a passenger. In those days without replacements the task of thirteen and a half players against fifteen was too much. Unfortunately, the Welsh Rugby Union took it very much to heart and did not invite Cyril Gadney to referee again until after the war! As one of the most honest of officials and the best of his day, this was rather sad.

A brave player was Glyn Davidge of Newport and a kindly one on the field. He had a big heart and once when playing against Cardiff at Rodney Parade, Cliff Morgan was the danger man and match-saver, and Newport went after him. The dapper outside-half was brought down by Davidge with the Newport pack hot on his heels. Here was the target they thought and he was due for a lesson but as they thundered close Davidge, a Wales and Lions number eight, whispered, 'Keep still Cliff or they'll bloody trample you to death!' Davidge suffered the hooves and it takes a big man to do that.

Glyn Davidge – 'The Protector'.

On 27 November 1909, W. J. Townsend Collins (Dromio) of the *South Wales Argus* criticised Llanelli for dirty play against Newport at Stradey Park. The club sued the *Argus* for libel in view of Collins' comments and then Newport cancelled fixtures for the 1910–11 season. The *Argus* were asked to pay a farthing damages and Llanelli appealed to the Welsh Rugby Union to ensure Newport fulfilled their fixture. Their appeal was upheld and the match was played in mid-week.

Because he always wrote about Newport, Collins was unfairly criticised by rival club supporters. He had only the sight of one eye and as his critics said, 'that one was black and amber' (the Newport colours). On one Welsh trip to Ireland in the 1920s, Dromio was travelling with the official party as a friend of committee man Harry Packer. It was a rough sea-crossing, and one wag suggested that if the players and officials covered one eye they would not suffer sea-sickness. All was well until one of the party discovered that Collins was sea-sick and, as he was known to have only one good eye, the whole party immediately surrendered to the waves!

It is of interest to compare gate receipts for big matches in the gap of seventy-five years. The 1905 Wales v New Zealand match yielded £2,650 which was a Welsh record at the time with a crowd of 40,000. The 1980 match between the two teams will yield £197,000 from a crowd of over 50,000. The largest attendance at a club match in Wales is 48,500 between Cardiff and Newport at the Arms Park on 17 February 1951, a match won by Newport. Since 1952, honorary treasurer K. M. Harris has seen the Welsh Rugby Union move out of the 'red' into becoming a healthy financial concern.

Cliff Morgan signs autographs two days before gaining his first cap in 1951.

In January 1961, the Welsh selectors assembled at Rodney Parade, Newport, to nominate the side to oppose England, after Wales had lost to South Africa in the 'flood match' of the previous December. They were an extremely long time at the job and eventually Wilfred Wooller and myself ascended the stairs to prompt them. To our surprise there was a strong smell of gas and the selectors were lolling about the table, half-conscious. We assisted then down to the club room and the fittest of them was the oldest member, David Jones, who had suffered the dust of the mines for many years. The team selected duly defeated England and the cry went up after the next match, a defeat at Murrayfield, 'Gas them again!'

K. M. Harris, honorary treasurer of the WRU since 1952 and president 1970–71. He is chairman of the Centenary Committee.

A really lovely story is that concerning former international referee Tommy Schofield of Bridgend; he of the big flat hat. He was introduced to King George V for the second time before the start of an international match at Twickenham, and after the King had shaken hands, Schofield replied, 'This is the second time Your Majesty has had the pleasure!'

'Jammy' Clinch, the notable Irish flanker of the 1920s and early 1930s was something of a character both on and off the field and many are the stories told of his interesting life as player and medical student, and later as a much loved GP in the valleys of Gwent. On one occasion, and there were many, he found himself under 'heavy fire' from an equally stern and unrelenting Welsh flank, Arthur Lemon, who unceremoniously laid Clinch low on the blindside of a maul (rucks were not referred to as such in those days) and when he came round, Clinch was heard to utter the challenge, 'Lemon, I know you did it, I'll squeeze every pip out of your bloody body!' After the match they drank together.

The early post-war visits to Paris were full of fun, and the eve of the match treat for the Welsh side was a visit to the Bal Tabarin, where the players were invited during the show to join the long-legged, scantily-dressed dancers on the stage. On one Saturday night, following the after-match dinner and a second well-timed visit to the Bal Tabarin, the players took to the stage just as it disappeared below ground. From the

David Jones (seated left at table) as chairman of selectors in 1949 with Enoch H. Rees, D. Hopkin Thomas, Ivor Jones and Vincent Griffiths.

cellars of Paris came shrieks of laughter, though presumably the players had made fair tackles, for the stage came up again with dancers and players arm in arm!

The Welsh Press party used to visit Paris in support of the team, well-organised with a president, a cashier, a secretary and an interpreter. Occasionally, a member would pass out and allow his face to fall in his soup. After being saved from 'drowning', he was put into a taxi and the driver liberally tipped to place him safely in the foyer of the Press hotel. One night a driver returned to the restaurant where the press were giving the *escargots* and *beaujolais* a bit of a hammering, and indicated that the party should inspect his cab. On the back seat was a glittering set of dentures and it took more than a few francs to restore the *entente cordiale*.

Three outstanding players who were the 'jolly' boys of the 1930s in Wales were undergraduates who believed in celebrating victory in the appropriate manner, and never failed in comparison with Boat Race night. One of the more amusing evenings or early mornings followed the very famous victory over New Zealand in December 1935. The Queen's Hotel at Cardiff was then the Welsh Rugby Union headquarters on big match weekends, later followed by the Royal Hotel and now the Angel Hotel. Long after the dinner the players celebrated until only the 'holy trinity', who had all played so well in the match, were left. The long counter in the centre bar was full of empty glasses left when the heroes of both sides had departed for bed, all tired and some more than a little unsteady. Our three heroes were still full of fun and one of the trio swept all the empty glasses on to a runner of carpet; another picked up the front and draped his shoulders with the 'regal train', and the third picked up the other end as the 'page in waiting' before all three marched off to the kitchens. The noise of the operation echoed through the hotel but greater noises were to follow.

There is a circular staircase from the foyer up to the top floor at the now closed Queen's Hotel and near the stairs on each floor in 1935 was a vase. The heroes climbed in slow time to the top, dropping a vase down to the foyer from each floor as they went. The noise brought the manager and his wife as near to the scene as possible without risking injury, and the manager's wife complete with hair curlers and dressing-gown, began screaming. Fortunately, the last vase was not dropped from the top floor and remained in the hotel as a symbol of the great 'party' after one of the greatest of all matches played at the Arms Park. Naturally, the Welsh Rugby Union made good the damage; Captain Rees was instructed to speak to our 'heroes', although none was dropped for the next match, and the vase remained until the hotel was closed a few years ago. There followed a sale of furnishings and I regret I was not able to bid for the vase and present it at the appropriate time to the anticipated Welsh Rugby Union museum, with the inscription, 'In honour of three close friends who were outstanding, on and off the field, in December 1935'.

Ray Prosser's descriptions of playing in matches are unique, and he has one word for Reggie Marques being crashed to earth in New Zealand often without the ball, 'Whoosh! The All Blacks spun him like a catherine wheel!' With his big tour friend, number eight Alan Ashcroft, they would sit looking at a mirror and sing, 'Mirror, mirror, on the wall who's the ugliest of us all!' Ray would shout, 'Ned' (the tour name for Ashcroft) and Ashcroft would shout 'Ray', and often they would make so much noise as to disturb the guests in their rooms. Then they would march down the hotel stairs, arm in arm, to where the Lions were dining and shout, 'We really are a handsome pair of b******s!'

Ray Prosser and Bryn Meredith were great friends on and off the field and Bryn has some superb stories to tell of Ray's comments in the front row of the scrum. However, Ray tells the best of them against himself, 'A chap in Timaru bonked me on the nose in a maul, and so I went looking for him but he saw me first and bonked me again, and this time he broke my nose. Those South Islanders are hard b******s!'

A biting incident occurred during the Wales v England match at Cardiff in 1965. An English forward claimed he was bitten and the referee stopped the match to speak to the Welsh captain, smiling Clive Rowlands. He asked the name of the culprit and the Welsh captain responded with his ready wit, 'I don't know ref, but it wasn't me, my dentures are in the dressing-room!' as he revealed a set of bare gums.

Clive Rowlands, the Welsh captain, who left his teeth in the dressing room!

A joint Pontypool Newport and Newbridge side was playing the Springboks at Pontypool Park and a Springbok was left lying on the ground as a ruck moved on. When play stopped the 'rub-a-dub' came running on while a rich Welsh voice bellowed, 'Nothing trivial, I 'ope!'

Gareth Edwards, who has a fine sense of rugby humour, was once reprimanded for speaking in Welsh by a South African referee in a test. The referee was not an expert and Edwards was giving him a little 'stick'. When the referee spoke to him, Edwards replied that he was giving his forwards secret instructions as were the Springboks in Afrikaans.

Gareth Edwards showing his commemorative cap to Phil Bennett and Gerald Davies, as the first player to make fifty appearances for Wales.

The famous Lions trio of 1955 who formed a formidable front-row, Courtenay and Bryn Meredith plus W. O. 'Billy' Williams, became bored with the South African front-row speaking in Afrikaans, and devised their own system by saying in Welsh to one another, because they were not fluent Welsh speakers, 'Good morning!', 'Merry Christmas!', 'Happy New Year!', 'Sit down!' and 'Good night!' It was good tactics because the Springboks thought the phrases indicated special moves. Dickie Jeeps at scrum-half didn't understand them but Welsh-speaking outside-half Cliff Morgan thoroughly enjoyed the joke.

Gareth Edwards was once squashed almost unconscious beneath a maul in the centre of Loftus Versfeld, on the hard cricket square, during a test match. Eventually the maul, which included some heavyweights, dispersed to leave Edwards prostrate on the ground in need of attention. The ambulance men arrived and eventually the recovering Edwards looked up into the blazing sun in a cloudless sky and uttered the memorable words, 'Don't move me, bury me!'

Finally, an amusing story of Wales playing at Twickenham in 1970. Twenty minutes from the end, Wales were trailing at 6–13 and Gareth

Edwards, the Welsh captain, was forced to leave the field through injury. One of the selectors rushed down to get the replacement, Ray Hopkins of Maesteg, ready to take the field once the duty medical officer had declared Edwards unfit. This duly took place and, on his way back to the committee box, the selector visited a toilet. Unfortunately, he locked himself in and could not get out until the match was over and the teams returned to the dressing-rooms. Thus the selector did not see Wales recover, Hopkins score a try, and England defeated by 17–13!

It became known as the match the selector did not see but although Hopkins did not receive a cap in the sense that he was selected for Wales, he holds two records. Chosen to tour New Zealand in 1971 as understudy to Edwards he again took the field as a replacement for his rival in the first test at Dunedin when Edwards was injured after ten minutes. Thus he remains the only player to have received an international cap and a test cap as a replacement. Hopkins joined the Rugby League later but was never as happy there as when 'standing in' for Edwards.

Welsh rugby still has a sense of humour even though the dedication in 1980 is far greater than it was in 1881, for characters come and go although each generation believes that there are not as many as there were. The game moves on into its second century which should prove every bit as colourful as the exciting first one.

6 THE CLUBS

In 1980, there are nineteen clubs in the list forming the basis of the Welsh Championship table and by common consent they are recognised as the leading clubs. The majority have existed for a hundred years or more, though some are more modern; still others have suffered trials and tribulations. Economic trends in Wales have affected various clubs and some that were great before the turn of the century have suffered from declining industrial wealth and growth in their areas and from migrating populations. Where coal was once the king and steel was made in the hills, coal production has been reduced in tonnage and in the number of workers employed in the industry while steel production has been moved to the coast and become highly mechanised.

There has been a diversification of industry and movements of population. The increased mobility of players has seen many move from club to club and fewer locals highlighting the ranks of the various clubs. Some have attracted players from far and wide, but now more than ever before it is possible for a player to achieve national recognition no matter of which of the top clubs he is a member.

The clubs that helped form the Welsh Rugby Union in 1880–81 have survived; some have gained in power, others have remained what they were one hundred years ago, still an essential part of the rugby family in Wales, and producing the odd player for senior clubs and later, perhaps, international honours. By the turn of the century the 'Big Four', Cardiff, Llanelli, Newport and Swansea, were the leaders and they still are, even if one of their number, like Mr Micawber, has fallen upon evil times and awaits better fortune.

In reviewing the clubs and their achievements, it is wise to do so alphabetically, for the rivalries are still great and pride of achievement an important thing. It would be possible to compile a whole book of interest upon each club, if not one as concise as that prepared for the Cardiff Club by the gentle veteran of the game and one of its more remarkable historians, Danny 'Massa' Davies, whose work of a lifetime was produced for the Club's Centenary. One is deeply conscious of the efforts made by the statisticians of all those Clubs who have celebrated their Centenaries.

ABERAVON

Founded: 1876. HQ: Talbot Athletic Ground. Colours: Red and black hoops.

Whenever there was a dull moment on any of the tours one shared with Vivian Jenkins and a discussion started as to the relative strength of clubs, he would sing 'Bravon, Bravon, you're going to beat Swansea today!', and this is the Aberavon Club's 'War Song' which has echoed through many a clubhouse when the 'Wizards' have had the scent of victory in their nostrils.

Aberavon, long known as 'Merlin's Wizards', celebrated their Centenary in 1976 and for them it had been one hundred years of good times and bad but in the main good, and today they remain exceedingly healthy, proud, noisy and ready for action. The club is unashamedly partisan, and possesses in Mrs Mainwaring a lady supporter and cheerleader better known in Wales than many players!

For Aberavon it all began in 1876 when three local sportsmen, Messrs Cooke and Martin and Dr Jack Jenkins founded the club and became its initial chairman, secretary and captain. It prospered because several new tinplate works were established in the area, although fixtures were few and

The Aberavon side of 1973–74 who were beaten in the WRU Cup Final by Llanelli 12–10. *At back:* K. Evans, R. Davies. *Standing:* M. Trigg, O. Alexander, W. T. Mainwaring, A. J. Martin, J. Owen, C. Williams. *Seated:* J. Griffiths (trainer), Kim Davies, I. Hall, M. Howells, P. Morgan (coach), A. Rees, M. Swain. *In front:* J. D. Bevan, R. C. Shell. This side included seven internationals with the coach.

far between at the start and the side did not travel far from its first playing field near the Port Talbot Docks.

An early hero was Bathuel Hancock, a relative of the club's present president, Lord Heycock, and since the first season the club has played on many grounds in the area before the present home of the Talbot Athletic Ground was occupied. It was destined to become the local rugby shrine before World War I. Aberavon soon celebrated the permanence of its tenure at the ground by winning the second Welsh Challenge Cup (the Welsh Rugby Union now has its third competition in operation) in 1913–14.

Humphrey Leyshon, W. R. Thomas and Lord Heycock remain the most ardent of the club's leaders in the 100 years but there have been many faithful helpers, none more so than the gentle forward of the 1920s–30s, Miah McGrath, the hairpin-slim fullback, T. O. James, and a host of others including the late David Phillips and the present secretary and Welsh Rugby Union and International Board member, Gwilym Treharne. Many matches have been played against major and minor touring teams and often in harness with neighbouring rivals, Neath, and none more memorable than that against the Springboks in 1931 which produced at least a moral victory.

In the 1920s and 1930s the club was a power in the land, proving worthy champions in several seasons, although since World War II its fortunes have fluctuated. From 1946 to 1963 it was only twice out of the top ten and was champion club in 1961 following half a dozen comparatively poor years and then runners-up in 1975 to Pontypool.

Starting with Dan Jones in 1897 and ending with Allan Martin in 1980, the club has provided forty-three international players for Wales and one for England with an unusual father–son combination of George Vickery (England) and Walter Vickery (Wales). The most capped player is Allan Martin (27) followed by Ned Jenkins (21). Since World War II there have been nineteen cap winners, and father and son combination, W. R. and Hywel Thomas, honoured as Welsh Rugby Union presidents.

In recent years since the resumption of the Welsh Rugby Union Challenge Cup, the club has reached two finals and several semi-finals, albeit without winning the trophy, while there have been three British Lions in Tony O'Connor, John Bevan and Allan Martin. In addition, local youth and schools rugby is in a healthy condition suggesting a secure future for the steel town club.

ABERTILLERY

Founded: 1901. HQ: Sports Club. Colours: Green and white hoops.

Several Gwent clubs were formed at the turn of the century and Abertillery as one of them, like its fellows, has suffered its ups and downs and is still struggling. Many players continue the trend of moving down the valleys attracted by the lure of the coastal clubs, or of moving as promising young players to where employment is available. Yet the top of the valley clubs survive and if outstanding players are not always available, there is the hard core of faithful workers, officials and followers who hold it all together.

There have been great days in the club's history such as when Dr Moran's first Wallabies were held to a draw (3–3) in 1908; when the club lost only by a point to the 1931 Springboks when in harness with Cross Keys, and the defeat of the Wallabies in 1957 while teamed with Ebbw Vale. Important days are worth remembering and for the valley clubs they are as good as a blood transfusion.

It is accepted that the first interesting rugby match in the town was that of October 1892 when the old town XV played Tredegar at the Gas Works Field and that two teams combined in 1901, the old Town XV and Abertillery Harlequins, to form the present club. It entered the Monmouthshire League, of which old timers speak with pride in the western valleys of the county, and was recognised by the Welsh Rugby Union in 1907 after the club had headed the League and earned the right to play against the Australian touring side in the following season on Christmas Day 1908. For the players, the day's traditional dinner was delayed until the evening and then they celebrated.

This match established the club among its senior fellows and it proceeded to supply an interesting list of players, mainly hard forwards, who served Wales well: Jim Webb, Bedwellty Jones, Hocker Thomas, Albert Fear, Bill Morris, W. J. Blakemore and George Parsons, followed by two of the club's most famous players in the British Lions – Haydn Morgan and Alun Pask. In the 1920s, one of the biggest and best of scrum-halves, W. C. 'Wick' Powell, started his career with the club, and a Scottish international, one of many doctors to settle in the Welsh Valleys, E. C. Fahmy, played for his country in 1920.

Twice was the club runner-up in the Championship before winning the title in 1931 and holding a ground record for four years, when no opponents could contain Abertillery's fiery pack of forwards. Well-known officials include L. W. Thomas, Bill Lloyd, Wilfred Rogers and Ron Jones. The club's ground is owned by the local authority and is one of the prettiest in Wales, especially when the surrounding trees carry the tints of autumn. The clubhouse is in the town and to drive in and out of Abertillery is an experience which immediately creates a vivid picture of valley life. The folk are friendly but hard competitors on the field of play. Support for the club is not as good now as it was in the 1930s when a visit to Abertillery was never undertaken optimistically by any club and when one match, against the reigning champions of the day, Pontypool, attracted a crowd of 30,000. Pontypool were led by a former Abertillery player, Cliff Axford, and his presence in the opposition inspired the locals to victory.

Since World War II the club has achieved a place in the top ten in eight seasons but the last few have proved difficult. Finding young players of promise, and keeping them, has become a major problem for top of the valley clubs. Abertillery battles on; but the struggle is not an easy one.

BRIDGEND

Founded: 1878. HQ: Brewery Field. Colours: Royal blue and white hoops.

Bridgend celebrated their Centenary season in the grand manner in the winter of 1978–79 by winning the Welsh Rugby Union/Schweppes Cup and coming second in the Western Mail Club Championship. This wiped out the sad memory of a stupid New Zealand prop trampling on their proud and defiant captain, J. P. R. Williams, when not in possession of the ball at the famous Brewery Field. In one hundred years of rugby, Bridgend has suffered a chequered career but since returning, finally, to the Brewery Field in 1958 it has been a success story all the way.

It is a club that has streamlined and modernised itself without losing its character, and boasts the longest serving, first-class honorary secretary in Durbar Lawrie, a friend of the people. Few administrators do more to keep the world acquainted with their club than Mr Lawrie, and his industry is not often matched by the secretaries of certain other clubs. Whatever is happening or has happened in the club, Mr Lawrie is aware of it.

The club began playing on the Old Mill Field in Tondu Road and then moved to the Quarella Field until after World War I, when it was decided to use the Brewery Field, a decision which must have delighted players past and present, since it is still argued that the team performs with greatest enthusiasm when playing towards the old brewery end! Greyhound racing captured this field in 1932 and the Bridgend caravan was off again to the Uxilla Field, which previously staged association football. A few years there, then back again to the Brewery Field, where the smell of the hops still remained, before an ill-fated rugby league venture took over the ground. Bridgend played 'home' fixtures at Cardiff and Aberavon and then used the Island Farm POW Camp and changed in dressing-rooms where once no less a campaigner than Field Marshal von Rundstedt used to change into his night attire. On to the Bandstand Field, before returning yet again to the Brewery Field to launch the most successful period in the club's history.

Since the 1960–61 season they have won the *Western Mail* Championship on four occasions and always been with the leaders, producing outstanding combinations, quality rugby and a host of players for Wales. Of the twenty-one players capped from the club, eleven have been

The Bridgend team which won the WRU/Schweppes Cup in 1978–79. *Standing:* C. Thomas (touch judge), D. J. Lloyd (coach), G. Jones, D. Brain, I. Stephens, R. Evans, Gareth Williams, L. Davies, M. James, S. P. Fenwick, S. Ellis, K. Rowlands (referee), C. Norling (touch judge), W. Griffiths (coach). *Seated:* K. Townley, V. Jenkins, I. Davies, G. Davies, J. P. R. Williams (capt.), L. Thomas, I. Lewis, Gerald Williams. *In front:* R. Llewellyn, A. Rose, C. Williams, R. O'Connell.

honoured since World War II, some of them outstanding performers, the like of J. P. R. Williams, Steve Fenwick, John Lloyd, Jeff Young and W. R. Evans. Of the years before, W. J. 'Bobby' Delahay ranks high for his all-round ability, plus the man who kicked-off to start international rugby at Twickenham in 1910, Ben Gronow, who became a rugby legend in his own lifetime.

The club has produced six Lions, five of them since World War II, and the post-war years must be regarded as the 'Golden Era' of the club although there were characters between the wars and none more important in the rugby world than the pint-sized administrator, T. D. 'Tommy' Scourfield who for many years was 'Mr Rugby' in the area, a member of the Welsh Rugby Union, an international referee and member of the International Board, and an expert in the laws of the game who hid beneath a giant, flat cap. Often nothing more was seen of him as he moved through the crowds than a pair of shoes and a flat hat! His word was law in the club, for being a member of the Board was the nearest thing to being crowned in the game. Now Bridgend drives on majestically; solvent, happy, important in the game, extremely well-administered and most capable on the field of play.

CARDIFF

Founded: 1876. HQ: Cardiff Arms Park. Colours: Blue and black hoops.

If not the greatest club in the world, as is claimed by its long-serving members, then Cardiff must be the most consistent as the records prove. One of the 'Big Four', it is *the* club that everyone, yes, just about everyone in the world wishes to defeat. Once in a while they achieve that ambition, and this in itself must be the true measure of the club's greatness. It matters more than Cardiff's post-war record in the club championship,

The Cardiff team which narrowly lost to New Zealand 10–8 in December 1905. *Standing:* J. L. Williams, J. Brown. E. Rumbelow, W. Neill, L. George, F. Smith, Gil Evans (referee). *Seated:* E. G. Nicholls, G. Northmore, P. F. Bush (capt.), R. T. Gabe, R. A. Gibbs. *In front:* R. Thomas, H. B. Winfield, R. David, J. Powell.

which produces an average of third place and only once in thirty-three seasons has it fallen lower than seventh position. Although they won the title five times in the first twelve years after World War II and never since, they have maintained a remarkable consistency of performance.

In the 1976–77 season the club celebrated its Centenary with true pomp and ceremony, after having played well over 3,000 first-class matches in the 100 years and having produced over 150 internationals; the most by any Welsh club. It also had a record number of ten in the same national side in 1948. It has been represented on every British Lions tour since 1904 with a total of twenty-eight players.

It has remained rather independent in attitude and approach, accepting praise and criticism with equal calm, and has endeavoured to maintain a committee composed of former players. For the greater part of its career, the club played on what is now the Arms Park national ground. This was its true home, but when the time came for the Welsh Rugby Union to have a home of its own, the late president of the Cardiff Club, Hubert Johnson, produced a plan that enabled the Union to take over the Arms Park while creating a club ground alongside it, on what was a splendid cricket ground. Cardiff opened its new club ground in 1970 and it has proved most popular although the club is still encouraged by the Welsh Rugby Union when major tours occur to play the opposition on the national ground. It boasted the oldest-surviving international until 1979 when Ewan Davies (the club's honorary solicitor) died at the age of ninety-two. Many of its internationals were honoured with the captaincy of their country.

The club has always run two sides, the 1st XV and the Athletic or 'Rags' XV. In recent years it has run a successful youth team but there was a stage in its history, between 1926 and 1931, when the club ran two first XVs. This was carried out as a financial experiment, following the purchase of the Cardiff Arms Park, in order to provide a first-class 'home' match every Saturday. Thus in 1926–27 the club created a record that will last for ever, one believes, by fulfilling eighty-one first-class fixtures!

Unlike its near-neighbour and perennial rival, Newport, it has never achieved an invincible year, although losing only once in a season on two occasions to Moseley in 1885–86 and to New Zealand in 1905–06 and only twice in the 1947–48 season (Pontypool and Penarth), with the respective captains being F. E. Hancock, Percy Bush and Haydn Tanner.

Many players have migrated to Cardiff down through the years, especially from West Wales; many to achieve their first caps after so doing, which created the saying, 'if you want a cap, join Cardiff'. Times have changed and the 'Big Four' in Wales have become the 'Big Ten'. Yet it remains important for every other club to beat Cardiff and this may be their way of offering a salute to a great club.

The outstanding Cardiff side of 1947–48. *Standing:* W. G. Jones, G. Evans, L. Manfield, W. E. Tamplin, R. Roberts, E. Jones, C. Davies. *Seated:* A. D. S. Bowes, D. H. Jones, Dr J. Matthews, H. Tanner (capt.), D. E. Davies (chairman), B. L. Williams, W. B. Cleaver, R. F. Trott. *In front:* M. James, L. Williams.

A group of Cardiff captains. *Standing:* Dr J. Matthews (1945–46), B. L. Williams (1949–50), W. E. Tamplin (1950–51), W. R. Willis (1952–53), M. Collins (1955–56), P. Goodfellow (1956–57), E. Thomas (1957–58), L. Williams (1960–61), D. J. Hayward (1963–64), H. M. Roberts (1964–65), K. A. Rowlands (1965–66), C. H. Norris (1967–68), J. P. O'Shea (1969–70). *Seated:* W. Wooller (1938–39), L. M. Spence (1936–37), T. Stone (1935–36), T. Lewis (1932–33), D. E. Davies (1925–26). (Twelve of these were international players.)

CROSS KEYS

Founded: 1900. HQ: Pandy Park. Colours: Black and white hoops.

Since World War II Cross Keys has not been the power in the land it was between the Wars, and it now faces a stern battle of survival year in, year out, but without the slightest thought of conceding the cause. Lying in the Western Valley of Monmouthshire, only a few miles north of Newport, it has suffered much from the siren call of the more glamorous clubs, yet for spirit none can better the 'Keys'. Friendly, workmanlike and proud, ready to accept the inevitability of its lot caused by the changing economic face of the valleys of South Wales and Monmouthshire. It has known great days and shared with other valley clubs in many a stern struggle against major sides from overseas, perhaps none as stirring as that of 1931 when in combination with Abertillery, they suffered defeat by a mere point at the hands of Bennie Osler's mighty Springboks.

It is suggested that the club was formed in the late 1890s, about 1897, and was known as the Cross Keys Harriers when recognised by the Welsh Rugby Union and granted official status, always a big event in the life of an emerging club. Its title was shortened to Cross Keys and it played its matches on a field in Mr Hoare's farm, later to become Pandy Field. Since those far-off first days the living has never been easy and the cash always in short supply, but the spirit superb. By 1909 the club had become the Monmouthshire League Champions. In many ways that competition was

The Cross Keys team of 1973–74. *Standing:* W. Jenkins (touch judge), B. Anthony, B. Allen, D. Eatwell, M. Hughes, G. Hewlett, L. Shipp, D. Cain, R. Badman (trainer), C. Thomas (referee). *Seated:* C. Evans, G. Bram, D. Thomas, W. Amos, W. James (capt.), P. Watkins, R. Roberts, R. Griffiths.

a survival course and only the strongest succeeded. This is not to suggest it was dirty, just plain hard!

Between the Wars the club blossomed and enjoyed its heyday; in 1922 it was the Champion Club and in 1922–23 when mighty Newport were invincible, Cross Keys had the power to share a pointless draw at Rodney Parade. No club did better that season, and soon the Cross Keys pack became known as the 'Terrible Eight' with opponents quaking at the knees even before the start of each match. The pack's pillars of fire and inspiration were Steve Morris, Ron Herrera and Fred Bowdler, all worthy internationals.

Through the 1930s the Cross Keys beacon shone brightly and the championship was won again in 1936 before Cardiff, with Wooller and Jones, took over. The Keys held a ground record for three years with Lion Russell Taylor and Walter Ward, Con Murphy and Trevor Williams providing the basis of a powerful pack. Before he went to Cardiff, local schoolmaster B. O. Male was capped from the club. After World War II it was harder, when promising players travelled down the valley to Newport although one, Rex Richards, was capped at prop before turning to professional sport as an aquatic expert.

Stuart Watkins and Brian Price, long-serving Newport and Wales players, started with Cross Keys, as did R. W. 'Bobby' Windsor, and they still come and go, benefitting by a short stay at the Keys. The club does not sit back and mourn the loss of such players but gets on with the job. It was one of the first clubs in Wales to install floodlighting, though it was all but a flickering candle, and a new system has since been installed to emulate its big brothers. Senior members recall the great days readily and even now a visiting club never finds it easy at Pandy Park in mid-winter when the mists shroud the neighbouring hills. Always the welcome in the clubhouse is warm, from an honest club that serves the game faithfully.

EBBW VALE

Founded: 1879. HQ: Eugene Cross Park. Colours: Red, green and white hoops.

The Combined Ebbw Vale and Newbridge side, captained by Eric Finney, which defeated the South African Combined Universities 6–5 at Ebbw Vale in February 1957.

One is led to believe that Ebbw Vale was founded in 1900 although rugby was played in the valley as far back as 1877 with teams bearing unique names like Bakehouse Rovers, Brierley Hill, the Lillywhites and the Crusaders who played on stony pitches and tips. They must have joined together at some stage and appeared as an Ebbw Vale team in the 1880s playing on Dobb's Field, south of the present ground. They joined the Monmouthshire League before the end of the nineteenth century and engaged in the struggle for survival.

Although unbeaten for two seasons a rent of £2 a match at the Bridgend field was too much and the club left the League for a period before returning in 1908. For several years there was the challenge of Rugby League in the town but it did not survive and disappeared before the outbreak of World War I. After the War a Welfare Scheme was started at the local steelworks and this launched the drive back to fame and fortune. The scheme is still in being and the club now boasts a first-class clubhouse and ground.

Alas, the steelworks closed down in 1928 and the club suffered hard times before a new steel complex was opened ten years later and the men who made the steel for the weapons of war worked hard and played hard and in 1939–40 they enjoyed an invincible season under a remarkable clubman Wally Talbot. After the War the club was strong enough to be accepted into the official championship as a fully fledged first-class club for the 1949–50 season. Since then it has enjoyed good fortune and much success and shared in many matches against major touring teams.

It has produced half a dozen spirited internationals in Graham Powell, David Nash, Denzil Williams, Graham Jones, Arthur Lewis, Clive Burgess and Paul Ringer and of these, Nash, Williams and Lewis were British Lions. The powerful Williams is the most-capped of Welsh props and Lewis is now the club's able coach. Ebbw Vale have been lucky with their former players, for many have remained to help as administrators and this has ensured an excellent club spirit.

GLAMORGAN WANDERERS

Founded: 1893. HQ: Memorial Ground, Ely. Colours: Cambridge blue, black and white.

The Glamorgan Wanderers side of 1969–70. *Standing:* R. Geddes, C. Mallows, P. Kallonas, M. Fudge, J. Davies, S. Williams, D. Lloyd (referee). *Seated:* R. Furness, P. Richards, H. Morgan, R. Brinning, K. Evans, T. O'Gorman (capt.), T. Coombes, D. Ewington, C. Lewis.

The Wanderers can claim to run more sides than any other first-class club in Wales and has a splendid community spirit in which all players are equal and share in the goodwill. Few players, if any, are turned away and one is always sure of a game – providing one is fit! Since its foundation in 1893 it has produced many characters who played for fun and until recent years refused to engage in the dedication of modern club football. Now it plays as well and as hard as any of its rivals; since it is well-coached and disciplined, and has a committee that works really hard to maintain good standards and improve amenities as cash permits.

Many of its members are distinguished professional men headed by a notable high court judge, Sir Tasker Watkins, VC. He was a more than useful outside-half in his playing days and like all members enjoys the warm friendly atmosphere that exists on and off the field.

The club was launched by a group of former pupils of Monkton House School, playing under the title of the Old Monktonians before changing to the Glamorgan Wanderers in 1913. Its first ground was alongside the Station Hotel at Llandaff, a pleasant suburb of the City of Cardiff, and then at the Polo Field, Whitchurch from 1919 to 1951 when a final move was made to the Memorial Ground at Ely, a western suburb of the city.

However, in 1927 a social section was formed with a clubhouse in the city centre and this became popular with all major touring sides in Wales. It was the first rugby social club in Wales and lasted until the 1970s. The first leading figure in the club was Cyril David as captain, chairman and president, and chairmen of note followed him in Tom Kerman, Lindsay Richards and Tasker Watkins, with hard-working secretaries in C. B. Boughton, Bill Maxwell and Ken Mathias.

Internationals have appeared in the club ranks, notably J. L. Williams and C. L. Davies, as well as 1930 British Lion Howard Poole and Ivor Nicholls, son of Gwyn Nicholls. The club's best season was in 1961–62 when it achieved fifth place in the championship table, to which it was admitted in 1957–58.

LLANELLI

Founded: 1872. HQ: Stradey Park. Colours: Scarlet.

One of the original 'Big Four' Welsh clubs, and still a major power in Welsh rugby, Llanelli is known throughout the world as the 'Sospans' and a side that continues to strike alarm into major touring teams when they take the field at the historic Stradey Park. It has played a notable part in the development of the game in Wales since it emerged as a club in the 1875–76 season, producing a host of notable players in its 105 years with almost 120 internationals among them. This is a magnificent record and although several players left the club to move to the East and play for Cardiff, they always remembered what they had learned in the West!

Club rivalries form the rich red blood that flows so proudly through Welsh rugby and Llanelli has a long record of struggles with the 'Swansea Jacks' and the Cardiff 'Blue and Blacks', while their encounters with the Aberavon 'Wizards' have caused many a 'Sospan' to boil over in enthusiasm. Once a report of a Llanelli v Newport match was the subject of a court case for libel with one penny damages. They take their rugby seriously in Llanelli and do a fine job as an essential stanchion in the Welsh rugby set-up.

The Llanelli team, complete with blazers and caps, which defeated the Australian touring 'Wallabies' at Stradey Park in October 1908. It was the first defeat of the tour as Llanelli won by a goal and a try to a try (8–3).

Owing much for my knowledge of Llanelli and its atmosphere to Rhys Gabe, my rugby tutor for many years, and being allowed the privilege of being a ball-boy at Stradey Park during pre-season training there in the 1920s as a relative of outside-half Dai John, I was able to study closely the scarlet giants of the day and none were more colourful than Albert Jenkins and Ivor Jones. In those years Llanelli was a town of tinplate and rugby; there was no escape!

Gabe told me of his boyhood heroes, Owen Badger, D. H. Bowen, D. J. Daniel, Ben Davies, C. B. Nicholl and Conway Rees, and they were giants; while amongst his own colleagues for Llanelli and Wales before he moved to the East were Willie Arnold, Tom Evans, J. Strand Jones, Harry Watkins and Jim Watts. Then between the Wars emerged players like Albert Jenkins, Ivor Jones, Dai and Arthur John, the two Bryn Evanses, Ernie Finch, Jim Lang, Archie Skym, Watcyn Thomas and Bill Clement.

After World War II, Llanelli turned from the men of the tinplate industry to those of steel and light industry and many from the broad farming acres west of the town. They suffered no shortage of players for as soon as a gap appeared there were two or more applicants waiting to join. Later players came from far and wide to join Llanelli in the 1970s, as the chance of gaining a cap from the Scarlets' ranks became more obvious. I still recall with pleasure and admiration hard forwards like Ossie Williams and Stan Williams, iron men, and a fullback as good as Terry Davies, an elusive scrum-half Onllwyn Brace, the amazing Lewis Jones, the strong

The Llanelli Cup-winning side of 1976 which defeated Swansea at the Cardiff Arms Park 16–4. *Standing:* T. Hudson (assistant coach), D. Nicholas, R. Hyndeman, E. R. Thomas, C. Thomas, H. Jenkins, P. May, A. James, R. Powell, K. Coslett, B. Peel (trainer), N. R. Gale (coach). *Seated:* C. Griffiths, R. W. Gravell, A. Crocker, D. L. Quinnell, P. Bennett (capt.), R. T. Bergiers, S. Williams, J. J. Williams.

and sound R. H. Williams, a superb craftsman at lock, and the man of all seasons in the game, Carwyn James. Recent years have produced Phil Bennett, Delme Thomas, J. J. Williams, Norman Gale, Barry Llewellyn, Roy Bergiers, Derek Quinnell and many others, not forgetting Barry John who started with the club.

Llanelli's history is a parade of great names but there have been some entertaining officials in F. L. Margrave, Jack Auckland, Elvet Jones, Bryn Evans, D. H. Thomas (Dai Hop), Harry Llewellyn, Handel Rogers and Ken Jones. Since the revival of the Welsh Rugby Union Cup Championship, Llanelli have won it on four consecutive occasions and appeared in five finals – a remarkable record!

They have miniature 'Sospans' on the top of the four uprights at Stradey Park and it is said that when the Llanelli club fails, Welsh rugby will end. 'It all starts at Llanelli, in the West!', and then they add, 'Of course, it is far better told in Welsh!' Ymlaen, Sospan!

LONDON WELSH

Founded: 1885. HQ: Old Deer Park. Colours: Scarlet.

Many hold the impression that the London Welsh Club became an important one when it took up residence at Old Deer Park in 1957 but it is now ninety-five years old and was started by a medical man who ran it in the early years from his surgery at 11 Hills Place. He was Dr Pryce-Jenkins, a kindly, enthusiastic and generous man and his idea was a little acorn that is now a very large and thriving oak at Old Deer Park, with London Welsh being one of the most successful of metropolitan clubs. Dr Pryce-Jenkins was a product of Llandovery College, many of whose former pupils have played for the 'Welsh', who developed his skill and

The London Welsh team of 1970–71 which just failed to win the Welsh Club Championship. *Standing:* C. Bosley (touch judge), P. Davey, J. P. R. Williams, I. C. Jones, M. G. Roberts, T. G. Evans, T. M. Davies, R. H. Phillips, A. Richards, K. Hughes. *Seated:* T. Davies, A. Gray, S. J. Dawes (capt.), J. Taylor, Trevor Davies, W. G. Hullin. (Ten of these players were or became Welsh internationals.)

love of the game at Cambridge University and Blackheath.

Vivian Jenkins, a former captain, prepared a detailed history of the club for a special publication honouring the move to Old Deer Park from Herne Hill in 1957, when the Prince of Wales opened the ground and watched a special match refereed by another club stalwart, Arthur Rees, who played with Jenkins for Wales in the 1930s. Tribute was paid to many characters and a co-founder with Pryce-Jenkins was Dr Rowley Thomas who was eighty-six years old when he died in 1949, and a remarkable all-round sportsman, playing six times for Wales as a forward. Vivian Jenkins puts forward the theory that as so many Welshmen were playing rugby in the London area for other clubs, they must have asked themselves 'Why not play together?'

A. J. Gould was present at the founding of the club and as always the influence of the 'great one' was for the benefit of Welsh rugby. There followed colourful days as famous international players spent some time in the London area and played for the club even though grounds were difficult to obtain. The club played at Herne Hill from 1919 to 1957 and during that period there were good years and bad but the spirit never wavered as players of quality continued to appear. The London Welsh was fortunate with its officials, patient and hard working, and one who provided me with a great deal of background and detail of its happy existence was the late Aneurin Jenkins who, when asked which player he thought to be the most colourful of all, had no hesitation in saying, 'There were many characters, but the chief of these must have been W. C. "Wick" Powell.' From the club was launched Captain Crawshay's Welsh XV in the 1920s and since arriving at Old Deer Park, the club has enjoyed unusual success. A host of international players, headed by John Dawes, gave a new image to London rugby, and the spirit permeated through to the Welsh XV. At the time the rivalry between the London Welsh and the leading indigenous clubs was considerable but it helped to create a return to the running game which highlighted the last decade.

The club has produced so many characters off the field, among them Viscount Tenby, Lloyd Owen, Wavy Thomas, Dick Ellis, Johnny Price, Ronnie Boon, Harry Bowcott, Vernon Davies, Bryn Michael, Roger Michaelson, Roy Ovens and many others. The new clubhouse at Old Deer Park has become a meeting-place for the Welsh and, come what may on the field, it should never look back and all at home will shout, 'Ymlaen, Cymru Llundain!'

MAESTEG

Founded: 1882. HQ: Rugby Clubhouse. Colours: Black with amber hoops.

Maesteg can boast of the most original club emblem, possibly, of any club in Britain, if not the world. It is '7777' and was launched when a local carpenter is alleged to have found the age of the deceased, at twenty-eight, too difficult for the coffin he was preparing and so he etched the four sevens. Believe it or not, and knowing the Llynfi Valley well I am prepared to accept it, since the carpenter must have had a wonderful sense of humour even on such a solemn occasion.

Although now nearly a hundred years old, until after World War II the club suffered a series of ups and downs, as have most valley clubs as their careers remain closely linked with the vagaries of economic conditions. The local cricket club came first and the rugby club later but it was allowed to play in the winter on the cricket ground. By 1914 it was reasonably strong and had produced a few internationals, including one, David Watts, of the 1914 'Terrible Eight'.

Between 1919 and 1939 there were hard times in the valley, especially during the two major coal strikes and the humour disappeared from the mouths of miners as did the green grass from the hills. Yet the club survived and characters like Enoch H. Rees, R. J. Pole, and Geraldus Rees were prominent survivors and leaders. After the War, new success was achieved as glittering as a new seam of hard coal from the Maesteg Deep Colliery, and in the 1949–50 season the club became Welsh champions with an unbeaten record.

Led by the redoubtable scrum-half Trevor Lloyd, whose bird-like cry of 'training is the thing, lads' carried him into the Welsh XV in 1953 and the Lions of 1955, Maesteg played forty-three matches, won thirty-seven and drew six. A superb pack of forwards and Lloyd as a tactical-kicking scrum-half, the equal of Clive Rowlands, saw to it that the opposition

The invincible Maesteg team of 1949–50, winners of the Welsh Club Championship. *Back row:* E. Pritchard, L. White, T. Davies, H. Mayled, D. M. James. *Standing:* I. Davies, W. Thomas, R. L. Jones, T. Lewis, D. G. Swain, M. Rees, S. Davies, R. Ley, T. Watkins. *Seated:* D. H. Jones, J. Drew, W. D. Williams, T. Lloyd (capt.), V. Callow, W. Major, J. W. D. Jenkins.

never assumed control. In 1979 they carried off the Merit Table title and are now businesslike and busy in their effort to stay in the top ten.

Known as the 'Old Parish' with a ground that is really at the top of a coal and iron ore tip, it has achieved a new clubhouse and complete respectability. Its rivalry with Aberavon and Bridgend is intense and if the struggles of the 1920s were fierce between hard and often hungry men, the close friendship of the Welsh valleys remains.

The club's president, Windsor Major, is a farmer from nearby historic Llangynwydd where the 'Maid of Cefn Edfyr' wrote her love letters in blood, and as a member of the 1950 Welsh Grand Slam side, he sees to it that Maesteg stands firm and shares in all the activities of Welsh club rugby.

NEATH

Founded: 1871. HQ: Gnoll Ground. Colours: All black.

It is suggested that rugby was first played in Wales in the Neath area and that the Cadoxton Hotel is the true site of the founding of the Welsh Rugby Union; the club claims to be the most senior of the major ones in Wales, and it doesn't pay to argue with a Neath supporter! Warm, robust and partisan are the 'Mourners' of Neath, and the club has played an important part in the game's development by its production of hard-working forwards. One notable Springbok captain, W. A. 'Billy' Millar of

The Neath team which won the WRU Cup in the first season of its launching in 1971–72. They defeated Llanelli 15–9. *Standing:* K. Collier, W. Davies, W. Williams, B. Davies, W. Lauder, B. Thomas, G. Shaw, W. D. Morris, M. Joseph (referee). *Seated:* G. Ball, J. Poole, M. Thomas, M. Davies (capt.), D. Parker, D. Jenkins, N. Rees.

the 1912–13 touring side, claimed that Neath provided the hardest forward opposition of the tour. 'They were d*** iron men!' he added – and not without good reason as his side licked their bruises. There have been long periods in the club's history when few sides relished a visit to the Gnoll because of the 'hot' reception on and off the field but that is how it enjoys its rugby; good, hearty, vigorous stuff, and it possesses a remarkable reputation for producing international players, administrators and referees.

Recalling the referees first, there have been Albert Freethy (the man who sent off All Black forward Cyril Brownlie before the Prince of Wales at Twickenham in 1925), Harold Phillips and Ivor David, all outstanding officials. The adminstrators are headed by Captain Walter Rees, secretary of the Welsh Rugby Union for thirty-two years, the dapper Theo Davies and Rayner Jones, while at the very beginning the migrant Scot, Dr T. P. Whittington, helped create the rugby and cricket clubs in the town. The two grounds are side by side and Dr W. G. Grace was once dismissed there before he had scored, and accepted it, only to return later and score a century.

The local grammar school was a true nursery of outstanding players of both games but is now hardly recognisable with its new Welsh title and one asks, why new lamps for famous old ones? Dr Whittington was the club's first international and in all there have been forty-five, with W. D. 'Dai' Morris, J. R. G 'Rees' Stephens, Brian Thomas, Roy John, Tom Arthur, Grahame Hodgson, Courtenay Meredith, Arthur Lemon and Glyn Stephens as the best of them. Wilson Lauder, a back-row forward, obtained eighteen Scottish caps between 1969 and 1977 and no less than twelve players made one appearance apiece for Wales and probably the most interesting of these was wing Dan Jones (who appeared against the 1927 Waratahs) as he scored fifty-nine tries in the 1928–29 season for Neath, said to be a Welsh club record.

In 1967 Neath were club champions and in 1972 won the Welsh Rugby Union challenge cup in the first year of the revived competition. In most seasons the club has produced a 'Terrible Eight', and it moves through the years proudly and fiercely partisan, but still with a warm welcome in the clubhouse.

NEWBRIDGE

Founded: 1888. HQ: Welfare Ground. Colours: Blue and black hoops.

Last season Newbridge, following a series of disasters and fires which would have destroyed the hopes and enthusiasm of most clubs, opened their new clubhouse and dressing-rooms; a magnificent achievement, indicative of the tenacity of rugby men and the spirit of the Welsh valleys. It really made Newbridge 'first-class' in the sense that they can now receive their major club guests in comfort.

Although the acceptance of Newbridge into the championship table did not occur until after World War II, it was founded in 1888 and was eventually recognised by the Welsh Rugby Union in 1907. Its early years were destined to be nomadic, moving from field to field, and the list is a long one; the Drill Hall field, Ty Hir Farm, Top Flats and in 1901 the Show Field followed by Waen Bwdr in 1904. This pitch had a notorious slope which confused opposing sides and by 1922 the Newbridge Welfare Association signed a 99-year lease for the present ground from the Newbridge–Abercarn Colliery Company.

Because the ground was virtually a quagmire, it required two years of unstinting effort by volunteers to make it a rugby pitch of sorts and it was only as a result of the 1926 Coal Strike that enough volunteer labour was available to complete the task. Yet life was still hard for the club in its brave efforts to improve its playing standards, and while World War II reduced the fortunes of many clubs it revived those of Newbridge who, between 1940 and 1944, recruited enough players to form a side strong enough to challenge Cardiff and Newport (who ran war-time sides composed of veterans and youngsters) and any Service side ready to visit Newbridge.

It was the break the club needed and they have remained in the 'big league' ever since the period of two important players, Norman Harris in the centre as captain and a second Bennie Osler in Glyn 'Spike' Meredith at outside-half. A strong, determined, hard working pack of forwards, mainly miners or men employed in vital or heavy industry for the war effort, provided the ball for Meredith to call the tune. This he did as the 'king of the castle'. After the war several young players developed, outstanding forwards like Don Hayward and Ray Cale, recognised by Wales and giving the club its final accolade. Then the Rugby League tore deep into the club's heart and it required all the energy and devotion of officials like former captain Ken Peregrine as chairman, and Dr Adam Buick as secretary, to enable the club to survive. Yet there were players who later served the club faithfully as did John Herbert, Gerry Gibbons, Les Davies, Robert Rossiter, the Shipp brothers (five of them), the Hughes brothers (including one international, Dennis), and the present England selector, dental surgeon Derek Morgan. Their spirit is alive in the new clubhouse and the future is bright for a club that deserves success.

NEWPORT

Founded: 1874. HQ: Rodney Parade. Colours: Black and amber hoops.

The last few seasons have not proved happy ones for Newport following an outstanding century of service to the game and Welsh rugby in particular. One trusts that it will soon revive on the field of play and prove as strong a force as it ever was in the past. Like Cardiff, its history is highlighted by its consistency on the field of play and its influence in the administrative corridors. For Newport, the Welsh Rugby Union's Centenary must evoke a greater feeling of pride than for any other club, for it was a Newport man, Richard Mullock, who set it all in motion and another Newport man, Horace Lyne, who was a front runner in the launching of the International Board.

It is affiliated to both the Welsh and English Unions and boasts of six seasons of invincibility; four of them consecutive from 1875 to 1879 when they played a total of fifty-two matches without defeat and again in 1891–92 and 1922–23, with the last two being the most notable achievements under the leadership respectively of T. C. Graham and Jack Wetter. Since World War II it has won the Club Championship on four occasions, been runners-up eight times and only twice outside the top ten, proof enough of the skill and consistency of its players.

Yet of all rugby clubs, its system is the oldest in style. The committee is elected by invitation, and it has withstood repeated attempts to have this system changed. Thus its leaders have always been senior, experienced administrators, cautious and conservative in approach. Occasionally there are minor eruptions, resignations and departures but, in its own way, the club has managed to keep pace with events and in addition to playing an important part in the launching of the Welsh Rugby Union and the International Board helped launch floodlit rugby and individual club tours to South Africa. It has supplied many members of the Welsh Rugby

The invincible Newport side of 1922–23. *Standing:* C. Mogford (trainer), E. Wetter, W. Radford, M. Williams, W. Friend, H. Packer (chairman), T. Roberts, J. Whitfield, G. Hathway, H. J. Davies, W. J. Martin (honorary secretary). *Seated:* T. Jones, W. Jones, A. R. Stock, R. Edwards (vice-capt.), J. J. Wetter (capt.), N. C. McPherson, Dr W. J. Roche, F. Baker, S. Skuse. *In front:* T. E. Vaughan, S. Manship, E. Dowdall, G. Andrews, J. V. Waite.

Union executive and many distinguished referees, with T. H. Vile, W. J. Parfitt, George Goldsworthy and Jack Wetter heading the list. Horace Lyne was the Welsh Rugby Union president for forty-one years and later followed by Vile and Parfitt.

Newport was formed originally in 1874 to play association football before a shortage of fixtures quickly forced it to adopt the union code with a first match against near neighbours and perpetual rivals, Cardiff. Newport won the match and since then the clubs have met 338 times with Cardiff still ahead in victories. It has beaten Newport four times in a season on four occasions but has never suffered the reverse, and this record by Cardiff and Newport's seasons of invincibility are banners carried high by rival groups of supporters!

In December 1878, Newport staged the first floodlit match in the game, against Cardiff at Rodney Parade, and it was called the 'electric light' match; almost an eighth wonder of the world except that it was reported each side experienced difficulty in finding each other's goal-line – a handicap that has not disappeared totally from the modern game!

Until recent years, Newport had always been well represented in the Welsh XV, has produced internationals for all four countries and once, in 1921, fielded a side composed entirely of internationals, a feat no other club has achieved. In 1893, Newport supplied nine players to the first Welsh Triple Crown side, a record that lasted until 1948 when Cardiff fielded ten. From Arthur Gould to David Watkins there have been so many outstanding performers in the black and amber jersey.

Again, the club's record against touring sides has been good; the 1905 All Blacks could only manage a 6–3 victory before the 1912 Springboks were beaten 9–3, followed by a 0–0 draw with the 1926 Maoris after the second All Blacks had escaped by 13–10 but honour was satisfied by a 3–3 draw with the 1945 Kiwis. The Wallabies were beaten 11–10 in 1957 and

The Newport XV which defeated Australia 11–0 in November 1957. *Standing:* G. Walters (referee), B. V. Meredith, B. Cresswell, I. Ford, G. Davidge, G. Whitson, D. Greenslade, R. T. Carter (touch judge). *Seated:* M. C. Thomas, K. J. Jones, L. H. Jenkins (capt.), J. Phillips, N. Morgan. *In front:* B. J. Jones, J. Hurrell, R. Burnett, B. Scrivens. (This team included thirteen internationals.)

then, at long last, the All Blacks 3–0 in 1963, followed by the Springboks again in 1969, 11–6.

Whatever their fortunes at the moment, the club can feel proud of its record and its contribution to the game, and if its leading administrators down through the years – Mullock, Lyne, Vile, Packer, Wetter, Snelling, Griffiths, Everson, Carter, Panting and Evans have appeared conservative in approach, they believed strictly in amateur rugby, as have their many great players, and this has required integrity and courage through the years.

PENARTH

Founded: 1879. HQ: Athletic Ground. Colours: Blue and white hoops.

Penarth's lot at the moment, like that of W. S. Gilbert's 'constabulary', may not be a happy one but nothing will destroy a club that has lived for a 100 years in the shadow of its powerful near-neighbour, Cardiff. It enjoyed its better days from the turn of the century to World War I when the town boasted half a dozen shipping and coal millionaires. Its once busy docks exporting coal and its pleasant seaside parade hold happy rugby memories and the Barbarians decided to make the Esplanade hotel on the sea front its home in 1900.

Since World War II it has been a hard struggle to survive, for once young players have been developed they have moved on, and this process will continue. Last winter the club celebrated its Centenary and the occasion was marked with the installation of floodlights in a bid to catch up with its big brothers. Yet there have been days when Penarth sides have risen gallantly to the occasion to overcome major sides, and victories over the Barbarians may have been limited but nevertheless happy ones.

Many clubs have tried to tempt the Barbarians away from their annual Good Friday match at Penarth but the illustrious tourists will 'not forsake thee' and ensure that the annual budget is balanced. The club was launched in 1879 as the result of an amalgamation of two local teams, the Bachelors' XV (composed of docksmen) and the Penarth Dreadnoughts (not reported as having any naval connections). In 1889 it produced its first international in R. M. Garrett, followed by George Rowles and then the try-scoring utility player, Reggie Gibbs and the Dyke brothers during the 'Golden Era'.

The Barbarians were first beaten in 1904 and again in 1905 and 1906, and although three narrow defeats followed there was a draw in 1910 and four successive wins in 1912, 1913, 1914 and 1920 with a draw in 1921. In that year the economic 'dive' occurred in the Cardiff and Penarth dockland; the 'millionaires' disappeared almost overnight and with them a great deal of Penarth's rugby glory. Continued Barbarians success was not halted until a draw in 1955 and then victory again in 1960 with Bernard 'Slogger' Templeman at the helm.

Individual players have often proved extremely loyal to the club and none more so than Jack Bassett, a Welsh captain in the 1930s, Bernard Templeman, the late John Heslop, Kevin Bush, Terry Smith and others while J. Lot Thorn is remembered as the club's most notable administrator. The motto for club officials is to 'serve without glory' and they do so cheerfully. Penarth has experienced more bad days than good but two victories remain for ever on the club's honours board. During the 1926–27 season, Penarth captured Llanelli's two-year-old ground record at the height of the Scarlets' power; and in order that the Penarth players could escape from their dressing-room in face of an army of irate fans, Llanelli officials hastily employed the town band to play 'See the Conquering Heroes Come!' in front of the retreating yet victorious Penarth side. The second notable victory was over Cardiff during the 1947–48 season, which enabled Penarth to share with Pontypool the honour of being the only clubs to beat Tanner's remarkable team. As Penarth say, 'Our great days are few and far between but when they occur they are great ones, and we live from one great day to another, however long be the intervals.' That is the story of Penarth's hundred years.

PONTYPOOL

Founded: 1901. HQ: Pontypool Park. Colours: Red, black and white hoops.

The outstanding Pontypool side of 1906–07.

It is difficult to imagine Pontypool as one of the younger leading Welsh clubs but it has packed a great deal of action into its seventy-nine years of existence. After thirteen years it became the champion club and again in 1921 and 1932. Since World War II it has achieved the distinction three times (in 1959, 1973 and 1975) and thus can claim a record as good as most clubs even though its fortunes have varied considerably in the last decade mainly due to the production of a magnificent, fire-eating pack without backs speedy enough to turn good possession into tries. As the present club coach, former Lion prop Ray Prosser comments, 'You cannot have everything, fine forwards *and* prima donnas behind!'

The club was launched at a public meeting at the Pontypool Town Hall, and derived from a combination of Pontypool Thursdays, Pontypool Saturdays and Pontymoel. The first secretary was a local surveyor, Ben J. Williams, followed by Charles Greening before Rowley Meredith took office in 1926 and all three did a notable job in establishing a club whose career has been (to say the least) a little stormy at times.

The first official match, at the Recreation Ground was against Cardiff

Romilly on 21 September 1901 and in 1904 they won the Monmouthshire League title, gold medals and all, duly presented at the Town Hall and accompanied by a grand feast with champagne at 10 shillings (50p) a bottle. Those really were the days!

Then came personalities who put the club 'on the map' as Welshmen love to say. The Jones brothers, D. P. (Ponty), Jack and Dr Tuan, sons of a local alderman, with Jack playing fourteen times for Wales in an era of great centres and touring twice with the British Lions, while acclaimed locally and overseas as a worthy No. 3 to Nicholls and Gabe. Other notables were Cliff Pritchard (a 1905 hero), Jack Evans and Bob Lloyd. When they were champions in 1914, Pontypool lost only seven matches out of forty-four. In 1921 they produced their own brand of a 'Terrible Eight' headed by England cap, Tommy Woods, which can claim to be the precursors of Cobner's pack of the 1970s.

Wing Cliff Richards and hooker Cecil Pritchard were outstanding in the 1920s and 1927 remains unique in Welsh rugby as Pontypool defeated two major touring sides in that year – the Maoris in January and the Waratahs in December at Pontypool Park before 20,00 excited and emotional men of Gwent, when centre Don Cormack scored the winning try. Waratahs like Breckenridge, Towers and Lawton, later told me how strong and fiery were the men of Pontypool; 1927 must be their greatest year. They scored a double over Cardiff in 1932 when Cullis and Axford were a wily pair of halves, and there followed several international players with perhaps Ray Prosser the most colourful and Graham Price the most-capped. As W. J. T. Collins wrote when the club celebrated its fiftieth birthday, 'Pontypool has never been cowed by records or reputations,' and no-one walks easily on to the pitch when visiting Pontypool Park. The welcome is loud and hard.

The four Pontypool members of the Triple Crown side celebrating the 1978 Grand Slam at Cardiff Castle. *Left to right:* A. G. 'Charlie' Faulkner, Graham Price, Terry Cobner, R. W. 'Bobby' Windsor.

In the 1970s Terry Cobner was captain for nine successive seasons and on several occasions, he and four members of his 'Terrible Eight' were in the Welsh side. All five made the 1977 Lions tour and helped match the All Blacks at forward.

Cobner, Price, Bobby Windsor, Charlie Faulkner and Jeff Squire (from Newport) produced their own brand of forward play that was forceful, hard and unrelenting. As Prosser says 'they were like All Blacks themselves' with Price the best tight-head prop of recent years. With Windsor and Faulkner, Price formed the first club trio to pack in the front-row for Wales and the Lions.

Sometimes the enthusiasm overflowed, but then they were never 'prima donnas' at forward as the cry went up to echo through the Park, 'Pooler, Pooler!' Tom Woods, Cliff Pritchard and Cecil Pritchard would have been proud of them, although many regard the 1959 Championship side as the club's most attractive with Ray Prosser, Malcolm Price and Benny Jones as the stars. They succeeded superb players like Ray Cale and Alan Forward to suggest there are always good and determined players in the club's ranks.

PONTYPRIDD

Founded: 1875. HQ: Sardis Road. Colours: Black and white hoops.

Suddenly, after years of struggle, Pontypridd reached the top and proved themselves in 1962–63 by winning the Welsh championship, and the Welsh Brewers Company with the *Western Mail* launched the club into the headlines by staging a celebration dinner in its honour which was to grow in popularity and become the 'high feast' of Welsh club rugby. The brainchild of former Pontypridd outside-half, Arwyn Owen, it has done much to lift the importance of the Welsh Club Championship. It was put on a proper footing and it is acknowledged that winning is the accolade of true consistency against all comers. Pontypridd has never looked back from that moment of triumph and in 1976, 1978 and 1979, through remarkable resilience, carried off the titles in three years out of four.

To Welshmen, Pontypridd is a famous town and the gateway to some of the most important valleys in the history of coal production but it is difficult to assess accurately when rugby began to be played there. Many townsmen have spent hours researching and the conclusion is that it was founded in the 1875–76 season. By 1878 it was moving along steadily and Cardiff were met a few years before the club became a founder member of the Welsh Rugby Union, an important step in rugby status. Unfortunately, no-one appears to have kept records of those early days but the club had two players, E. Treharne and T. Williams, in the first Welsh team

The Pontypridd team which won the Welsh Club Championship and were Cup finalists in 1978–79. *Standing:* H. Evans (coach), C. Norling (touch judge), M. Alexander, R. Lot, J. Luff, M. Shellard, C. Seldon, R. Penberthy, D. Shellard, C. Riley, L. Walsh, D. Rees, K. Rowlands (referee), C. Thomas (touch judge). *Seated:* A. Thomas, W. Evans, R. Morgan, J. Poole, T. P. David (capt.), S. Lewis, C. Bolderson, S. Flynn, J. Hazzard, T. Andrews (trainer), J. Smith (coach). *In front:* R. Dyer, K. Salmon.

against Ireland in 1882. As they say in the town, 'We were there at the beginning!'

The famous stone bridge was there over the River Taff long before the club, a monument to the art of construction before the days of mechanised building. They are as proud of the Taff Bridge in Pontypridd as the citizens of Sydney are of their mighty bridge, and many players and spectators have crossed the River Taff in search of rugby football. First matches were played at Taff Vale Park, and then the People's Park before a return to Taff Vale (incidentally, the name of the railway that served the town before the amalgamation), and on to Ynysangharad Park in 1908. Alas, in 1973 a new road snatched a corner of the ground and there was a brief spell at Taff Vale Park again before the move to its spacious new headquarters at Sardis Road, officially opened in January 1974. There the club will stay and former administrator Ack Llewellyn, headman in the lively years 1900–1914, would have enjoyed the new set-up and the fact that the club has been the 'King' of rugby in recent years. There were many able men before and after him and the workers of recent years who set the club moving into the big league include Alfred John, Howard Hicks, D. W. Davies, Sam Simon, Desmond Jones, Stan Thomas, Eddie Jones, Graham Gittings, W. J. A. Evans, Cliff James and Hugh McVicker.

There have been players, too, giving noble service and none more than Bob Penberthy who has played more matches for the club than any other, while the internationals include E. Treharne, T Williams, E. George, D. G. McGregor, F. Hawkins, Glyn Davies, Russell Robins, Danny Harris, Gareth Payne, and Tom David. One believes that the club will produce many more in the next century.

SWANSEA

Founded: 1872. HQ: St Helen's ground. Colours: All white.

The Swansea team of 1895–96. *Standing:* Ted Poole (trainer), R. S. Jenkin, W. Grey, J. Williams, S. Jackson, Smith, Gil Evans, W. Bowen (umpire). *Seated:* F. Gordon, W. Crocker, R. Oldham, A. M. Jenkin (capt.), F. Crocker, R. Thomas, R. Messer, J. Morgans. *In front:* J. Prescott, S. Rice.

The fourth member of the original 'Big Four' and a big club in every way, one of the great ones in the game, Swansea has defeated all the major touring teams and is immensely proud of its long history of more than a hundred years. Whatever have been its fortunes, and it had to wait from 1913 until 1978 to win another major prize in Welsh rugby, it has always been a top club with a long list of fine players and important occasions at the historic St Helen's ground.

It is one of the oldest of the major clubs, only one year younger than Neath and, like many others in the British Isles, was originally formed to play association football, playing its first match in this code against Neath in November 1872. However, there proved little enthusiasm for the round ball and in 1874, the club turned to the oval ball and engaged in the 'fierce' game of rugby football, winning its first match against Llandovery, a team believed to have been a combination of masters and pupils from the College. Its first field was Mount Pleasant, then the Primrose Field (what a delicate name for a rugby ground!) and on to St Helen's which remained as Swansea's own until the lease was surrendered (sadly I feel) during World War II to the Swansea Corporation who have benefited financially from the deal and cared for the historic turf.

Swansea was the scene of the original formation of the Welsh Rugby Union and the club's first president was industrialist Sir John Llewellyn, who became president in 1895. The first secretary was C. C. Chambers and he was followed by a noble line in F. E. Perkins, W. Griffiths, E. C. Perkins, R. S. Palmer, a loyal war-time secretary in C. B. Jones, T. C. Prosser and now the long-serving David Price. The first international produced was G. L. Morris in 1882 with the legendary W. J. Bancroft appearing in 1889 and remaining until 1901 without a break. From 1890 to 1910, Swansea enjoyed twenty years of consistent success and many of its great players in this era have been discussed in earlier chapters as contributing much to the success of the national XV. Many of them remain household names. The Bancrofts, the Jameses, Owen and Trew, were outstanding for club and country and there have been many more since with Geoffrey Wheel, last season's club captain, and David Richards maintaining Swansea's colourful contribution in the current Welsh XV. There have been others, uncapped players who gave much to the club as did Genny Gordon and Jack Elwyn Watkins, both inspiring captains, Gordon leading an invincible side in 1904–05.

The club's record against touring teams has been excellent, with victories over Australia (1908 and 1966), South Africa (1912) and New Zealand (1935). A highlight of the club's career has been the ability of its teams to rise to the occasion, especially against touring sides and the Barbarians who visit St Helen's every Easter Monday to share in matches that are full of fire and points. The club has contributed its share of British Lions, starting with Tom Bevan and Bill Jowett in 1904, followed by Edgar Morgan, Rowe Harding, David Parker (one of the club's outstanding personalities), Haydn Tanner, Eddie Morgan, W. O. Williams, R. C. C. Thomas, Alun Thomas, Terry Davies, John Faull and Dewi Bebb while Mervyn Davies, a Swansea man, rejoined the club after becoming a Lion; finally Geoffrey Wheel who, although selected in 1977, could not travel.

The Swansea team which won the WRU/Schweppes Cup in 1977–78. *Standing:* C. Norling (referee), W. R. Blyth, P. Thomas, A. Mages, P. Jones, R. Moriarty, B. G. Clegg, P. D. Llewellyn, H. Rees, M. Keyworth, T. P. Evans, C. P. G. Thomas (touch judge). *Seated:* C. Thomas (touch judge), G. Jones, A. Donovan, D. Richards, G. A. D. Wheel, A. Meredith (capt.), J. Herdman, D. James, H. Davies, H. Hopkins. *In front:* G. Jenkins, R. Woodward.

St Helen's was the site of the first home international played by Wales in 1882 and remained an international venue until 1954 and the match against Scotland. It was in this match that K. J. Jones (Newport) led his country when he equalled the existing record of the most-capped Welsh player (Swansea's R. M. Owen) with thirty-five appearances. It was a sad day for Swansea, but the larger seating capacity at Cardiff was decisive together with the fact that it was privately-owned and eventually became the property of the Welsh Rugby Union. Yet the atmosphere at St Helen's remains unique, if partisan, since anyone born a mile outside Swansea towards Port Talbot is said to come from the East. The town has become a city and is naturally proud of its new status in the civic and rugby sense. Alas, there are but few now who remember, 'My Bancroft and my Trew, long ago!'

TREDEGAR

Founded: 1893. HQ: Recreation Ground. Colours: Red, black and white hoops.

When Lord Tredegar presented a patch of land to the iron town of Tredegar in the early 1890s for the benefit of the town's recreation facilities, he lit the flame of rugby enthusiasm in the area, just over the hill from Ebbw Vale, and the birthplace of Aneurin Bevan. At the time David Lloyd George was complaining about the virus of 'footballism' in Gwent, and a local enthusiast Jim Davies, a rugby fanatic, was busy spreading the virus. Davies was known locally as the 'footballer' and while some records suggest that a Tredegar Harriers side played Newport in 1881, it was Mr Davies who officially formed the club in 1893 but, alas, it lasted no more than two years as Davies, with other iron workers and colliers, moved to the Dowlais Club, who arranged a coach and pair for their travel to Dowlais each Saturday.

Fortunately, they returned in due course to re-form the club and establish the pitch now known as the Tredegar Recreation Ground, with a clubhouse some hundred yards from it after World War II. In the years before World War I, Tredegar helped to establish the Monmouthshire League and soon gained admission into the Welsh Rugby Union. By the start of the war, the club was a power in Gwent as the iron works and collieries worked at full blast. One player, Cyril Mawbray, is reported as having lost thirteen teeth, knocked out against Blaina, and two days later was in action against Machen. Another notable Tredegar player of the period was Percy Jones, who later joined Newport and was a member of the 1914 Welsh team's 'Terrible Eight'.

The days of the depression suffered during the 1920s and 1930s saw Tredegar experience a hard time as enthusiasm and success fell away.

During World War II the club was kept alive by a Home Guard side while the Recreation Ground deteriorated and when the club resumed it was in competition with the local greyhounds galloping round the touch-lines. The locals regarded it as an excellent method of disturbing the concentration of opponents. It is not reported if they actually laid bets during the matches. To help the rehabilitation of the club, a Guards Regiment sent them a set of rugby boots and by 1950 the club had fully recovered its poise. It won the Monmouthshire Championship and the Ben Francis Cup, and Aneurin Bevan was the guest speaker at the club's celebration dinner. Next followed the establishment of the present excellent clubhouse as a rugby social club breaking new ground in the valleys of Gwent. It was opened in 1955 and was followed by a stand on the Recreation Ground provided by the local council before, at long last, Tredegar could claim to be a first-class club. In 1960 it was admitted into the *Western Mail* Championship Table and since then it has played its part in the continuing life and enjoyment of Welsh club rugby.

SOUTH WALES POLICE

Founded: 1897. HQ: Waterton Cross, Bridgend. Colours: Scarlet and royal blue.

The police officers of South Wales have made a worthy contribution to the game since a remarkable enthusiast launched the club at the end of the last century. This was Colonel Lionel Lindsay, who at the time had just been appointed Chief Constable of the Glamorgan force. He was a tremendous enthusiast who if interviewing a big, strong, intelligent applicant would question him about his rugby prowess and physical strength for the game!

His team became famous through the valleys of Glamorgan and was said to have played against the strikers and the soldiers during the Tonypandy Riots of 1910, because it was a 'peace keeping' unit and designed to preserve friendship with the citizens. As a result, local sides often used to 'take it out' of the police officers trying to play rugby, as the matches provided an excellent opportunity for such activities.

When a small boy I recall the worthy Chief Constable halting a match between Pontypridd and the Glamorgan Police because it was becoming too involved, as there were some lively constables in the Pontypridd team. During the 1920s the team was at its strongest and against England in 1926 the Welsh pack included six police officers. The match was drawn – but it was hard!

After World War II there was a temporary lapse as the forces were rebuilt but by 1951 they had resumed in the best of health. In 1969 the South Wales Police Rugby Football Club was formed following the reorganisation of the force and Rod Morgan, a splendid prop forward, was the fixture secretary at the time. He served for twenty-one years (1957–78) until becoming a member of the Welsh Rugby Union executive, and was soon appointed as a Welsh selector. For the 1978–79 season he was chairman of the national selection committee and the first serving police officer to be honoured by Wales. The club plays in the Welsh Championship and runs an excellent cadets team coached by former international, Ian Hall.

APPENDIX: RECORDS

WELSH INTERNATIONAL PLAYERS

Key: E—England, S—Scotland, I—Ireland, F—France, NZ—New Zealand, SA—South Africa, A or Aust—Australia, NSW—New South Wales, M—Maoris, R—Replacement

Alexander, E. P. (*Cambridge Univ.*), S. 85; E.S. 86; E.I. 87.
Alexander, W. H. (*Llwynypia*), I.E. 98; E.S.I. 99; S.I. 1901.
Allen, C. P. (*Oxford Univ.*), E.S. 84.
Andrews, F. G. (*Swansea*), E.S. 84.
Andrews, F. (*Pontypool*), SA. 1912; E.S.I. 1913.
Andrews, G. E. (*Newport*), E.S. 1926; E.F.I. 1927.
Anthony, L. (*Neath*), E.S.F. 1948.
Arnold, W. (*Llanelli*), S. 1903.
Arthur, C. S. (*Cardiff*), I.M. 88; E. 91.
Arthur, T. (*Neath*), S.I.F. 1927; E.S.I.F. 1929, 1930, 1931; SA. 1931; E.S. 1933.
Ashton, C. (*Aberavon*), E.S.I. 1959, E.S.I. 1960; I. 1962.
Attewell, L. (*Newport*), E.S.F. 1921.

Badger, O. (*Llanelli*), E.S.I. 95; E. 96.
Baker, A. (*Neath*), I. 1921; E.S.I.F. 1923.
Baker, A. M. (*Newport*), S.F. 1909; S. 1910.
Bancroft, J. (*Swansea*), E.S.I.F. 1909, 1910; E.F.I. 1911; E.S.I. 1912; I. 1913; E.S.F. 1914.
Bancroft, W. J. (*Swansea*), S.E.I. 90, 91, 92, 93, 94, 95, 96; E. 97; E.I. 98; E.S.I. 99, 1900, 1901.
Barlow, T. M. (*Cardiff*), I. 84.
Barrell, R. (*Cardiff*), S.I.F. 1929; I. 1933.
Bartlett, J. D. (*Llanelli and L. Welsh*), S. 1927; E.S. 1928.
Bassett, A. (*Aberavon and Cardiff*), I. 1934; E.S.I. 1935; E.S. 1938.
Bassett, J. (*Penarth*), E.S.I.F. 1929; E.S.I. 1930; E.S.I.F.SA. 1931; E.S.I. 1932.
Bayliss, G. (*Pontypool*), S. 1933.
Bebb, D. (*Swansea*), E.S.I.F. 1959; E.S.I.F. SA 1960; E.S.I.F. 1961; I.E.S.F. 1962; E.F. NZ. 1963; E.S.F.SA. 1964; E.I.S.F. 1965; F. 1966; A. 1966; E.S.I.F. 1967.
Beckingham, G. (*Cardiff*), E.S. 1953; F. 1958.
Bennett, Ivor (*Aberavon*), I. 1937.
Bennett, Phil, (*Llanelli*), F. (R) 1969; SA. S.F. 1970; S. (R), N.Z. 1972; E.S.I.F. A. 1973; S.I.F.E. 1974; S. (R) I. 1975; E.S.I.F. 1976; I.F.E.S. 1977; E.S.I.F. 1978.
Bennett, P. (*Cardiff Quins*) E.S. 91; S.I. 92.
Bergiers, R. T. E. (*Llanelli*) E.S.F. NZ. 1972; E.S.I.F.A. 1973; E. 1974; I. 1975.
Bevan, Griff. (*Llanelli*), E. 1947.
Bevan, J. A. (*Cambridge Univ.*), E. 81.
Bevan, J. C. (*Cardiff*), E.S.I.F. 1971; E.S.F. NZ. 1972; E.S. 1973.
Bevan, J. D. (*Aberavon*), F.E.S.A. 1975.
Bevan, Sid. (*Swansea*), I. 1904.
Beynon, Ben. (*Swansea*), E.S. 1920.
Beynon, E. (*Swansea*), I.F. 1925.
Biggs, N. (*Cardiff Univ.*), M. 88; I. 89; I. 92; E.S.I. 93; E.I. 94.
Biggs, S. (*Cardiff*), E.S. 95; S. 96; E. 97; E.I. 98; S.I. 99; I. 1900.
Birch, J. (*Neath*), S.F. 1911.
Birt, F. W. (*Newport*), E.S. 1911; E.S.I.SA. 1912; E. 1913.
Bishop, E. H. (*Swansea*), S. 89.
Blackmore, J. (*Abertillery*), E. 1909.
Blake, J. (*Cardiff*), E.S.I. 99, 1900, 1901.
Blakemore, R. E. (*Newport*), E. 1947.
Bland, A. F. (*Cardiff*), E.S.I. 87; M.S.I. 88; E.S.I. 90.
Blyth, L. (*Swansea*), SA. 1951; E.S. 1952.
Blyth, W. R. (*Swansea*), E. 1974; S. (*sub.*) 1975; F.E.S.I. 1980.
Boon, R. W. (*Cardiff*), S.F. 1930; E.S.I.F. SA. 1931; E.S.I. 1932; E.I. 1933.
Booth, J. (*Pontymister*), I. 98.
Boots, G. (*Newport*), I.E. 98; I. 99; E.S.I. 1900, 1901, 1902, 1903; E. 1904.
Boucher, A. W. (*Newport*), E.S.I. 92, 93; E. 94; E.S.I. 95; E.I. 96; E. 97.
Bowcott, H. M. (*Cardiff*), S.I.F. 1929; E. 1930; E.S. 1931; E.I. 1933.
Bowdler, F. A. (*Cross Keys*), NSW. 1927; E.S.I.F. 1928, 1929; E. 1930; SA. 1931; E.S.I. 1932; I. 1933.
Bowen, C. (*Llanelli*), E.S.I. 96; E. 97.
Bowen, D. H. (*Llanelli*), E. 83; E.S. 86; E. 87.
Bowen, G. E. (*Swansea*), S.I. 87, 88.

Bowen, W. (*Swansea*), S.F. 1921; E.S.I.F. 1922.
Bowen, Wm. (*Swansea*), E.S. 86; E.S.I. 87; M. 88; S.I. 89; E.S.I. 90; E.S. 91.
Brace, D. O. (*Newport and Llanelli*), E.S.I.F. 1956; E. 1957; S.I.F. 1960; I. 1961.
Braddock, K. J. (*Newbridge*), A. 1966; S.I. 1967.
Bradshaw, K. (*Bridgend*), E.S.I.F.SA. 1964, E.S.I.F. 1966.
Brewer, T. J. (*Newport and L. Welsh*), E. 1950; E.S. 1955.
Brice, A. (*Aberavon and Cardiff*), E.S.I. 99, 1900, 1901, 1902, 1903, 1904.
Bridie, R. (*Newport*), I. 82.
Britton, G. R. (*Newport*), S. 1961.
Broughton, A. (*Treorchy*), NSW. 1927; S. 1929.
Brown, Archie (*Newport*), I. 1921.
Brown, J. (*Cardiff*), I. 1925.
Brown, Jack (*Cardiff*), E.S.I. 1907; E.S.F. 1908; E. 1909.
Burcher, D. H. (*Newport*), I.F.E.S. 1977.
Burgess, R. C. (*Ebbw Vale*), I.F.E.S. 1977.
Burnett, R. (*Newport*), E. 1953.
Burns, J. (*Cardiff*), F.I. 1927.
Bush, P. F. (*Cardiff*), NZ. 1905; E. 1906; SA. 1906; I. 1907; E.S. 1908; S.I. 1910.
Butler, E. T. (*Pontypool*), F.E.S.I. 1980.

Cale, W. R. (*Newbridge and Pontypool*), E.S.I. 1949; E.S.I.F. 1950.
Cattell, A. (*Llanelli*), E. 82; S. 83.
Challinor, C. (*Neath*), E. 1939.
Clapp, T. J. S. (*Nantyglo and Newport*), I. 82; E.S. 83; E.S.I. 84; E.S. 85; S. 86; E.S.I. 87; S.I. 88.
Clarke, J. (*Cardiff*), E. 82.
Clarke, S. S. (*Neath*), I. 82; I. 87.
Cleaver, W. B. (*Cardiff*), E.S.F.I.A. 1947; E.S.F.I. 1948; I. 1949; E.S.I.F. 1950.
Clegg, B. (*Swansea*), F. 1979.
Clement, W. H. (*Llanelli*), E.S.I. 1937, 1938.
Cobner, T. J. (*Pontypool*), S.I.F.E. 1974; F.E.S.I.A. 1975; E.S. 1976; F.E.S. 1977; E.S.I.F.A. (1st Test), 1978.
Coldrick, A. P. (*Newport*), E.S.I. 1911; E.S.F. 1912.
Coleman, E. (*Newport*), E.S.I. 1949.
Coles, F. C. (*Pontypool*), S.I.F. 1960.
Collins, J. (*Aberavon*), A.E.S.F. 1958; E.S.I.F. 1959; E. 1960; F. 1961.
Collins, T. (*Mountain Ash*), I. 1923.
Cook, T. (*Cardiff*), S.I. 1949.
Cope, W. (*Cardiff*), S. 96.
Cornish, F. H. (*Cardiff*), E. 97; E.I. 98; I. 99.
Cornish, R. A. (*Cardiff*), E.S. 1923; E. 1924; E.S.F. 1925; E.S.I.F. 1926.
Coslett, K. (*Aberavon*), E.S.F. 1962.
Cowey, B. T. V. (*Newport*), E.S.I. 1934; E. 1935.
Cresswell, B. (*Newport*), E.S.I.F. 1960.
Cummins, W. (*Treorchy*), E.S.I.F 1922.
Cunningham, L. J. (*Aberavon*), E.S.I.F. 1960; E.S.F.I. 1962; NZ 1963; E.S.I.F. SA. 1964.

Daniel, D. J. (*Llanelli*), S. 91; E.S.I. 94; E.I. 98; E.I. 99.
Daniel, L. (*Newport*), S. 1970.
Darbyshire, G. (*Bangor*), E. 81.
Dauncey, F. H. (*Newport*), E.S.I. 96.
Davey, Claude (*Swansea*), F. 1930; E.S.I.F. SA 1931; E.S.I. 1932; E.S. 1933; E.S.I. 1934, 1935; NZ. 1935; S. 1936; E.I. 1937, 1938.
David, R. (*Cardiff*), I. 1907.
David Tom (*Llanelli and Pontypridd*), F.A. 1973; I.F. 1976.
Davidge, G. (*Newport*), F. 1959; S.I.F. SA 1960; E.S.I. 1961; F. 1962.
Davies, Rev. Alban (*Swansea and Llanelli*), S.I.F. 1913; E.S.F.I. 1914.
Davies, A. C. (*London Welsh*), I. 89.
Davies, B. (*Llanelli*), E. 95, 96.
Davies, Bailey (*Llanelli*), E. 1907.
Davies, C. H. A. (*Cardiff and Llanelli*), I. 1957; A.E.S.I. 1958; S.A. 1960; E. 1961.
Davies, C. L. (*Cardiff*), E.S.I. 1956.
Davies, Cecil Rhys (*Bedford and Cardiff High School*), E. 1934.
Davies, Cliff (*Cardiff*), S.F.I.A. 1947; E.S.F.I. 1948; F. 1949; E.S.I.F. 1950; E.S.I. 1951.
Davies, Daph. (*Bridgend*), I. 1921, 1925.
Davies, D. Brian (*Llanelli*), I. 1962; E.S. 1963.
Davies, D. G. (*Cardiff*), E.S. 1923.
Davies, D. H. (*Neath*), S. 1904.
Davies, D. Hunt (*Aberavon*), E. 1924.
Davies, D. Idwal (*Swansea*), E. 1939.
Davies, D. J. (*Neath*), I. 1962.
Davies, D. M. (*Somerset Police*), E.S.I.F. 1950; E.S.I.F. SA. 1951; E.S.I.F. 1952; I.F. NZ. 1953; E. 1954.
Davies, E. (*Aberavon*), A. 1947; I. 1948.
Davies, Evan (*Maesteg*), NZ 1919.
Davies, Ewan (*Cardiff*), E.F. 1912.
Davies, George (*Swansea*), E.S.I. 1900, 1901, 1905.
Davies, Glyn (*Pontypridd*), S.AUST. 1947; E.S.F.I. 1948; E.S.F. 1949; E.S. 1951.
Davies, Graham (*Llanelli*), F.I. 1921; F. 1925.
Davies, Gwyn (*Cardiff*), F. 1928; E. 1929; S. 1930
Davies, H. (*Swansea*), I.E. 98; S.I. 1901.
Davies, H. J. (*Aberavon*), E.S. 1959.
Davies, Harold (*Newport*), S. 1924.
Davies, Howard (*Swansea and Llanelli*), S.I. 1939; E.S.F.I. 1947.
Davies, Howel (*Neath*), E.S. 1912.
Davies, J. H. (*Aberavon*), I. 1923.
Davies, I. T. (*Llanelli*), S.F.I. 1914.
Davies, Len (*Llanelli*), F.S. 1954; I. 1955.
Davies, Leslie (*Swansea*), S.I. 1939.
Davies, Lyn (*Bridgend*), E.S.I. 1966.
Davies, M. J. (*Oxford Univ.*), S.I. 1939.
Davies, N. Glyn (*London Welsh*), E. 1955.
Davies, R. H. (*London Welsh*), S.I.F. 1957; A. 1958; E.S. 1962.
Davies, Stan. (*Treherbert*), I. 1923.
Davies, Terry (*Swansea and Llanelli*), E.S.I.F. 1953; E.S.I.F. 1957; A.E.S.F. 1958; E.S.I.F. 1959; E.S.A. 1960; E.S.F. 1961.
Davies, T. G. R. (*Cardiff, and London Welsh*), A. 1966; E.S.I.F. 1967; E.S. 1968; S.I.F. NZ. (1st and 2nd Tests) A. 1969; E.S.I.F. 1971; E.S.F. NZ. 1972; E.S.I.F.A. 1973; S.F.E. 1974; F.E.S.I. 1975; E.S.I.F. 1976; I.F.E.S. 1977; E.S.I.A. (1st and 2nd Tests) 1978.

Davies, T. Mervyn (*London Welsh and Swansea*), S.I.F.E. NZ. (1st and 2nd Tests) A. 1969; SA.S.E.I.F. 1970; E.S.I.F. 1971; E.S.F. NZ. 1972; E.S.I.F.A. 1973; S.I.F.E. 1974.; F.E.S.I.A. 1975; E.S.I.F. 1976.
Davies, W. Gareth (*Cardiff*), A. (1st and 2nd Tests), NZ. 1978; S.I.F.E. 1979; F.E.S. 1980.
Davies, W. (*Cardiff*), S. 96.
Davies, Will (*Swansea*), SA. 1931; E.S.I. 1932.
Davies, Willie (*Aberavon*), S.I. 1912.
Davies, W. T. H. (*Swansea*), I. 1936; E.I. 1937; E.S.I. 1939.
Davis, Clive (*Newbridge*) A. (2nd Test) 1978.
Davis, W. E. N. (*Cardiff*), E.S.I. 1939.
Dawes, S. J. (*London Welsh*), I.F.SA. 1964; E.S.I.F. 1965; A. 1966; I.F. 1968; E.NZ. (2nd test) A. 1969; SA.S.E.I.F. 1970; E.S.I.F. 1971.
Day, H. T. (*Newport*), I. 92; S.E. 93; S.I. 94.
Day, H. C. (*Newport*), S.I.F. 1930; E.S. 1931.
Day, T. (*Swansea*), E.S.I.F.SA. 1931; E.S.I. 1932; S.I. 1934; E.S.I. 1935.
Deacon, J. T. (*Swansea*), I. 91; E.S.I. 92.
Delahay, W. J. (*Bridgend*), E.S.I.F. 1922, 1923; NZ. 1924; E.S.I.F. 1925, 1926, 1927.
Devereux, D. (*Neath*), A.E.S. 1958.
Dobson, G. (*Cardiff*), S. 1900.
Dobson, T. (*Cardiff*), E.I. 98; E.S. 99
Donovan, A. (*Swansea*), A. (2nd Test) 1978.
Douglas, W. M. (*Cardiff*), E.S. 86, 87.
Dowell, W. (*Newport and Pontypool*), E.S.I. 1907; E.S.I.F. 1908.
Dyke, J. C. M. (*Penarth*), SA. 1906.
Dyke, L. M. (*Cardiff*), I. 1910; S.I.F. 1911.

Edwards, A. B. (*London Welsh*), E.S. 1955.
Edwards, Ben. (*Newport*), I. 1951.
Edwards, D. (*Glynneath*), E. 1921.
Edwards, Gareth (*Cardiff*), F.E.NZ. 1967; E.S.I.F. 1968; S.I.F.E.NZ. (1st and 2nd Tests) A. 1969; SA.S.E.I.F. 1970; E.S.I.F. 1971; E.S.F.NZ. 1972; E.S.I.F.A. 1973; S.I.F.E. 1974; F.E.S.I.A. 1975; E.S.I.F. 1976; I.F.E.S. 1977; E.S.I.F 1978.
Elliott, J. E. (*Cardiff*), I. 94; E.I. 98.
Elsey, W. J. (*Cardiff*), E. 95.
Evans, A. C. (*Pontypool*), E.I.F. 1924.
Evans, Bryn (*Swansea*), S. 1933.
Evans, Bryn (*Llanelli*), E.S. 1933; E.S.I. 1936; E. 1937.
Evans, Bryn E. (*Llanelli*), E. 1920; E.S.I.F. 1922.
Evans, Colin (*Pontypool*), E. 1960.
Evans, D. (*Penygraig*), S.I. 96; E. 97; E. 98.
Evans, D. B. (*Swansea*), E. 1926.
Evans, Dan (*Cheshire and Barry*), E. 1934.
Evans, D. P. (*Llanelli*), SA. 1960.
Evans, D. W. (*Cardiff*), S.I. 89; E.I. 90, E. 91.
Evans, Emrys (*Llanelli*), E. 1937; S.I. 1939.
Evans, Frank (*Llanelli*), S. 1921.
Evans, Gareth (*Newport*), F. (R), 1977; F.A. (R, 2nd Test) 1978.
Evans, G. (*Cardiff*), E.S.F.I.A. 1947; E.S.F.I. 1948; E.S.I. 1949.
Evans, Iorwerth (*London Welsh*), S.I. 1934.
Evans, Islwyn (*Swansea*), E.S.I.F. 1922.
Evans, J. (*Llanelli*), S.I. 96; E. 97.
Evans, J. (*Blaina*), E. 1904.
Evans, J. (*Pontypool*), E.S.I. 1907.
Evans, J. D. (*Cardiff*), I.F. 1958.
Evans, J. Elwyn (*Llanelli*), S. 1924.
Evans, John R. (*Newport*), E. 1934.
Evans, O. J. (*Cardiff*), E.S. 87; S.I. 88.
Evans, Peter (*Llanelli*), E.F. 1951.
Evans, Rosser (*Cardiff*), S. 89.
Evans, Ron. (*Bridgend*), S.I.F. 1963.
Evans, R. T. (*Newport*), F.I. 1947; E.S.I.F. 1950, 1951.
Evans, Tom (*Llanelli*), I. 1906; E.S.I. 1907; I.A. 1908; E.S.I.F. 1909, 1910, 1911.
Evans, Tom (*Swansea*), I. 1924.
Evans, T. G. (*London Welsh*), SA.S.E.I. 1970; E.S.F. 1972.
Evans, T. P. (*Swansea*), F.E.S.I.A. 1975; E.S.I.F. 1976; I. 1977.
Evans, Viv (*Neath*), I.F.S. 1954.
Evans, Wynne (*Llanelli*), A. 1958.
Evans, W. F. (*Rhymney*), I. 82; S. 83.
Evans, W. G. (*Brynmawr*), I. 1911.
Evans, W. H. (*Llwynypia*), E.S.F.I. 1914.
Evans, W. J. (*Pontypool*), S. 1947.
Evans, W. R. (*Cardiff and Bridgend*), A.E.S.I.F. 1958; SA. 1960; E.S.I.F. 1961; E.S.I. 1962.
Evans, W. Rice (*Swansea*), S. 90; E.S. 91.
Everson, W. A. (*Newport*), S. 1926.

Faulkner, A. G. (*Pontypool*), F.E.S.I.A. 1975; E.S.I.F. 1976; E.S.I.F.A. (1st and 2nd Tests), NZ. 1978; S.I.F. 1979.
Faull, J. (*Swansea*), I.F. 1957; A.E.S.I.F. 1958; E.S.I. 1959; E.F. 1960.
Fear, A. (*Newport*), S.I. 1934, 1935.
Fender, N. (*Cardiff*), I.F. 1930; E.S.I.F. 1931.
Fenwick, S. P. (*Bridgend*), F.E.S.A. 1975; E.S.I.F. 1976; I.F.E.S. 1977; E.S.I.F.A. (1st and 2nd Tests), NZ. 1978; S.I.F.E. 1979; F.E.S.I. 1980.
Finch, E. (*Llanelli*), F.NZ. 1924; I.F. 1925; F. 1926; NSW. 1927; I. 1928.
Finlayson, A. A. J. (*Cardiff*), I.F.E. 1974.
Fitzgerald, D. (*Cardiff*), S.I. 94.
Ford, Ian (*Newport*), E.S. 1959.
Ford, F. J. V. (*Welch Regt. and Newport*), E. 1939.
Forward, A. (*Pontypool*), S.SA. 1951; E.S.I.F. 1952.
Fowler, I. (*Llanelli*), NZ. 1919.
Francis, G. (*Llanelli*), NZ. 1919; S. 1924.

Gabe, R. T. (*Llanelli and Cardiff*), I. 1901; E.S.I. 1902, 1903, 1904, 1905; NZ. 1905; E.I.SA. 1906; E.S.I. 1907; E.S.I.F. 1908.
Gale, N. R. (*Swansea and Llanelli*), I. 1960; E.S.I.NZ. 1963; E.S.I.F.SA. 1964; E.S.I.F. 1965, 1966; A. 1966; E.NZ. 1967; E. 1968; NZ. (1st (R) and 2nd Tests) A. 1969.
Gallacher, Stuart (*Llanelli*), F. 1970.
Garrett, R. M. (*Penarth*), M. 88; S. 89; E.S.I. 90; S.I. 91; E. 92.
Geen, W. P. (*Newport*), SA. 1912; E.I. 1913.
George, E. (*Pontypridd*), S.I. 95; E. 96.
Gething, Glyn (*Neath*), F. 1913.
Gibbs, R. A. (*Cardiff*), S.I. 1906; E.S. 1907; E.S.I.F. 1908, 1910, 1911.

Girling, B. E. (*Cardiff*), E. 81.
Goldsworthy, S. (*Swansea*), I. 84; E.S. 85.
Gore, J. (*Blaina*), I.F.NZ. 1924; E. 1925.
Gore, W. (*Newbridge*), S.F.I. 1947.
Gould, A. J. (*Newport*), E.S. 85, 86; E.S.I. 87; S. 88; I. 89; E.S.I. 90, 92, 93; E.S. 94; E.S.I. 95, 96; E. 97.
Gould Bert (*Newport*), I. 92; S.I. 93.
Gould Bob (*Newport*), E.I. 82; S. 83; E.S.I. 84; E.S. 85; E. 86; E.S. 87.
Graham, T. C. (*Newport*), I. 90; S.I. 91; E.S. 92; E.S.I. 93; E.S. 94, 95.
Gravell, R. W. R. (*Llanelli*), F.E.S.I.A. 1975; E.S.I.F. 1976; E.S.I.F.A. (1st and 2nd Tests), NZ. 1978; S.I. 1979.
Gray, A. J. (*London Welsh*), E.S. 1968.
Greenslade, D. (*Newport*), S. 1962.
Greville, H. (*Llanelli*), A. 1947.
Griffin, Dr. A. (*Edinburgh Univ.*), S. 83.
Griffiths, Clive (*Llanelli*), E.(R) 1979.
Griffiths, D. (*Llanelli*), M. 88; I. 89.
Griffiths, G. (*Llanelli*), I. 89.
Griffiths, Gareth (*Cardiff*), E.S.I.F.NZ. 1953; S.I.F. 1954; I.F. 1955; E.S. 1957.
Griffiths, V. M. (*Newport*), S.I.F. 1924.
Gronow, B. (*Bridgend*), F.E.S.I. 1910.
Gwilliam, J. A. (*Newport and Edinburgh Wands.*), A. 1947; I. 1948; E.S.I.F. 1949, 1950; E.S.I.SA. 1951; E.S.I.F. 1952; E.I.F.NZ. 1953; E. 1954.
Gwynn, D. (*Swansea*), E. 83; S. 87; E.I. 90; E.S. 91.
Gwynn, W. H. (*Swansea*), E.S.I. 84; E.S. 85.

Hall, Ian (*Aberavon*), NZ. 1967; SA.S.E. 1970; S. 1971; S.I.F. 1974.
Hancock, F. E. (*Cardiff*), I. 84; E.S. 85; S. 86.
Hannan, J. (*Newport*), M. 88; S.I. 89; E.S.I. 90; E. 91; E.S.I. 92, 93, 94, 95.
Harding, A. F. (*Cardiff and London Welsh*), E.S.I. 1902, 1903, 1904, 1905; NZ. 1905; E.S.I.SA. 1906; I. 1907; E.S. 1908.
Harding, G. F. (*Newport*), E. 81; I.E. 82; S. 83.
Harding, W. Rowe (*Swansea*), E.S.I.F. 1923; I.F.NZ. 1924; I.F. 1925; E.I.F. 1926; E.S.I.F. 1927; E. 1928.
Harding, Theo. (*Newport*), M. 88; S.I. 89.
Harris, D. J. E. (*Pontypridd and Cardiff*), I.F. 1959; S.I.F.SA. 1960; E.S. 1961.
Harris, Tal. (*Aberavon*), NSW. 1927.
Hathway, G. (*Newport*), I.F. 1924.
Havard, Rev. W. T. (*Llanelli*), NZ. 1919.
Hawkins, F. (*Pontypridd*), I.F. 1912.
Hayward, Don. (*Newbridge*), E.F. 1949; E.S.I.F. 1950, 1951, 1952; SA. 1951.
Hayward, David (*Cardiff*), E.NZ. 1963; S.I.F.SA. 1964.
Hayward, G. (*Swansea*), S.I.F.A. 1908; E. 1909.
Hellings, R. (*Llwynypia*), E. 97; E.I. 98; S.I. 99; E.I. 1900; E.S. 1901.
Herrera, R. C. (*Cross Keys*), S.I.F. 1925; E.S.I.F. 1926; E. 1927.
Hiams, H. (*Swansea*), I.F. 1912.
Hickman, Arthur (*Neath*), E. 1930; S. 1933.
Hiddlestone, D. (*Neath*), E.S.I.F. 1922; NZ. 1924.
Hill, A. F. (*Cardiff*), S. 85; E.S. 86; M.S.I. 88; S. 89; S.I. 90; E.S.I. 93, 94.
Hinam, S. (*Cardiff*), I. 1925; E.S.I.F. 1926.
Hinton, J. T. (*Cardiff*), I. 84.
Hirst, G. L. (*Newport*), S. 1912, 1913; E.S.F.I. 1914.
Hodder, W. (*Pontypool*), E.S.F. 1921.
Hodges, J. J. (*Newport*), E.S.I. 99, 1900; E.S. 1901; E.S.I. 1902, 1903; E.S. 1904; E.S.I.NZ. 1905; E.S.I. 1906.
Hodgson, G. T. R. (*Neath*), I. 1962; E.S.I.F.NZ. 1963; E.S.I.F.SA. 1964; S.I.F. 1966; I. 1967.
Hollingdale, B. (*Swansea*), SA. 1912; E. 1913.
Hollingdale, T. (*Neath*), NSW. 1927; E.S.I.F. 1928; E. 1930.
Holmes, T. (*Cardiff*), A. (2nd Test), N.Z. 1978; S.I.F.E. 1979; F.E.S.I. 1980.
Hopkin, W. H. (*Newport*), S. 1937.
Hopkins, Phil. (*Swansea*), A. 1908; E.I. 1909; E. 1910.
Hopkins, Ray (*Maesteg*), E. (R), 1970.
Hopkins, T. (*Swansea*), E.S.I.F. 1926.
Hopkins, W. J. (*Aberavon*), E.S. 1925.
Howell, Bryn (*Llanelli*), E. 1934.
Howells, Geoff (*Llanelli*), E.S.I.F. 1957.
Howells, W. H. (*Swansea*), S.I. 88.
Hughes, Dennis (*Newbridge*), NZ. 1967; NZ. (2nd Test) 1969; SA.S.E.I. 1970.
Hughes, Gomer (*Penarth*), E.S.I. 1934.
Hughes, H. (*Cardiff*), S. 87, 89.
Hughes, Keith (*Camb. Univ. and London Welsh*), I. 1970; A. 1973; S. 1974.
Hullin, W. (*Cardiff*), S. 1967.
Hurrell, J. E. (*Newport*), F. 1959.
Hutchinson, F. (*Neath*), I. 94; S.I. 96.
Huxtable, R. (*Swansea*), F.I. 1920.
Huzzey, H. V. P. (*Cardiff*), E.I. 98; E.S.I. 99.
Hybart, A. J. (*Cardiff*), E. 87.

Ingledew, H. M. (*Cardiff*), I. 90; E.S. 91.
Isaacs, I. (*Cardiff*), E.S. 1933.

Jackson, T. H. (*Swansea*), E. 95.
James, Boyo (*Bridgend*), E. 1968.
James, Carwyn (*Llanelli*), A.F. 1958.
James, David (*Swansea*), I. 91; S.I.92; E. 99.
James, D. R. (*Treorchy*), F.I. 1931.
James, Evan (*Swansea*), S. 90; I. 91; S.I. 92; E. 99.
James, Maldwyn (*Cardiff*), A. 1947; E.S.F.I. 1948.
James, T. O. (*Aberavon*), I. 1935; S. 1937.
James, W. P. (*Aberavon*), E.S. 1925.
Jarman, H. (*Newport*), E.S.I. 1910; E. 1911.
Jarrett, K. S. (*Newport*), E. 1967; E.S. 1968; S.I.F.E.NZ. (1st and 2nd Tests); A. 1969.
Jeffery, J. J. (*Newport*), NZ. 1967.
Jenkins, Albert (*Llanelli*), E.S.I.F. 1920; S.F. 1921; F. 1922; E.S.I.F. 1923; NZ. 1924; S.I. 1928.
Jenkins, A. M. (*Swansea*), I. 95; E. 96.
Jenkins, D. (*Treorchy*), E.S.I.F. 1926.
Jenkins, D. R. (*Swansea*), NSW. 1927; E. 1929.
Jenkins, E. M. (*Aberavon*), S.I.F.NSW. 1927; E.S.I.F. 1928; F. 1929; E.S.I.F. 1930, 1931; SA. 1931; E.S.I. 1932.

Jenkins, E. (*Newport*), S.I. 1910.
Jenkins, J. C. (*London Welsh*), SA. 1906.
Jenkins, L. (*Aberavon*), S.F. 1923.
Jenkins, Leighton (*Newport*), I. 1954; E.S.I.F. 1956.
Jenkins, V. G. J. (*London Welsh and Bridgend*), E.I. 1933; S.I. 1934; E.S.NZ. 1935; E.S.I. 1936; E. 1937; E.S. 1938; E. 1939.
Jenkins, W. (*Cardiff*), I.F. 1912; S.I. 1913.
John, A. (*Llanelli*), I. 1925; E.S.I. 1928.
John, B. (*Llanelli and Cardiff*), A. 1966; S.NZ. 1967; E.S.I.F. 1968; S.I.F.E.NZ. (1st and 2nd Tests), A. 1969; SA.S.E.I. 1970; E.S.I.F. 1971; E.S.F. 1972.
John, D. E. (*Llanelli*), F.I. 1923; E.S.I. 1928.
John, E. R. (*Neath*), E.S.I.F. 1950, 1951; SA. 1951; E.S.I.F. 1952, 1953; NZ. 1953; E. 1954.
John, G. (*St. Luke's Coll., Exeter*), E.F. 1954.
John, J. H. (*Swansea*), E.S.I.F. 1926, 1927.
Johnson, T. (*Cardiff*), E.F.I. 1921; E.S.F. 1923; E.S.NZ. 1924; E.S.F. 1925.
Johnson, W. D. (*Swansea*), E. 1953.
Jones, A. H. (*Cardiff*), E.S. 1933.
Jones, Bedwellty (*Abertillery*), E.S.F.I. 1914.
Jones, Bert (*Llanelli*), S.I. 1934.
Jones, Bob (*Llwynypia*), I. 1901.
Jones, B. J. (*Newport*), I.F. 1960.
Jones, Charles, W. (*Bridgend*), E.S.F. 1920.
Jones, Cliff (*Cambridge and Cardiff*), E.S.I. 1934, 1935; NZ. 1935; E.S.I. 1936, 1938.
Jones, Dan (*Neath*), NSW. 1927.
Jones, Dan (*Aberavon*), E. 97.
Jones, David (*Swansea*), E.F.I. 1947; E.S.I.F. 1949.
Jones, David (*Treherbert*), E.S.I. 1902, 1903, 1905; NZ. 1905; E.S.SA. 1906.
Jones, David (*Newport*), E.S.I.F. 1926; E. 1927.
Jones, Des (*Llanelli*), E. 1948.
Jones, D. K. (*Llanelli and Cardiff*), E.S.F.I. 1962; E.F.NZ. 1963; E.S.SA. 1964; E.S.I.F. 1966.
Jones, David, P. (*Pontypool*), I. 1907.
Jones, D. N. Rocyn (*Cambridge*), I. 1925.
Jones, Edgar (*Llanelli*), F. 1930; E.S.I. 1933; E. 1935.
Jones, Elvet (*Llanelli*), S. 1939.
Jones, Graham (*Cardiff*), S. 1930; I. 1933.
Jones, Graham (*Ebbw Vale*), S.I.F. 1963.
Jones, G. R. Rees (*Oxford and London Welsh*), E.S. 1934; I.NZ. 1935; E. 1936.
Jones, Harold (*Neath*), E.S. 1929.
Jones, Harry (*Penygraig*), S.I. 1902.
Jones, Howel (*Neath*), I. 1904.
Jones, Howie (*Swansea*), I.F. 1930.
Jones, Iorwerth (*Llanelli*), NSW, 1927; E.S.I.F. 1928.
Jones, Ivor (*Llanelli*), E.S. 1924; S.I.F.NSW. 1927; E.S.I.F. 1928, 1929; E.S. 1930.
Jones, I. C. (*London Welsh*), I. 1968.
Jones, J. (*Aberavon*), E. 1901.
Jones, J. A. (*Cardiff*), S. 83.
Jones, Jim (*Aberavon*), NZ. 1919; E.S. 1920; S.F.I. 1921.
Jones, Joe (*Swansea*), F. 1924.
Jones, J. P. (*Newport and Pontypool*), A. 1908; E.S.I.F. 1909; E.F. 1910, 1912; I.F. 1913, 1920; E. 1921.
Jones, J. Strand (*Llanelli*), E.S.I. 1902; E.S. 1903.
Jones, Ken (*Monmouth and London Welsh*), E. 1934.
Jones, Ken (*Newport*), E.S.I.F.A. 1947; E.S.F.I. 1948, 1949, 1950, 1951; SA. 1951; E.S.I.F. 1952, 1953; NZ. 1953; E.S.I.F. 1954, 1955, 1956; S. 1957.
Jones, K. D. (*Cardiff*), SA. 1960; E.S.I. 1961; E.F. 1962; E.S.I.NZ. 1963.
Jones, Lewis (*Llanelli*), E.S.I.F. 1950; E.S.SA. 1951; E.I.F. 1952.
Jones, Marsden (*Cardiff*), E. 1921; NZ. 1924.
Jones, P. Baker (*Newport*), S. 1921.
Jones, Percy (*Newport and Pontypool*), SA. 1912; E.S.F. 1913; E.S.F.I. 1914.
Jones, R. (*Swansea*), I. 1901; E. 1902; E.S.I 1904; E. 1905; I.F.A. 1908; E.S.I.F. 1909; E.F. 1910.
Jones, R. (*London Welsh*), E. 1929.
Jones, R. B. (*Cambridge*), E.S. 1933.
Jones, R. E. (*Coventry*), F.E. 1967; S.I.F. 1968.
Jones, Robert (*Northampton*), E.S.F. 1926.
Jones, Roy (*Swansea*), NSW. 1927; F. 1928.
Jones, T. B. (*Newport*), I.E. 82; S. 83; S. 84; E.S. 85.
Jones, Tom (*Newport*), E.S.I.F. 1922; E.S. 1924.
Jones, J. 'Tuan' (*Pontypool*), S. 1913.
Jones, W. (*Cardiff*), E.I. 98.
Jones, W. I. (*Llanelli*), E.S.I.F. 1925.
Jones, W. J. (*Llanelli*), I. 1924.
Jones, W. K. (*Cardiff*), NZ. 1967; E.S.I.F. 1968.
Jones, Wyndham (*Mountain Ash*), I. 1905.
Jones-Davies, T. E. (*London Welsh*), E.I. 1930; E.S. 1931.
Jordan, H. M. (*Newport*), E.S. 85; S. 89.
Joseph, W. (*Swansea*), E.S.I. 1902, 1903; E.S. 1904; E.S.I.NZ. 1905; E.S.I.SA. 1906.
Jowett, F. (*Swansea*), E. 1903.
Judd, S. (*Cardiff*), E.S.I.F.NZ. 1953; E.S.F. 1954; E:S. 1955.
Judson, J. H. (*Llanelli*), E. 82; S. 83.

Kedzlie, Q. D. (*Cardiff*), S.I. 88.
Keen, L. (*Aberavon*), F.E.S.I. 1980.
Knill, F. M. D. (*Cardiff*), F. (R), 1976.

Lane, Stuart (*Cardiff*), A. (1st Test (R), and 2nd Test) 1978; I. (R) 1979; S.I. 1980.
Lang, J. (*Llanelli*), F.I. 1931; S.I. 1934; E.S.I.NZ. 1935; E.S.I. 1936; E. 1937.
Law, V. J. (*Newport*), I. 1939.
Lawrence, S. (*Bridgend*), S.I. 1925; S.I.F. 1926; E. 1927.
Legge, W. G. (*Newport*), I. 1937, 1938.
Leleu, J. (*London Welsh and Swansea*), E.S. 1959; F.SA. 1960.
Lemon, A. (*Neath*), I. 1929; S.I.F. 1930; E.S.I.F.SA. 1931; E.S.I. 1932; I. 1933.
Lewis, Arthur (*Ebbw Vale*), F. 1970; E.I.F. 1971; E.S.F. 1972; E.S.I.F. 1973.
Lewis, A. R. (*Abertillery*), E.S.I.F.A. 1966; I. 1967.
Lewis, Bryn (*Swansea*), I. 1912, 1913.
Lewis, J. M. C. (*Cardiff*), E. 1912; S.I.F. 1913; E.S.F.I. 1914; I. 1921; E.S. 1923.
Lewis, C. P. (*Llandovery*), I.E. 82; S. 83; E.S. 84.

Lewis, D. H. (*Cardiff*), E.S. 86.
Lewis, E. J. (*Llandovery*), E. 81.
Lewis, Howell (*Swansea*), S.I.F. 1913; E. 1914.
Lewis, J. (*Llanelli*), I. 87.
Lewis, Mark (*Treorchy*), F. 1913.
Lewis, Tom (*Cardiff*), E. 1926; E.S. 1927.
Lewis, W. (*Llanelli*), F. 1925.
Lewis, Geoff W. (*Richmond*), E.S. 1960.
Lewis, Windsor H. (*London Welsh*), I. 1926; E.I.F.NSW. 1927; F. 1928.
Llewelyn, Barry (*Newport and Llanelli*), SA.S.E.I.F. 1970; E.S.I.F. 1971; E.S.F.NZ. 1972.
Llewellyn, P. D. (*Swansea*), I.F.A. 1973; S.E. 1974.
Llewellyn, W. (*Llwynypia*), E.S.I. 99, 1900, 1901, 1902; I. 1903; E.S.I. 1904, 1905; NZ. 1905.
Lloyd, D. J. (*Bridgend*), E.S.I.F.A. 1966; S.I.F.E. 1967; S.I.F. 1968; S.I.F.E.NZ. (1st Test) A. 1969; F. 1970; E.S.F. 1972; E.S. 1973.
Lloyd, E. (*Llanelli*), S. 95.
Lloyd, G. L. (*Newport*), I. 96; S.I. 99; E.S. 1900; E.S. 1901; S.I. 1902; E.S.I. 1903.
Lloyd, Percy (*Llanelli*), S.E. 90; E.I. 91.
Lloyd, R. (*Pontypool*), S.I.F. 1913; E.S.F.I. 1914.
Lloyd, T. C. (*Neath*), F. 1909; I.F. 1913; E.S.F.I. 1914.
Lloyd, T. (*Maesteg*), I.F. 1953.
Lockwood, T. W. (*Newport*), E.S.I. 87.
Long, Eddie (*Swansea*), E.S.I. 1936; E.S. 1937; S.I. 1939.
Lyne, H. S. (*Newport*), S. 83; E.S.I. 84; E. 85.

Maddocks, H. T. (*London Welsh*), E.S.I. 1906; E.S. 1907; F. 1910.
Maddocks, K. (*Neath*), E. 1957.
Main, D. R. (*London Welsh*), E.S.I.F. 1959.
Mainwaring, H. J. (*Swansea*), F. 1961.
Mainwaring, W. T. (*Aberavon*), S.I.F.E.NZ. 1967; E. 1968.
Major, W. (*Maesteg*), F. 1949; S. 1950.
Male, B. O. (*Cross Keys, Pontypool and Cardiff*), F. 1921; S. 1923; S.I. 1924; E.S.I.F. 1927; S.I.F. 1928.
Manfield, L. (*Mountain Ash and Cardiff*), S.I. 1939; A. 1947; E.S.F.I. 1948.
Mann, B. B. (*Cardiff*), E. 81.
Mantle, J. (*Newport*), E.SA. 1964.
Margrave, F. L. (*Llanelli*), E.S. 84.
Martin, A. J. (*Aberavon*), A. 1973; S.I. 1974; F.E.S.I.A. 1975; E.S.I.F. 1976; I.F.E.S. 1977; E.S.I.F.A. (1st and 2nd Tests); NZ. 1978; S.I.F.E. 1979; F.E.S.I. 1980.
Martin, W. J. (*Newport*), I.F. 1912; NZ. 1919.
Mathias, R. (*Llanelli*), F. 1970.
Matthews, Rev. A. A. (*Lampeter*), S. 86.
Matthews, Chris. (*Bridgend*), I. 1939.
Matthews, Jack (*Cardiff*), E.A. 1947; E.S.F. 1948; E.S.I.F. 1949, 1950, 1951.
McCall, B. E. W. (*Welch Regt. and Newport*), E.S.I. 1936.
McCarley, A. (*Neath*), E.S.I. 1938.
McCutcheon, W. (*Swansea*), S. 91; E.S. 92; E.S.I. 93; E. 94.
Meredith, A. (*Devonport Serv's*), E.S.I. 1949.
Meredith, B. V. (*Newport*), I.F.S. 1954; E.S.I.F. 1955, 1956, 1957; A.E.S.I. 1958; E.S.I.F. 1959; E.S.F. 1960; SA. 1960; E.S.I. 1961; E.S.F.I. 1962.
Meredith, C. C. (*Neath*), S.NZ. 1953; E.I.F.S. 1954, 1955; E.I. 1956; E.S. 1957.
Meredith, J. (*Swansea*), S.I. 88; E.S. 90.
Merry, G. E. (*Pill Harriers*), I.F. 1912.
Michael, G. (*Swansea*), E.S.F. 1923.
Michaelson, R. C. B. (*Aberavon*), E. 1963.
Miller, F. (*Mountain Ash*), I. 96; E.S.I. 1900, 1901.
Mills, F. (*Swansea and Cardiff*), E.S.I. 92, 93, 94, 95; E. 96.
Moore, W. J. (*Bridgend*), I. 1933.
Morgan, C. Henry (*Llanelli*), I.F. 1957.
Morgan, C. I. (*Cardiff*), I.F.SA. 1951; E.S.I. 1952; S.I.F.NZ. 1953; E.S.I. 1954; E.S.I.F. 1955, 1956, 1957, 1958.
Morgan, D. (*Swansea*), S. 85; E.S. 86; E.S.I. 87; I. 89.
Morgan, Dai (*Llanelli*), I. 95; E. 96.
Morgan, D. R. (*Llanelli*), E.S.F.I. 1962, 1963; NZ. 1963.
Morgan, E. (*Llanelli*), I. 1920; E.S.F. 1921.
Morgan, E. (*London Welsh*), E.S.I. 1902; I. 1903; E.S.I. 1904, 1905; NZ. 1905; E.S.I.SA. 1906; F. 1908.
Morgan, Eddie (*Swansea*), E.S.I. 1938; E. 1939.
Morgan, Edgar (*Swansea*), E.S.F.I. 1914.
Morgan, F. L. (*Llanelli*), E.S.I. 1938; E. 1939.
Morgan, H. J. (*Abertillery*), E.S.I.F. 1958; I.F. 1959; E. 1960; E.S.I.F. 1961, 1962; S.I.F. 1963; E.S.I.F. 1965, 1966; A. 1966.
Morgan, H. P. (*Newport*), E.S.I.F. 1956.
Morgan, Ivor (*Swansea*), A. 1908; E.S.I.F. 1909, 1910; E.I.F. 1911; S. 1912.
Morgan, Jack (*Llanelli*), SA. 1912; E. 1913.
Morgan, N. (*Newport*), S.I.F. 1960.
Morgan, P. (*Llanelli*), S.(R)I. 1980.
Morgan, P. E. J. (*Aberavon*), E.S.F. 1961.
Morgan, T. (*Llanelli*), I. 89.
Morgan, W. Guy (*Cambridge and Swansea*), I.F. 1927; E.S.I.F. 1929; I.F. 1930.
Morgan, W. L. (*Cardiff*), S. 1910.
Morley, J. C. (*Newport*), E.S.I.F. 1929; E.I. 1930; E.S.F.I.SA. 1931; E.S.I. 1932.
Morris, G. L. (*Swansea*), I.E. 82; S. 83; E.S. 84.
Morris, H. (*Cardiff*), F. 1951; I.F. 1955.
Morris, Ivor (*Swansea*), E.S. 1924.
Morris, R. R. (*Swansea and Bristol*), S. 1933, 1937.
Morris, S. (*Cross Keys*), E.S.I.F. 1920, 1922, 1923; E.S.F.NZ. 1924; E.S.F. 1925.
Morris, W. (*Abertillery*), NZ. 1919; F. 1920; I. 1921.
Morris, William (*Llanelli*), S.I. 96; E. 97;
Morris, W. D. (*Neath*), F.E. 1967; E.S.I.F. 1968; S.I.F.E.NZ. (1st and 2nd Tests) A. 1969; SA.S.E.I.F. 1970; E.S.I.F. 1971; E.S.F.NZ. 1972; E.S.I.A. 1973; S.I.F.E. 1974.
Morris, W. J. (*Newport*), S. 1965; F. 1966
Morris, W. J. (*Pontypool*), S.I. 1963.
Murphy, C. (*Cross Keys*), E.S.I. 1935.

Nash, D. (*Ebbw Vale*), SA. 1960; E.S.I.F. 1961; F. 1962.
Neill, W. (*Cardiff*), S.I. 1904; E.S.I. 1905; E.I.

1907; E.S.I.F. 1908.
Newman, C. H. (*Newport*), E. 81; I.E. 82; S. 83; E.S. 84, 85; E. 86, 87.
Nicholas, T. J. (*Cardiff*), NZ. 1919.
Nicholl, C. B. (*Llanelli*), I. 91; E.S.I. 92, 93; E.S. 94; E.S.I. 95, 96.
Nicholls, D. W. (*Llanelli*), I. 94.
Nicholls, E. G. (*Cardiff*), S.I. 96; E. 97; E.I. 98; E.S.I. 99; S.I. 1900; E.S.I. 1901, 1902; I. 1903; E. 1904; I.NZ. 1905; E.S.I.SA. 1906.
Nicholls, F. E. (*Cardiff Harlequins*), I. 92.
Nicholls, Howard (*Cardiff*), I. 1958.
Nicholls, S. H. (*Cardiff*), M. 88; S.I.89; S. 91.
Norris, C. H. (*Cardiff*), F. 1963; F. 1966;.
Norton, W. B. (*Cardiff*), I.E. 82; S. 83; E.S.I. 84.

O'Connor, A. (*Aberavon*), SA. 1960; E.S. 1961; F.I. 1962.
O'Connor, R. (*Aberavon*), E. 1957.
O'Shea, J. P. (*Cardiff*), S.I. 1967; S.I.F. 1968.
Oliver, G. (*Pontypool*), E.S.I.F. 1920.
Osborne, W. T. (*Mountain Ash*) E.S.I. 1902, 1903.
Ould, W. J. (*Cardiff*), E.S. 1924.
Owen Albert, (*Swansea*), E. 1924.
Owen, G. (*Newport*), I.F. 1955; E.S.I.F. 1956.
Owen, R. M. (*Swansea*), I. 1901; E.S.I. 1902, 1903, 1904, 1905; NZ. 1905; E.S.I.SA. 1906; E.S. 1907; I.F.A. 1908; E.S.I.F. 1909; E.F. 1910; E.S.I.F. 1911; E.S. 1912.

Packer, H. (*Newport*), E. 91; S.I. 95; E.S.I. 96; E. 97.
Palmer, Frank (*Swansea*), E.S.I. 1922.
Parfitt, F. C. (*Newport*), E.S.I. 93, 94; S. 95; S.I. 96.
Parker, D. (*Swansea*), I.F.NZ. 1924; E.S.I.F. 1925; I.F. 1929; E. 1930.
Parker, T. (*Swansea*), NZ. 1919; E.S.I. 1920; E.S.F.I. 1921, 1922; E.S.F. 1923.
Parker, W. (*Swansea*), E.S. 99.
Parsons, G. (*Newport*), E. 1947.
Pascoe, D. (*Bridgend*), F.I. 1923.
Pask, A. E. I. (*Abertillery*), F. 1961; E.S.F.I. 1962, 1963; NZ. 1963; E.S.I.F.SA. 1964; E.S.I.F. 1965, 1966; A. 1966; S.I. 1967.
Payne, G. W. (*Pontypridd*), E.S.I. 1960.
Payne, H. (*Swansea*), NZ. 1935.
Peacock, H. (*Newport*), S.I.F. 1929, 1930.
Peake, E. (*Chepstow*), E. 81.
Pearson, T. W. (*Cardiff and Newport*), E.I. 91; E.S. 92; S.I. 94; E.S.I. 95; E. 97; E.I. 98; E. 1903.
Pegge, E. V. (*Neath*), E. 91.
Perrett, F. (*Neath*), SA. 1912; E.S.I.F. 1913.
Perrins, Vic (*Newport*), SA.S. 1970.
Perry, W. (*Neath*), E. 1911.
Phillips, Alan (*Cardiff*), E. 1979; F.E.S.I. 1980.
Phillips, Bryn (*Aberavon*), E.S.I.F. 1925; E. 1926.
Phillips, Harry (*Newport*), E.S.I.F.NSW. 1927; E.S.I.F. 1928.
Phillips, H. (*Swansea*), F. 1952.
Phillips, L. A. (*Newport*), E.S.I. 1900; S. 1901.
Phillips, Percy (*Newport*), E. 92; E.S.I. 93; E.S. 94.
Phillips, W. D. (*Cardiff*), E. 81; I. 82; E.S.I. 84.
Plummer, R. C. S. (*Newport*), S.I.F.SA. 1912; E. 1913.
Pook, T. (*Newport*), S. 95.
Powell, Graham (*Ebbw Vale*), I.F. 1957.
Powell, J. (*Cardiff*), I. 1906.
Powell, J. (*Cardiff*), I. 1923.
Powell, W. J. (*Cardiff*), E.S.I.F. 1920.
Powell, R. W. (*Newport*), S.I. 88.
Powell, W. C. (*London Welsh*), S.I.F. 1926; E.I.F. 1927; S.I.F. 1928; E.S.I.F. 1929; S.I.F. 1930; E.S.I.F.SA. 1931; E.S.I. 1932, 1935.
Price, B. (*Newport*), I.F. 1961; E.S. 1962; E.S.F.NZ. 1963; E.S.I.F.SA. 1964; E.S.I.F. 1965, 1966; A. 1966; E.S.I.F. 1967; S.I.F.NZ. (1st and 2nd Tests) A. 1969.
Price, G. (*Pontypool*), F.E.S.I.A. 1975; E.S.I.F. 1976; I.F.E.S. 1977; E.S.I.F.A. (1st and 2nd Tests), NZ. 1978; S.I.F.E. 1979; F.E.S.I. 1980.
Price, M. (*Pontypool*), E.S.I.F. 1959, 1960; E. 1962.
Price, R. E. (*Weston*), S.I. 1939.
Price, T. G. (*Llanelli*), E.S.I.F. 1965; E.A. 1966; S.F. 1967.
Priday, A. J. (*Cardiff*), I. 1958; I. 1961.
Pritchard, Cliff (*Newport and Pontypool*), S.I. 1904; NZ. 1905; E.S. 1906.
Pritchard, C. M. (*Newport*), I. 1904; E.S.NZ. 1905; E.S.I.SA. 1906; E.S.I. 1907; E. 1908; E.F. 1910.
Pritchard, Cecil (*Pontypool*), E.S.I.F. 1928, 1929.
Prosser, D. R. (*Neath*), S.I. 1934.
Prosser, Glyn, (*Neath*), E.S.I. 1934; NZ. 1935.
Prosser, J. (*Cardiff*), I. 1921.
Prosser, R. (*Pontypool*), S.F. 1956; E.S.I.F. 1957; A.E.S.I.F. 1958; E.S.I.F. 1959, 1960; SA. 1960; I.F. 1961.
Prothero, G. J. (*Bridgend*), S.I.F. 1964; E.S.I.F. 1965, 1966.
Pryce-Jenkins, T. J. (*London Welsh*), S.I. 88.
Pugh, C. (*Maesteg*), E.S.I.F.NZ. 1924; E.S. 1925.
Pugsley, J. (*Cardiff*), E.S.I. 1910; E.S.I.F. 1911.
Pullman, J. (*Neath*), F. 1910.
Purdon, F. (*Newport*), E. 81; I.E. 82; S. 83.

Quinnell, D. L. (*Llanelli*), F. (R), NZ. 1972; E.S.A. 1973; S.F. 1974; E. (R), 1975; I. (R), F.E.S. 1977; E.S.I.F.A. (1st Test) NZ. 1978; S.I.F.E. 1979.

Radford, W. (*Newport*), I. 1923.
Ralph, A. R. (*Newport*), F.I.SA. 1931; E.S.I. 1932.
Ramsey, S. H. (*Treorchy*), E. 96; E. 1904.
Randell, R. (*Aberavon*), I.F. 1924.
Raybould, W. H. (*London Welsh*), S.I.F.E.NZ. 1967; I.F. 1968; SA.E.I.F. (R) 1970.
Rees, Aaron (*Maesteg*), NZ. 1919.
Rees, Alan (*Maesteg*), E.S.F. 1962.
Rees, A. M. (*London Welsh*), E. 1934; E.S.I.NZ. 1935; E.S.I. 1936, 1937; E.S. 1938.
Rees, B. I. (*London Welsh*), S.I.F. 1967.
Rees, Clive (*London Welsh*), I. 1974; A. 1975; NZ. 1978.
Rees, Doug (*Swansea*), S.I.F. 1968.
Rees, J. Conway (*Llanelli*), S. 92; E. 93, 94.
Rees, Dan (*Swansea*), E. 1900; E.S. 1903, 1905.
Rees, E. B. (*Swansea*), NZ. 1919.
Rees, H. (*Cardiff*), S.I. 1937; E.S.I. 1938.

Rees H. Elgan (*Neath*), S.I.F.E. 1979; F.E.S.I. 1980.
Rees, J. Idwal (*Swansea*), E.S.I. 1934; S.NZ. 1935; E.S.I. 1936, 1937, 1938.
Rees, Joe (*Swansea*), E.S.I.F. 1920; E.S.I. 1921; E. 1922; E.I.F. 1923; E. 1924.
Rees, L. (*Cardiff*), I. 1933.
Rees, Peter (*Llanelli*), F.I. 1947.
Rees, P. M. (*Newport*), E.S.I. 1961; I. 1964.
Rees, Tom (*Newport*), S.I.NZ. 1935; E.S.I. 1936; E.S. 1937.
Rees, T. A. (*Llandovery*), E. 81.
Rees, T. E. (*London Welsh*), I.F. 1926; NSW. 1927; E. 1928.
Reeves, F. (*Cross Keys*), F.I. 1920; E. 1921.
Rhapps, J. (*Penygraig*), E. 97.
Richards, Bryan (*Swansea*), F. 1960.
Richards, Cliff (*Pontypool*), E.S.I.F. 1922; I. 1924.
Richards, D. S. (*Swansea*), F.E. 1979; F.E.S.I. 1980.
Richards, E. S. (*Swansea*), E. 85; S. 87.
Richards, Gwyn (*Cardiff*), S. 1927.
Richards, Idris (*Cardiff*), E.S.F. 1925.
Richards, Ken (*Bridgend*), SA. 1960; E.S.I.F. 1961.
Richards, M. C. R. (*Cardiff*), I.F. 1968; S.I.F.E.NZ. (1st and 2nd Tests) A. 1969.
Richards, Rees (*Aberavon*), S.I.F. 1913.
Richards, Rex (*Cross Keys*), F. 1956.
Richards, T. L. (*Maesteg*), I. 1923.
Richardson, J. (*Aberavon*), A. (R 2nd Test) 1978; E. 1979.
Rickard, A. (*Cardiff*), F. 1924.
Ring, J. (*Aberavon*), E. 1921.
Ringer, P. (*Ebbw Vale and Llanelli*), NZ. 1978; S.I.F.E. 1979; F.E. 1980.
Roberts, Cyril (*Neath*), I.F. 1958.
Roberts, E. (*Llanelli*), E. 86; I. 87.
Roberts, E. D. A. (*London Welsh*), E. 1930.
Roberts, E. J. (*Llanelli*), S.I. 88; I. 89.
Roberts, H. M. (*Cardiff*), SA. 1960; E.S.I.F. 1961; S.F. 1962; I. 1963.
Roberts, J. (*Cardiff*), E.S.I.F.NSW. 1927; E.S.I.F. 1928, 1929.
Roberts, M. G. (*London Welsh*), E.S.I.F. 1971; I.F. 1973; S. 1975; E. 1979.
Roberts, T. (*Risca and Newport*), S.F.I. 1921; E.S.I.F. 1922; E.S. 1923.
Roberts, Willie (*Cardiff*), E. 1929.
Robins, J. D. (*Birkenhead Park*), E.S.I.F. 1950, 1951; E.I.F. 1953.
Robins, R. (*Pontypridd*), S. 1953; S.F. 1954; E.S.I.F. 1955; E.F. 1956; E.S.I.F. 1957.
Robinson, I. R. (*Cardiff*), F.E. 1974.
Roderick, W. B. (*Llanelli*), I. 84.
Rosser, M. (*Penarth*), S.F. 1924.
Rowlands, C. F. (*Aberavon*), I. 1926.
Rowlands, D. C. T. (*Pontypool*), E.S.I.F.NZ. 1963; E.S.I.F.SA. 1964; E.S.I.F. 1965.
Rowlands, Gwyn (*Cardiff*), NZ. 1953; E.F. 1954; F. 1956.
Rowlands, J. (*Lampeter*), E. 85.
Rowlands, K. A. (*Cardiff*), F.I. 1962; I. 1963; I.F. 1965.
Rowles, G. R. (*Penarth*), E. 92.

Samuel, D. (*Swansea*), I. 91, 93.
Samuel, F. (*Mountain Ash*), S.I.F. 1922.
Samuel, J. (*Swansea*), I. 91.
Scourfield, T. (*Torquay*), F. 1930.
Scrine, F. (*Swansea*), E.S. 99; I. 1901.
Shanklin, J. L. (*London Welsh*), F. 1970; NZ. 1972; I.F. 1973.
Shaw, G. (*Neath*), NZ. 1972; E.S.I.F.A. 1973; S.I.F.E. 1974; I.F. 1977.
Shea, Jerry (*Pill Harriers and Newport*), NZ. 1919; E.S. 1920; E. 1921.
Shell, R. C. (*Aberavon*), A. (R), 1973.
Simpson, H. J. (*Cardiff*), E.S.I. 84.
Skrimshire, R. T. (*Newport*), E.S.I. 99.
Skym, A. (*Llanelli and Cardiff*), E.S.I.F. 1928, 1930, 1931; S.A. 1931; E.S.I. 1932, 1933; E. 1935.
Smith, J. S. (*Cardiff*), E.I. 84; E. 85.
Sparks, B. (*Neath*), I. 1954; E.F. 1955; E.S.I. 1956; S. 1957.
Spiller, W. (*Cardiff*), S.I. 1910; E.S.I.F. 1911; E.F.SA. 1912; E. 1913.
Squire, J. (*Newport and Pontypool*), I.F. 1977; E.S.I.F.A. (1st Test) NZ. 1978; S.I.F.E. 1979; F.E.S.I. 1980.
Stadden, W. H. (*Cardiff*), I. 84; E.S. 86; I. 87; M.S. 88; E.S. 90.
Stephens, G. (*Neath*), E.S.I.F.SA. 1912; E.S.I.F. 1913; NZ. 1919.
Stephens, Rev. J. G. (*Llanelli*), E.S.I.F. 1922.
Stephens, J. R. G. (*Neath*), E.S.F.I. 1947; I. 1948; S.I.F 1949; F.SA. 1951; E.S.I.F. 1952, 1953; NZ. 1953; E.I. 1954; E.S.I.F. 1955; S.I.F. 1956; E.S.I.F. 1957.
Stock, A. (*Newport*), F.NZ. 1924; E.S. 1926.
Stone, P. (*Llanelli*), F. 1949.
Summers, R. H. B. (*Haverfordwest*), E. 81.
Sweet-Escott, R. B. (*Cardiff*), S. 91; I. 94, 95.

Tamplin, W. E. (*Cardiff*), S.I.F.A. 1947; E.S.F. 1948.
Tanner, H. (*Swansea and Cardiff*), NZ. 1935; E.S.I. 1936, 1937, 1938, 1939; E.S.F.I. 1947, 1948, 1949.
Tarr, D. J. (*Swansea*), NZ. 1935.
Taylor, A. R. (*Cross Keys*), I. 1937, 1938; E. 1939.
Taylor, C. G. (*Blackheath*), E.S.I. 84; E.S. 85, 86; E.I. 87.
Taylor, J. (*London Welsh*), S.I.F.E.NZ. 1967; I.F. 1968; S.I.F.E.NZ. (1st Test) A. 1969; F. 1970; E.S.I.F. 1971; E.S.F.NZ. 1972; E.S.I.F. 1973.
Thomas, Alan (*Newport*), NZ. 1963; E. 1964.
Thomas, Alun G. (*Cardiff and Llanelli*), E.S.I.F. 1952; S.I.F. 1953; E.I.F. 1954; S.I.F. 1955.
Thomas, B. (*Neath*), E.S.I.F.NZ. 1963; E.S.I.F.SA. 1964; E. 1965; E.S.I. 1966; NZ. 1967; S.I.F.E.NZ. (1st and 2nd Tests) 1969.
Thomas, Bob (*Swansea*), E.S.I. 1900; E. 1901.
Thomas, C. J. (*Newport*), M.I. 88; S.I. 89; E.S.I. 90; E.I. 91.
Thomas, C. (*Bridgend*), E.S. 1925.
Thomas, David, (*Aberavon*), I. 1961.
Thomas, D. (*Swansea*), S.I. 1930; E.S.I. 1932; E.S. 1933; E. 1934; E.S.I. 1935.
Thomas, Denzil (*Llanelli*), I. 1954.

Thomas, Dick (*Mountain Ash*), SA. 1906; I.F. 1908; S. 1909.
Thomas, D. J. (*Swansea*), E. 1904; A. 1908 E.S.I. 1910; E.S.I.F. 1911; E. 1912.
Thomas, D. L. (*Neath*), E. 1937.
Thomas, E. (*Newport*), S.I. 1904; S.I.F. 1909; F. 1910.
Thomas, Gethin (*Llanelli*), E.S.I.F. 1923.
Thomas, George (*Newport*), M. 88; I. 90; S. 91.
Thomas, Harold (*Llanelli*), F. 1912.
Thomas, Harold (*Neath*), E.S.I. 1936, 1937.
Thomas, H. W. (*Swansea*), SA. 1912; E. 1913.
Thomas, Ifor (*Bryncethin*), E. 1924.
Thomas, L. C. (*Cardiff*), E.S. 85.
Thomas, M. C. (*Newport*), F. 1949; E.S.I.F. 1950, 1951; SA. 1951; E.S.I.F. 1952; E. 1953; E.S.I.F. 1956; E.S. 1957; E.S.I.F. 1958; I.F. 1959.
Thomas, Melbourne (*Bridgend and St. Bart's Hospital*), NZ. 1919; S.F.I. 1921; F. 1923; E. 1924.
Thomas, R. C. C. (*Swansea*), F. 1949; I.F. 1952; S.I.F.NZ. 1953; E.S.I.F. 1954; S.I. 1955; E.S.I. 1956; E. 1957; A.E.S.I.F. 1958; E.S.I.F. 1959.
Thomas, Rees (*Pontypool*), F.I. 1909; S.F. 1911; E.S.SA 1912; E. 1913.
Thomas, R. L. (*London Welsh*), S.I. 89; I. 90; E.S.I. 91; E. 92.
Thomas, S. (*Llanelli*), E.S. 90; I. 91.
Thomas, Watcyn (*Llanelli and Swansea*), E.S.I.F. 1927; E. 1929; E.S.SA. 1931; E.S.I. 1932, 1933.
Thomas, W. D. (*Llanelli*), A. 1966; S.I.F. 1968; E.NZ. (2nd Test) A. 1969; SA.S.E.I.F. 1970; E.S.I.F. 1971; E.S.F.NZ. 1972; E.S.I.F. 1973; E. 1974.
Thomas, W. J. (*Cardiff*), F. 1961; F. 1963.
Thomas, W. H. (*Llandovery and London Welsh*), S. 85; E.S. 86, 87; S.I. 88; E.I. 90; S.I. 91.
Thomas, W. Ll. (*Newport*), S. 94; E.I. 95.
Thomas, W. T. (*Abertillery*), E. 1930.
Thomson, J. (*Cross Keys*), E. 1923.
Towers, W. H. (*Swansea*), I. 87; M. 88.
Travers, G. (*Pill Harriers and Newport*), E.S.I. 1903; 1905; NZ. 1905; E.S.I.SA. 1906; E.S.I. 1907; E.S.I.F.A. 1908; E.S.I. 1909; S.I.F. 1911.
Travers, W. (*Newport*), S.I. 1937; E.S.I. 1938, 1939; E.S.I.F. 1949.
Treharne, E. (*Pontypridd*), E. 81; E. 82.
Trew, W. J. (*Swansea*), E.S.I. 1900; E.S. 1901; S. 1903, 1905, 1906; E.S. 1907; E.S.I.F.A. 1908; E.S.I.F. 1909; E.S.F. 1910; E.S.I.F. 1911; S. 1912; S.F. 1913.
Trott, R. F. (*Cardiff*), E.S.F.I. 1948, 1949.
Truman, H. (*Llanelli*), E. 1934, 1935.
Trump, L. (*Newport*), E.S.I.F. 1912.
Turnbull, B. R. (*Cardiff*), I. 1925; E.S. 1927; E.F. 1928; S. 1930.
Turnbull, M. J. (*Cardiff*), E.I. 1933.

Uzzell, H. (*Newport*), E.S.I.F. 1912; S.I.F. 1913; E.S.F.I. 1914, 1920.
Uzzell, J. (*Newport*), NZ. 1963; E.S.I.F. 1965.

Vickery, W. (*Aberavon*), E.S.I. 1938; E. 1939.
Vile, T. H. (*Newport*), E.S. 1908; I. 1910; I.F.SA. 1912; E. 1913; S. 1921.
Vincent, H. C. (*Bangor*), I. 82.

Waldron, R. (*Neath*), E.S.I.F. 1965.
Waller, P. D. (*Newport*), A. 1908; E.S.I.F. 1909; F. 1910.
Walters, Nathaniel 'Danny' (*Llanelli*), E. 1902.
Wanbon, R. (*Aberavon*), E. 1968.
Ward, W. (*Cross Keys*), S.I. 1934.
Warlow, J. (*Llanelli*), I. 1962.
Watkins, D. (*Newport*), E.S.I.F.NZ. 1963; E.S.I.F.SA. 1964; E.S.I.F. 1965, 1966; E.I.F. 1967.
Watkins, Eddie (*Neath*), E.S.I.F. 1924.
Watkins, E. (*Blaina*), S.I.F. 1926.
Watkins, E. (*Cardiff*), NZ. 1935; S.I. 1937; E.S.I. 1938; E.S. 1939.
Watkins, H. (*Llanelli*), S.I. 1904; E.S.I. 1905; E. 1906.
Watkins, L. (*Llandaff*), E. 81.
Watkins, S. J. (*Newport*), S.I.F. 1964; E.S.I.F. 1965, 1966; A. 1966; E.S.I.F.NZ. 1967; E.S. 1968; S.I.F.E.NZ. (1st Test) 1969; E.I. 1970.
Watkins, W. (*Newport*), F. 1959.
Watt, W. J. (*Llanelli*), E. 1914.
Watts, D. (*Maesteg*), E.S.F.I. 1914.
Watts, J. (*Llanelli*), E.S.I. 1907; E.S.I.F.A. 1908; S.I.F. 1909.
Watts, Wallace (*Newport*), E.S.I. 92, 93, 94; E.I. 95; E. 96.
Weaver, D. (*Swansea*), E. 1964.
Webb, J. (*Abertillery*), S. 1907; E.S.I.F.A. 1908; E.S.I.F. 1909, 1910, 1911; E.S. 1912.
Webb, J. E. (*Newport*), M. 88; S. 89.
Wells, G. (*Cardiff*), E.S. 1955; I.F. 1957; A.E.S. 1958.
Westacott, D. (*Cardiff*), I. 1906.
Wetter, H. (*Newport*), SA. 1912; E. 1913.
Wetter, J. (*Newport*), S.F.I. 1914; E.S.F.I. 1920; E. 1921; I.NZ. 1924.
Wheel, G. (*Swansea*), I.E.(R) 1974; F.E.I.A. 1975; E.S.I.F. 1976; I.E.S. 1977; E.S.I.F.A.(1st and 2nd Tests), NZ. 1978; S.I. 1979; F.E.S.I. 1980.
Wheeler, P. J. (*Aberavon*), NZ. 1967; E. 1968.
Whitfield, J. (*Pill Harriers and Newport*), NZ. 1919; E.S.I.F. 1920; E. 1921; E.S.I.F. 1922; S.I. 1924.
Whitson, G. (*Newport*), F. 1956; S.I. 1960.
Williams, Bleddyn (*Cardiff*), E.S.F.I.A. 1947; E.S.F.I. 1948; E.S.I. 1949; I.SA. 1951; S. 1952; E.S.I.F.NZ. 1953; S. 1954; E. 1955.
Williams, Bryn (*Llanelli*), S.I.F. 1920.
Williams, C. (*Llanelli*), NZ. 1924; E. 1925.
Williams, C. D. (*Cardiff and Neath*), F. 1955; F. 1956.
Williams, Clive (*Aberavon*), E.S. 1977; F.E.S.I. 1980.
Williams, D. Brynmor (*Newport*), A. (1st Test) 1978.
Williams, D. (*Ebbw Vale*), E.S.I.F. 1963, 1964; S.A. 1964; E.S.I.F. 1965; E.S.I.A. 1966; E.F.NZ. 1967; E. 1968; S.I.F.E.NZ.(1st and 2nd Tests) A. 1969; SA. S.E.I. 1970; E.S.I.F. 1971.
Williams, Eddie (*Neath*), NZ. 1924; F. 1925.
Williams, Evan (*Aberavon*), E.S. 1925.

Williams, Frank L. (*Cardiff*), S.I.F. 1929; E.S.I.F. 1930; I.F.SA. 1931; E.S.I. 1932; I. 1933.

Williams, Gerwyn (*London Welsh*), I.F. 1950; E.S.I.F.SA. 1951; E.S.I.F. 1952; NZ. 1953; E. 1954.

Williams, Griff (*Aberavon*), E.S.I. 1936.

Williams, Jack (*Blaina*), E.S.I.F. 1920; S.F.I. 1921.

Williams, J. F. (*London Welsh*), I.NZ. 1905; S.SA. 1906.

Williams, John J. (*Llanelli*), F.(R)A. 1973; S.I.F.E. 1974; F.E.S.I.A. 1975; E.S.I.F. 1976; I.F.E.S. 1977; E.S.I.F.A.(1st and 2nd Tests), NZ. 1978; S.I.F.E. 1979.

Williams, J. L. (*Cardiff*), SA. 1906; E.S.I. 1907, 1908; A. 1908; E.S.I.F. 1909; I. 1910; E.S.I.F. 1911.

Williams, J. P. R. (*London Welsh*), S.I.F.E.NZ. (1st and 2nd Tests) A. 1969; SA.S.E.I.F. 1970; E.S.I.F. 1971; E.S.F.NZ. 1972; E.S.I.F.A. 1973; S.I.F. 1974; F.E.S.I.A. 1975; E.S.I.F. 1976; I.F.E.S. 1977; E.S.I.F.A. (1st and 2nd Tests), NZ. 1978; S.I.F.E. 1979.

Williams, Lloyd (*Cardiff*), S.I.F. 1957; E.S.I.F. 1958; E.S.I. 1959; F. 1961; E.S. 1962.

Williams, Les (*Llanelli and Cardiff*), E.S.F.I.A. 1947; I. 1948; E. 1949.

Williams, M. (*Newport*), F. 1923.

Williams, Ossie (*Llanelli*), E.S.A. 1947; E.S.F.I. 1948.

Williams, Ray (*Llanelli*), S. 1954; F. 1957; A. 1958.

Williams, R. D. G. (*Cambridge Univ.*), E. 81.

Williams, R. F. (*Cardiff*), SA. 1912; E.S. 1913; I. 1914.

Williams, R. H. (*Llanelli*), S.I.F. 1954; S.I.F. 1955; E.S.I. 1956; E.S.I.F. 1957; A.E.S.I.F. 1958; E.S.I.F. 1959; E. 1960.

Williams, Sid (*Aberavon*), E.S.I. 1939.

Williams, Stan. (*Llanelli*), E.S.F.I. 1947; S.F. 1948.

Williams, Tom (*Pontypridd*), I. 82.

Williams, T. (*Swansea*), S.I. 88.

Williams, Tom (*Swansea*), I. 1912; F. 1913; E.S.F.I. 1914.

Williams, Trevor (*Cross Keys*), S.I.NZ. 1935; E.S.I. 1936; S.I. 1937.

Williams, Tudor (*Swansea*), F. 1921.

Williams, W. (*Crumlin*), E.S.I.F. 1927.

Williams, W. A. (*Newport*), I.F. 1952; E. 1953.

Williams, W. E. O. (*Cardiff*), S.I. 87; S. 89; E.S. 90.

Williams, W. H. (*Pontymister*), E.S.I. 1900; E. 1901.

Williams, W. O. (*Swansea*), F.SA. 1951; E.S.I.F. 1952, 1953; NZ. 1953; E.S.I.F. 1954, 1955; E.S.I. 1956.

Williams, W. P. J. (*Neath*), I.F. 1974.

Willis, R. (*Cardiff*), E.S.I.F. 1950, 1951; SA. 1951; E.S. 1952; S.NZ. 1953; E.S.I.F. 1954, 1955.

Wiltshire, M. L. (*Aberavon*), NZ. 1967; E.S.F. 1968.

Windsor, R. W. (*Pontypool*), A. 1973; S.I.F.E. 1974; F.E.S.I.A. 1975; E.S.I.F. 1976; I.F.E.S. 1977; E.S.I.F.A. (1st and 2nd Tests), NZ. 1978; S.I.F. 1979.

Winfield, H. B. (*Cardiff*), I. 1903; E.S.I. 1904; NZ. 1905; E.S.I. 1906; S.I. 1907; E.S.I.F.A. 1908.

Winmill, S. (*Cross Keys*), E.S.F.I. 1921.

Wooller, W. (*Rydal School, Sale and Cardiff*), E.S.I. 1933, 1935; NZ. 1935; E.S.I. 1936, 1937; S.I. 1938; E.S.I. 1939.

Young, G. A. (*Cardiff*), E.S. 86.

Young, J. (*Harrogate and London Welsh*), S.I.F. 1968; S.I.F.E.NZ.(1st Test) 1969; E.I.F. 1970; E.S.I.F. 1971; E.S.F.NZ. 1972; E.S.I.F. 1973.

LEADING WELSH CAP-HOLDERS

	Matches		*Matches*		*Matches*
G. O. Edwards	53	S. P. Fenwick	27	J. J. Hodges	23
J. P. R. Williams ...	52	A. J. Gould	27	R. H. Williams	23
T. G. R. Davies ...	46	H. J. Morgan	27	Jeff Young	23
K. J. Jones	44	W. C. Powell	27	S. J. Dawes	22
Mervyn Davies	38	M. C. Thomas	27	R. Prosser	22
Denzil Williams	36	A. E. I. Pask	26	D. L. Quinnell	22
R. M. Owen	35	J. Taylor	26	B. L. Williams	22
D. I. Bebb	34	R. C. C. Thomas ...	26	W. O. Williams	22
B. V. Meredith	34	S. J. Watkins	26	T. J. Davies	21
W. D. Morris	34	G. Wheel	26	E. M. Jenkins	21
W. J. Bancroft	33	N. R. Gale	25	Brian Thomas	21
B. Price	32	B. John	25	D. Watkins	21
J. R. G. Stephens ...	32	H. Tanner	25	W. R. Willis	21
A. J. Martin	31	G. Travers	25	A. F. Harding	20
J. J. Williams	30	Delme Thomas	25	W. Llewellyn	20
Phil Bennett	29	R. T. Gabe	24	A. Skym	20
C. I. Morgan	29	D. J. Lloyd	24	J. Webb	20
W. J. Trew	29	E. Gwyn Nicholls ...	24	T. J. Cobner	19
G. Price	28	E. C. Davey	23	A. G. Faulkner	19
R. W. Windsor	28	J. A. Gwilliam	23	J. Hannan	19

E. R. John	19
S. Morris	19
T. Arthur	18
J. Bancroft	18
A. B. Brice	18
W. J. Delahay	18
Tom Evans	18
R. W. Gravell	18
W. Wooller	18
D. M. Davies	17
Rowe Harding	17
J. Matthews	17
J. L. Williams	17
J. G. Boots	16
Cliff Davies	16
R. A. Gibbs	16
W. W. Joseph	16
Ivor Jones	16
E. Morgan	16
J. Squire	16
J. Bassett	15
F. A. Bowdler	15
Don Hayward	15
A. F. Hill	15
G. T. R. Hodgson	15
R. Jones	15
C. B. Nicholl	15
T. Parker	15
H. Uzzell	15
H. B. Winfield	15
T. J. S. Clapp	14
W. B. Cleaver	14
L. J. Cunningham	14
J. P. Jones	14
D. K. Jones	14
Albert Jenkins	14
V. G. J. Jenkins	14
C. C. Meredith	14
J. C. Morley	14
C. M. Pritchard	14
J. Idwal Rees	14
D. C. T. Rowlands	14
Watcyn Thomas	14
F. L. Williams	14
A. W. Boucher	13
W. Bowen	13
T. Day	13
W. R. Evans	13
C. W. Jones	13
D. Jones	13
A. Lemon	13
Barry Llewelyn	13
F. Mills	13
Ivor Morgan	13
T. W. Pearson	13
A. M. Rees	13
J. Roberts	13
R. J. Robins	13
Alun Thomas	13
Gerwyn Williams	13
L. H. Williams	13
R. W. Boon	12
Gwyn Evans	12
J. Faull	12
T. C. Graham	12
G. M. Griffiths	12
T. Johnson	12
J. Lang	12
G. Ll. Lloyd	12
Joe Rees	12
G. Shaw	12
W. Travers	12
W. H. Watts	12
Jack Whitfield	12

WALES 'B' SELECTIONS

Key: A—Argentine; C—Canada. All other appearances are against France. R—Replacement.
Note: Two matches were played against France in 1972; one in second half of season 1971–72 the other in first half of season 1972–73.

Alexander, Ogwyn (*Aberavon*), 1972, 1974, 1975.
Arthur, David (Maesteg), 1978.

Barry, David (*Newport*), A. 1978.
Baxter, Lyn (*Cardiff*), C. 1971, 1972 (R).
Bergiers, R. T. E. (*Llanelli*), 1972.
Bevan, J. D. (*Aberavon*), 1974.
Blyth, Roger (*Swansea*), 1973.
Burcher, D. H. (*Newport*), 1976.
Burgess, Clive (Ebbw Vale), 1976.
Butler, Eddie (*Pontypool*), 1977, 1979.

Charles, Chris (*Llanelli*), 1973 (R).
Clegg, B. G. (*Swansea*), 1975, 1977.
Cobner, T. J. (*Pontypool*), 1973.

Daniels, Pat (*Cardiff*), 1978, 1979.
David, T. P. (*Pontypridd and Llanelli*), C. 1971, 1971, 1972, 1972.
Davies, Alan (*S. W. Police*), 1978.
Davies, Alun (*Llanelli*), 1979.
Davies, Barrie (*Neath*), C. 1971.
Davies, Geoff (*Bridgend*), A. 1978.
Davies, Jeff (*Swansea*) C.1971, 1971.
Davies, Martyn (*Neath*), C. 1971, 1971, 1972.
Davies, Robert (*Maesteg*), 1970.
Davies, Richie (*Aberavon*), 1976.
Davies, Terry (*London Welsh*), 1972.
Davies, Wynne (*Neath*), 1974, 1975, 1976.
Davis, Clive (*Newbridge*), 1977 (R).
Donovan, Alun (*Swansea*), 1977.
Donovan, A. (*Maesteg*), 1979.
Dowling, M. J. (*Newbridge*), 1979.
Dyer, R. (*Swansea*), 1979.

Ellis-Jones, Rhodri (*London Welsh*), 1977. A. 1978.
Evans, Alun (*Newport*), 1974.
Evans, Gwyn *Maesteg*), 1977 (R), 1979.
Evans, T. P. (*Swansea*), 1974.

Faulkner, A. G. (*Pontypool*), 1974.
Fenwick, S. P. (*Bridgend*), 1974.
Finlayson, A. J. (*Cardiff*), 1972.
Floyd, Ron (*Pontypool*), 1974, 1975.

Gallacher, Stuart (*Llanelli*), 1970.
Gravell, Ray (*Llanelli*), 1972, 1974.
Griffiths, Clive (*Llanelli*), 1978.
Griffiths, David (*Bridgend*), C.1971.
Griffiths, Jeff (*Aberavon*), 1978.

Haines, Del (*Newport*), 1970, C. 1971, 1972.
Hill, Andy (*Llanelli*), 1973, 1975.
Hopkins, Ray (*Maesteg*), 1970.
Howcroft, Cliff (*London Welsh*), 1976.
Howls, Gareth (*Ebbw Vale*), 1971, 1972, 1976, 1977, 1978, A. 1978.
Hughes, Keith (*Llanelli*), 1970.
Hutchings, Neil (*Aberavon*), A. 1978, 1978.

James, Mel (*Swansea*), C. 1971.
James, Keith (*Cardiff*), 1972.
Jenkins, David (*Neath and Swansea*), 1973, 1974.

Jenkins, G. (*Swansea*), 1979.
Jenkins, Gareth (*Llanelli*), 1975.
Jenkins, Hefin (*Llanelli*), C. 1971, 1971, 1972, 1973, 1974, 1975.
Jenkins, Viv (*Bridgend*), 1971.
John, Clive (*Llanelli*), 1970, 1971.
Jones, Dawson (*Abertillery*), A. 1978.
Jones, Lyn (*Ebbw Vale and Newport*), 1971, 1972, 1974.
Juliff, Brian (*Pontypridd*), 1976.

Keen, L. (*Aberavon*), 1979.
Knill, Mike (*Cardiff*), 1975.

Lane, Roger (*Cardiff*), 1972, 1973.
Lane, Stuart (*Cardiff*), 1977.
Lang, N. (*Bridgend*), 1971, C. 1971, 1972.
Leach, M. (*Waterloo*), 1979.
Lewis, Alun (*London Welsh*), 1978.
Lewis, Arthur (*Ebbw Vale*), 1970.
Lewis, Dai (*Neath*), A. 1978.
Lewis, Ian (*Bridgend*), 1973.
Lewis, P. (*Pontypool*), 1979.
Llewellyn, David (*London Welsh*), 1972.
Lloyd, D. J. (*Bridgend*), 1970.

McCreedy, Jim (*Newbridge*), 1978.
Manfield, John (*London Welsh*), 1977.
Martin, A. J. (*Aberavon*), 1972, 1973.
Morgan, Peter (*Llanelli*), A. 1978, 1978.
Moriarty, Richard (*Swansea*), A. 1978.

Neville, C. (*Llandudno*), 1974 (R).
Nicholas, David (*Llanelli*), 1975.
Norster, R. (*Cardiff*), 1979.

Perkins, John (*Pontypool*), 1977, 1978.
Phillips, Alan (*Cardiff*), 1977, 1978.
Phillips, Phil (*Maesteg*), 1975, 1976.
Phillips, Bob (*London Welsh*), 1970, C. 1971, 1971, 1972.
Price, Graham (*Pontypool*), 1973, 1974.

Quinell, D. L. (*Llanelli*), 1971.

Rees, Elgan (*Neath*), 1974, 1975, 1976, 1977, A. 1978, 1978.
Rees, Norman (*Neath*), C. 1971, 1971, 1972.
Richards, David (*Swansea*), 1975, 1976, 1977.
Richardson, John (*Aberavon*), 1977.
Ringer, Paul (*Ebbw Vale*), A. 1978.
Roberts, John (*Neath*), 1970.
Roberts, Mike (*London Welsh*), 1970.
Robinson, Ian (*Cardiff*), 1972.

Seldon, Chris (*Pontypridd*), A. 1978, 1978.
Shaw, Glyn (*Neath*), 1972, 1972.
Shell, R. C. (*Aberavon*), 1972, 1973.
Stephens, I. (*Bridgend*), 1979.
Sutton, Steve (*Pontypool*), A. 1978, 1978.
Squire, Jeff (*Newport*), 1976.
Swain, Malcolm (*Moseley*), 1972, 1977.

Thomas, Bernard (*Llanelli*), 1973.
Thomas, Lyndon, (*Bridgend*), 1973.
Thomas, Richie (*London Welsh*), 1976.
Thomas, Roy (*Swansea and Llanelli*), 1970, 1974, 1975.
Tovey, Alan (*Ebbw Vale*), C. 1971, 1971.

Upton, Billy (*Maesteg*), 1970.

Wallace, Gerry (*Cardiff*), 1973.
Walsh, Ian (*Pontypridd*), 1977, A. 1978.
Watkins, Mike (*Cardiff*), 1976, 1979.
Wheel, G. A. D. (*Swansea*), 1973.
Williams, Brynmor (*Cardiff and Newport*), 1976, 1977.
Williams, Clive (*Aberavon*), 1975, 1976.
Williams, Gareth (*Bridgend*), A. 1978, 1978, 1979.
Williams, Gerald (*Bridgend*), A. 1978.
Williams, J. J. (*Bridgend*), C. 1971, 1972, 1972.
Williams, Robin (*Pontypool*), 1970, 1971, 1972.
Williams, Selwyn (*Llanelli*), 1975.
Williams, Walter (*Neath*), 1970, C. 1971, 1971, 1972, 1972.
Windsor, R. W. (*Pontypool*), 1972, 1973.

WELSH CLUB CHAMPIONS

(*Since* 1946–47)

1946–47	Neath	1963–64	Bridgend
1947–48	Cardiff	1964–65	Newbridge
1948–49	Cardiff	1965–66	Bridgend
1949–50	Maesteg	1966–67	Neath
1950–51	Newport	1967–68	Llanelli
1951–52	Ebbw Vale	1968–69	Newport
1952–53	Cardiff	1969–70	Bridgend
1953–54	Ebbw Vale	1970–71	Bridgend
1954–55	Cardiff	1971–72	London Welsh
1955–56	Newport	1972–73	Pontypool
1956–57	Ebbw Vale	1973–74	Llanelli
1957–58	Cardiff	1974–75	Pontypool
1958–59	Pontypool	1975–76	Pontypridd
1959–60	Ebbw Vale	1976–77	Llanelli
1960–61	Aberavon	1977–78	Pontypridd
1961–62	Newport	1978–79	Pontypridd
1962–63	Pontypridd	1979–80	Swansea

NATIONAL SEVENS CHAMPIONS

1966 Pontypool Utd, beat UC Swansea 11–8 (*Aberavon*)
1967 Cardiff Coll. of Ed. beat Amman Utd. 11–10 (*Aberavon*)
1968 Llanelli beat Glynneath 13–8 (*Aberavon*)
1969 Cardiff beat Neath 11–3 (*Cardiff*)
1970 Cardiff beat Newbridge 14–10 (*Cardiff*)
1971 Llanelli beat Aberavon 23–8 (*Cardiff*)
1972 Cardiff beat Bridgend 21–14 (*Cardiff*)
1973 Bridgend beat Cardiff 28–24 (*Cardiff*)
1974 Bridgend beat Cardiff*22–18 (*Cardiff*)
1975 Cardiff beat Bridgend *20–16 (*Cardiff*)
1976 Cardiff beat Bridgend 28–22 (*Pontypridd*)
1977 Bridgend beat Cardiff 18–8 (*Aberavon*)
1978 Bridgend beat Maesteg 22–18 (*Penygraig*)
1979 Swansea beat Llanelli 42–6 (*Llanelli*)
1980 Swansea beat Newport 16–12 (*Pontypool*)
*Indicates extra time

WRU CHALLENGE CUP WINNERS

1971–72 Neath beat Llanelli 15–9
1972–73 Llanelli beat Cardiff 30–7
1973–74 Llanelli beat Aberavon 12–10
1974–75 Llanelli beat Aberavon 15–6
1975–76 Llanelli beat Swansea 16–4
1976–77 Newport beat Cardiff 16–15
1977–78 Swansea beat Newport 13–9
1978–79 Bridgend beat Pontypridd 18–12
1979–80 Bridgend beat Swansea 15–9

SNELLING SEVENS CHAMPIONS

1954 Newport beat Ebbw Vale 6–0 (*Newport*)
1955 Cardiff beat Newport 8–3 (*Newport*)
1956 Newport beat Penarth 5–3 (*Swansea*)
1957 Newport beat Abertillery 11–8 (*Swansea*)
1958 Ebbw Vale beat Newport 10–5 (*Cardiff*)
1959 Newport beat Pontypool 6–3 (*Newport*)
1960 Llanelli beat Penarth 14–10 (*Cardiff*)
1961 Newport beat Pontypool 8–3 (*Cardiff*)
1962 Newport beat Neath 19–3 (*Swansea*)
1963 Newport beat Bridgend 8–0 (*Cardiff*)
1964 Neath beat Cardiff 10–5 (*Cardiff*)
1965 Newport beat Newbridge 9–8 (*Swansea*)
1966 Cardiff beat Newport 23–20* (*Cardiff*)
1967 Newport beat Cardiff 21–15 (*Cardiff*)
1968 Bridgend beat Pontypool 25–5 (*Cardiff*)
1969 Cardiff beat Llanelli 18–15 (*Cardiff*)
1970 Neath beat Ebbw Vale 18–8 (*Cardiff*)
1971 Llanelli beat Newport 31–10 (*Cardiff*)
1972 Cardiff beat Bridgend 15–4 (*Cardiff*)
1973 Llanelli beat Newbridge 52–6 (*Cardiff*)
1974 Bridgend beat Swansea 30–14 (*Cardiff*)
1975 Bridgend beat Cardiff 32–12 (*Cardiff*)
1976 Cardiff beat Newport 18–8 (*Cardiff*)
1977 Cardiff beat Newport 24–16 (*Cardiff*)
1978 Bridgend beat Cardiff 38–16 (*Cardiff*)
1979 Llanelli beat Ebbw Vale 26–16 (*Cardiff*)
*Indicates extra time

SILVER BALL WINNERS

1956–57	Taibach	1968–69	Cardiff Coll. of Ed.
1957–58	Welsh Acads.	1969–70	Cardiff Coll. of Ed.
1958–59	Maesteg Celtic	1970–71	Senghenydd
1959–60	Seven Sisters	1971–72	Senghenydd
1960–61	Glynneath	1972–73	Abercynon
1961–62	Glynneath	1973–74	Kenfig Hill
1962–63	Glynneath	1974–75	Taffs Well
1963–64	Llantwit Major	1975–76	Pyle
1964–65	Llantwit Major	1976–77	Abercynon
1965–66	Cwmgwrach	1977–78	Pyle
1966–67	Cardiff Athletic	1978–79	Bridgend Sports
1967–68	Cardiff Athletic	1979–80	Bridgend Sports

WELSH INTERNATIONAL RESULTS

AGAINST ENGLAND

Matches played 85
Wales 40 wins, England 34, 11 drawn

1880–81 **ENGLAND** 7G, 1DG, 6T to 0 (*Blackheath*).
1881–82 No Match.
1882–83 **ENGLAND** 2G, 4T, to 0 (*Swansea*).
1883–84 **ENGLAND** 1G, 2T to 1G (*Leeds*).
1884–85 **ENGLAND** 1G, 4T to 1G, 1T (*Swansea*).
1885–86 **ENGLAND** 1GM, 2T to 1G (*Blackheath*).
1886–87 **DRAWN** no score (*Llanelli*).
1887–88 and 1888–89 No Matches.
1889–90 **WALES** 1T (1) to 0 (*Dewsbury*).
1890–91 **ENGLAND** 2G, 1T (7) to 1G (3) (*Newport*).
1891–92 **ENGLAND** 3G, 1T (17) to 0 (*Blackheath*).
1892–93 **WALES** 1G, 1PG, 2T (12) to 1G, 3T (11) (*Cardiff*).
1893–94 **ENGLAND** 4G, 1GM (24) to 1T (3) (*Birkenhead*).
1894–95 **ENGLAND** 1G, 3T (14) to 2T (6) (*Swansea*).
1895–96 **ENGLAND** 2G, 5T (25) to 0 (*Blackheath*).
1896–97 **WALES** 1G, 2T (11) to 0 (*Newport*).
1897–98 **ENGLAND** 1G, 3T (14) to 1DG, 1T (7) (*Blackheath*).
1898–99 **WALES** 4G, 2T (26) to 1T (3) (*Swansea*).
1899–1900 **WALES** 2G, 1PG (13) to 1T (3) (*Gloucester*).
1900–01 **WALES** 2G, 1T (13) to 0 (*Cardiff*).
1901–02 **WALES** 1PG, 2T (9) to 1G, 1T (8) (*Blackheath*).
1902–03 **WALES** 3G, 2T (21) to 1G (5) (*Swansea*).
1903–04 **DRAWN.** ENGLAND 1G, 1PG, 2T (14) to WALES 2G, 1GM (14) (*Leicester*).
1904–05 **WALES** 2G, 5T (25) to 0 (*Cardiff*).
1905–06 **WALES** 2G, 2T (16) to 1T (3) (*Richmond*).
1906–07 **WALES** 2G, 4T (22) to 0 (*Swansea*).
1907–08 **WALES** 3G, 1DG, 1PG, 2T (28) to 3G, 1T (18) (*Bristol*).
1908–09 **WALES** 1G, 1T (8) to 0 (*Cardiff*).
1909–10 **ENGLAND** 1G, 1PG, 1T (11) to 2T (6) (*Twickenham*).
1910–11 **WALES** 1PG, 4T (15) to 1G, 2T (11) (*Swansea*).
1911–12 **ENGLAND** 1G, 1T (8) to 0 (*Twickenham*).
1912–13 **ENGLAND** 1G, 1DG, 1T (12) to 0 (*Cardiff*).
1913–14 **ENGLAND** 2G (10) to 1G, 1DG (9) (*Twickenham*).
1919–20 **WALES** 1G, 2DG, 1PG, 1T (19) to 1G (5) (*Swansea*).
1920–21 **ENGLAND** 1G, 1DG, 3T (18) to 1T (3) (*Twickenham*).
1921–22 **WALES** 2G, 6T (28) to 2T (6) (*Cardiff*).
1922–23 **ENGLAND** 1DG, 1T (7) to 1T (3) (*Twickenham*).
1923–24 **ENGLAND** 1G, 4T (17) to 3T (9) (*Swansea*).
1924–25 **ENGLAND** 1PG, 3T (12) to 2T (6) (*Twickenham*).
1925–26 **DRAWN** 1T (3) each (*Cardiff*).
1926–27 **ENGLAND** 1G, 1PG, 1GM (11) to 1PG, 2T (9) (*Twickenham*).
1927–28 **ENGLAND** 2G (10) to 1G, 1T (8) (*Swansea*).
1928–29 **ENGLAND** 1G, 1T (8) to 1T (3) (*Twickenham*).
1929–30 **ENGLAND** 1G, 1PG, 1T (11) to 1T (3) (*Cardiff*).
1930–31 **DRAWN.** ENGLAND 1G, 2PG (11) WALES 1G, 1GM, 1T (11) (*Twickenham*).
1931–32 **WALES** 1G, 1DG, 1PG (12) to 1G (5) (*Swansea*).
1932–33 **WALES** 1DG, 1T (7) to 1T (3) (*Twickenham*).
1933–34 **ENGLAND** 3T (9) to 0 (*Cardiff*).
1934–35 **DRAWN.** ENGLAND 1PG (3) WALES 1T (3) (*Twickenham*).
1935–36 **DRAWN** no score (*Swansea*).
1936–37 **ENGLAND** 1DG (4) to 1T (3) (*Twickenham*).
1937–38 **WALES** 1G, 2PG, 1T (14) to 1G, 1T (8) (*Cardiff*).
1938–39 **ENGLAND** 1T (3) to 0 (*Twickenham*).
1946–47 **ENGLAND** 1G, 1DG (9) to 2T (6) (*Cardiff*).
1947–48 **DRAWN.** ENGLAND 1PG (3) WALES 1T (3) (*Twickenham*).

(Dropped goal revalued to 3 pts.)

1948–49 **WALES** 3T (9) to 1DG (3) (*Cardiff*).
1949–50 **WALES** 1G, 1PG, 1T (11) to 1G (5) (*Twickenham*).
1950–51 **WALES** 4G, 1T (23) to 1G (5) (*Swansea*).
1951–52 **WALES** 1G, 1T (8) to 2T (6) (*Twickenham*).
1952–53 **ENGLAND** 1G, 1PG (8) to 1PG (3) (*Cardiff*).
1953–54 **ENGLAND** 3T (9) to 1PG, 1T (6) (*Twickenham*).
1954–55 **WALES** 1PG (3) to 0 (*Cardiff*).

1955–56 **ENGLAND** 1G, 1T (8) to 1PG (3) (*Twickenham*).
1956–57 **ENGLAND** 1PG (3)to 0 (*Cardiff*).
1957–58 **DRAWN.** ENGLAND 1T(3) WALES 1PG (3) (*Twickenham*).
1958–59 **WALES** 1G (5) to 0 (*Cardiff*).
1959–60 **ENGLAND** 1G, 2PG, 1T (14) to 2PG (6) (*Twickenham*).
1960–61 **WALES** 2T (6) to 1T (3) (*Cardiff*).
1961–62 **DRAWN** no score (*Twickenham*).
1962–63 **ENGLAND** 2G, 1DG (13) to 1PG, 1T (6) (*Cardiff*).
1963–64 **DRAWN** 2T each (*Twickenham*).
1964–65 **WALES** 1G, 1DG, 2T (14) to 1PG (3) (*Cardiff*).
1965–66 **WALES** 1G, 2PG (11) to 1PG, 1T (6) (*Twickenham*).
1966–67 **WALES** 5G, 2PG, 1DG (34) to 4PG, 3T (21) (*Cardiff*).
1967–68 **DRAWN.** ENGLAND 1G, 1PG, 1T (11) to IG, IDG, IT (11) (*Twickenham*).
1968–69 **WALES** 3G, 2PG, 1DG, 2T (30) to 3PG (9) (*Cardiff*).
1969–70 **WALES** 1G, 1DG, 3T (17) to 2G, 1PG (13) (*Twickenham*).
1970–71 **WALES** 2G, 2DG, 1PG, 1T (22) to 1PG, 1T (6) (*Cardiff*).
(Try upgraded to 4 pts.)
1971–72 **WALES** 1G, 2PG, (12) to 1PG (3) (*Twickenham*).
1972–73 **WALES** 1G, 1PG, 4T (25) to 2PG, 1DG (9) (*Cardiff*).
1973–74 **ENGLAND** 1G, 2PG, 1T (16) to 1G, 2PG (12) (*Twickenham*).
1974–75 **WALES** 1G, 2PG, 2T (20) to 1T (4) (*Cardiff*).
1975–76 **WALES** 3G, 1PG, (21) to 3PG (9) (*Twickenham*).
1976–77 **WALES** 2PG, 2T (14) to 3PG (9) (*Cardiff*).
1977–78 **WALES** 3PG (9) to 2PG (6) (*Twickenham*).
1978–79 **WALES** 2G, 1DG, 3T (27) to 1PG (3) (*Cardiff*).
1979–80 **ENGLAND** 3PG (9) to 2T (8) (*Twickenham*).

AGAINST SCOTLAND

Matches played 84
Wales 48 wins, Scotland 34, 2 drawn

1882–83 **SCOTLAND** 3G to 1G (*Edinburgh*).
1883–84 **SCOTLAND** 1DG, 1T to 0 (*Newport*).
1884–85 **DRAWN** no score (*Glasgow*).
1885–86 **SCOTLAND** 2G, 1T to 0 (*Cardiff*).
1886–87 **SCOTLAND** 4G 8T to 0 (*Edinburgh*).
1887–88 **WALES** 1T to 0 (*Newport*).
1888–89 **SCOTLAND** 2T to 0 (*Edinburgh*).
1889–90 **SCOTLAND** 1G, 2T (5) to 1T (1) (*Cardiff*).
1890–91 **SCOTLAND** 1G, 2DG, 5T (15) to 0 (*Edinburgh*).
1891–92 **SCOTLAND** 1G, 1T (7) to 1T (2) (*Swansea*).
1892–93 **WALES** 1PG, 3T (9) to 0 (*Edinburgh*).
1893–94 **WALES** 1DG, 1T (7) to 0 (*Newport*).
1894–95 **SCOTLAND** 1G (5) to 1GM (4) (*Edinburgh*).
1895–96 **WALES** 2T (6) to 0 (*Cardiff*).
1896–97 and 1897–98 No Match.
1898–99 **SCOTLAND** 1GM, 2DG, 3T (21) to 2G (10) (*Edinburgh*).
1899–1900 **WALES** 4T (12) to 1T (3) (*Swansea*).
1900–01 **SCOTLAND** 3G, 1T (18) to 1G, 1T (8) (*Inverleith*).
1901–02 **WALES** 1G, 3T (14) to 1G (5) (*Cardiff*).
1902–03 **SCOTLAND** 1PG, 1T (6) to 0 (*Inverleith*).
1903–04 **WALES** 3G, 1PG, 1T (21) to 1T (3) (*Swansea*).
1904–05 **WALES** 2T (6) to 1T (3) (*Inverleith*).
1905–06 **WALES** 3T (9) to 1PG (3) (*Cardiff*).
1906–07 **SCOTLAND** 2T (6) to 1PG (3) (*Inverleith*).
1907–08 **WALES** 2T (6) to 1G (5) (*Swansea*).
1908–09 **WALES** 1G (5) to 1PG (3) (*Inverleith*).
1909–10 **WALES** 1G, 3T (14) to 0 (*Cardiff*).
1910–11 **WALES** 2G, 1DG, 6T (32) to 1DG, 2T (10) (*Inverleith*).
1911–12 **WALES** 2G, 2DG, 1T (21) to 2T (6) (*Swansea*).
1912–13 **WALES** 1G, 1T (8) to 0 (*Inverleith*).
1913–14 **WALES** 2G, 2DG, 1PG, 1T (24) to 1G (5) (*Cardiff*).
1919–20 **SCOTLAND** 2PG, 1T (9) to 1G (5) (*Inverleith*).
1920–21 **SCOTLAND** 1G, 1PG, 2T (14) to 2DG (8) (*Swansea*).
1921–22 **DRAWN.** SCOTLAND 1PG, 2T (9) WALES 1G 1DG (9) (*Inverleith*).
1922–23 **SCOTLAND** 1G, 2T (11) to 1G, 1PG (8) (*Cardiff*).
1923–24 **SCOTLAND** 4G, 1PG, 4T (35) to 2G (10) (*Inverleith*).
1924–25 **SCOTLAND** 1G, 1DG, 5T (24) to 1G, 1PG, 2T (14) (*Swansea*).
1925–26 **SCOTLAND** 1G, 1PG (8) to 1G (5) (*Murrayfield*).
1926–27 **SCOTLAND** 1G (5) to 0 (*Cardiff*).
1927–28 **WALES** 2G, 1T (13) to 0 (*Murrayfield*).
1928–29 **WALES** 1G, 3T (14) to 1DG, 1PG (7) (*Swansea*).
1929–30 **SCOTLAND** 1G, 1DG, 1T (12) to 1G, 1DG (9) (*Murrayfield*).

1930–31 **WALES** 2G, 1T (13) to 1G, 1T (8) (*Cardiff*).
1931–32 **WALES** 1PG, 1T (6) to 0 (*Murrayfield*).
1932–33 **SCOTLAND** 1G, 1PG, 1T (11) to 1T (3) (*Swansea*).
1933–34 **WALES** 2G, 1T (13) to 1PG, 1T (6) (*Murrayfield*).
1934–35 **WALES** 1DG, 2T (10) to 2T (6) (*Cardiff*).
1935–36 **WALES** 2G, 1T (13) to 1T (3) (*Murrayfield*).
1936–37 **SCOTLAND** 2G, 1T (13) to 2T (6) (*Swansea*).
1937–38 **SCOTLAND** 1G, 1PG (8) to 2T (6) (*Murrayfield*).
1938–39 **WALES** 1G, 1PG, 1T (11) to 1PG (3) (*Cardiff*).
1946–47 **WALES** 2G, 1PG, 3T (22) to 1G, 1PG (8) (*Murrayfield*).
1947–48 **WALES** 1G, 1PG, 2T (14) to 0 (*Cardiff*).

(Dropped goal revalued to 3 Pts.)

1948–49 **SCOTLAND** 2T (6) to 1G (5) (*Murrayfield*).
1949–50 **WALES** 1DG, 1PG, 2T (12) to 0 (*Swansea*).
1950–51 **SCOTLAND** 2G, 1DG, 1PG, 1T (19) to 0 (*Murrayfield*).
1951–52 **WALES** 1G, 2PG (11) to 0 (*Cardiff*).
1952–53 **WALES** 1PG, 3T (12) to 0 (*Murrayfield*).
1953–54 **WALES** 1PG, 4T (15) to 1T (3) (*Swansea*).
1954–55 **SCOTLAND** 1G, 1DG, 1PG, 1T (14) to 1G, 1T (8) (*Murrayfield*).
1955–56 **WALES** 3T (9) to 1PG (3) (*Cardiff*).
1956–57 **SCOTLAND** 1DG, 1PG, 1T (9) to 1PG, 1T (6) (*Murrayfield*).
1957–58 **WALES** 1G, 1T (8) to 1PG (3) (*Cardiff*).
1958–59 **SCOTLAND** 1PG, 1T (6) to 1G (5) (*Murrayfield*).
1959–60 **WALES** 1G, 1PG (8) to 0 (*Cardiff*).
1960–61 **SCOTLAND** 1T (3) to 0 (*Murrayfield*).
1961–62 **SCOTLAND** 1G, 1T (8) to 1DG (3) (*Cardiff*).
1962–63 **WALES** 1DG, 1PG (6) to 0 (*Murrayfield*).
1963–64 **WALES** 1G, 1PG, 1T (11) to 1T (3) (*Cardiff*).
1964–65 **WALES** 1G, 2PG, 1T (14) to 2DG, 2PG (12) (*Murrayfield*).
1965–66 **WALES** 1G, 1T (8) to 1PG (3) (*Cardiff*).
1966–67 **SCOTLAND** 1G, 1DG, 1T (11) to 1G (5) (*Murrayfield*).
1967–68 **WALES** 1G (5) to 0 (*Cardiff*).
1968–69 **WALES** 1G, 2PG, 2T (17) to 1PG (3) (*Murrayfield*).
1969–70 **WALES** 3G, 1T (18) to 1DG, 1PG, 1T (9) (*Cardiff*).
1970–71 **WALES** 2G, 1PG, 2T (19) to 4PG, 2T (18) (*Murrayfield*).

(Try upgraded to 4 Pts.)

1971–72 **WALES** 3G, 3PG, 2T (35) to 1G, 2PG (12) (*Cardiff*).
1972–73 **SCOTLAND** 1G, 1T (10) to 3PG (9) (*Murrayfield*).
1973–74 **WALES** 1G (6) to 0 (*Cardiff*).
1974–75 **SCOTLAND** 3PG, 1DG (12) to 2PG 1T (10) (*Murrayfield*).
1975–76 **WALES** 2G, 3PG, 1DG, 1T (28) to 1G (6) (*Cardiff*).
1976–77 **WALES** 2G, 2PG (18) to 1G, 1DG (9) (*Murrayfield*).
1977–78 **WALES** 1DG, 1PG, 4T (22) to 2PG, 2T (14) (*Cardiff*).
1978–79 **WALES** 1G, 3PG, 1T (19) to 3PG, 1T (13) (*Murrayfield*).
1979–80 **WALES** 1G, 1PG, 2T (17) to 1G (6) (*Cardiff*).

AGAINST IRELAND

Matches played 82
Wales 50 wins, Ireland 27, 5 drawn

1881–82 **WALES** 2G, 2T to 0 (*Dublin*).
1882–83 No match.
1883–84 **WALES** 1DG, 2T to 0 (*Cardiff*).
1884–85 and 1885–86 No matches.
1886–87 **WALES** 1DG, 1T to 3T (*Birkenhead*).
1887–88 **IRELAND** 1G, 1DG, 1T to 0 (*Dublin*).
1888–89 **IRELAND** 2T to 0 (*Swansea*).
1889–90 **DRAWN** 1G each (3) (*Dublin*).
1890–91 **WALES** 1G, 1DG (6) to 1DG, 1T (4) (*Llanelli*).
1891–92 **IRELAND** 1G, 2T (9) to 0 (*Dublin*).
1892–93 **WALES** 1T (2) to 0 (*Llanelli*).
1893–94 **IRELAND** 1PG (3) to 0 (*Belfast*).
1894–95 **WALES** 1G (5) to 1T (3) (*Cardiff*).
1895–96 **IRELAND** 1G, 1T (8) to 1DG (4) (*Dublin*).
1896–97 No Match.
1897–98 **WALES** 1G, 1PG, 1T (11) to 1PG (3) (*Limerick*).
1898–99 **IRELAND** 1T (3) to 0 (*Cardiff*).
1899–1900 **WALES** 1T (3) to 0 (*Belfast*).
1900–01 **WALES** 2G (10) to 3T (9) (*Swansea*).
1901–02 **WALES** 1G, 1DG, 2T (15) to 0 (*Dublin*).
1902–03 **WALES** 6T (18) to 0 (*Cardiff*).
1903–04 **IRELAND** 1G, 3T (14) to 4T (12) (*Belfast*).
1904–05 **WALES** 2G, (10) to 1T (3) (*Swansea*).
1905–06 **IRELAND** 1G, 2T (11) to 2T (6)

(*Belfast*).
1906–07 **WALES** 2G, 1DG, 1PG, 4T (29) to 0 (*Cardiff*).
1907–08 **WALES** 1G, 2T (11) to 1G (5) (*Belfast*).
1908–09 **WALES** 3G, 1T (18) to 1G (5) (*Swansea*).
1909–10 **WALES** 1DG, 5T (19) to 1T (3) (*Dublin*).
1910–11 **WALES** 2G, 1PG, 1T (16) to 0 (*Cardiff*).
1911–12 **IRELAND** 1G, 1DG, 1T (12) to 1G (5) (*Belfast*).
1912–13 **WALES** 2G, 1PG, 1T (16) to 2G, 1PG (13) (*Swansea*).
1913–14 **WALES** 1G, 2T (11) to 1T (3) (*Belfast*).
1919–20 **WALES** 3G, 1DG, 3T (28) to 1DG (4) (*Cardiff*).
1920–21 **WALES** 1PG, 1T (6) to 0 (*Belfast*).
1921–22 **WALES** 1G, 2T (11) to 1G (5) (*Swansea*).
1922–23 **IRELAND** 1G (5) to 1DG (4) (*Dublin*).
1923–24 **IRELAND** 2G, 1T (13) to 1DG, 2T (10) (*Cardiff*).
1924–25 **IRELAND** 2G, 1PG, 2T (19) to 1T (3) (*Belfast*).
1925–26 **WALES** 1G, 2T (11) to 1G, 1PG (8) (*Swansea*).
1926–27 **IRELAND** 2G, 1PG, 2T (19) to 1G, 1DG (9) (*Dublin*).
1927–28 **IRELAND** 2G, 1T (13) to 2G (10) (*Cardiff*).
1928–29 **DRAWN** 1G (5) each (*Belfast*).
1929–30 **WALES** 1PG, 3T (12) to 1DG, 1PG (7) (*Swansea*).
1930–31 **WALES** 1G, 1DG, 2T (15) to 1T (3) (*Belfast*).
1931–32 **IRELAND** 4T (12) to 1DG, 2T (10) (*Cardiff*).
1932–33 **IRELAND** 1DG, 1PG, 1T (10) to 1G (5) (*Belfast*).
1933–34 **WALES** 2G, 1T (13) to 0 (*Swansea*).
1934–35 **IRELAND** 2PG, 1T (9) to 1PG (3) (*Belfast*).
1935–36 **WALES** 1PG (3) to 0 (*Cardiff*).
1936–37 **IRELAND** 1G (5) to 1PG (3) (*Belfast*).
1937–38 **WALES** 1G, 1PG 1T (11) to 1G (5) (*Swansea*).
1938–39 **WALES** 1DG, 1T (7) to 0 (*Belfast*).
1946–47 **WALES** 1PG, 1T (6) to 0 (*Swansea*).
1947–48 **IRELAND** 2T (6) to 1T (3) (*Belfast*).
(Dropped goal revalued to 3 pts.)
1948–49 **IRELAND** 1G (5) to 0 (*Swansea*).
1949–50 **WALES** 2T (6) to 1PG (3) (*Belfast*).
1950–51 **DRAWN.** WALES 1PG (3) IRELAND 1T (3) (*Cardiff*).
1951–52 **WALES** 1G, 1PG, 2T (14) to 1PG (3) (*Dublin*).
1952–53 **WALES** 1G (5) to 1T (3) (*Swansea*).
1953–54 **WALES** 1DG, 3PG (12) to 2PG. 1T (9) (*Dublin*).
1954–55 **WALES** 3G, 1PG, 1T (21) to 1PG (3) (*Cardiff*).
1955–56 **IRELAND** 1G, 1DG, 1PG (11) to 1PG (3) (*Dublin*).
1956–57 **WALES** 2PG (6) to 1G (5) (*Cardiff*).
1957–58 **WALES** 3T (9) to 1PG, 1T (6) (*Dublin*).
1958–59 **WALES** 1G, 1T (8) to 1PG, 1T (6) (*Cardiff*).
1959–60 **WALES** 2G (10) to 2PG, 1T (9) (*Dublin*).
1960–61 **WALES** 2PG, 1T (9) to 0 (*Cardiff*).
1961–62 **DRAWN.** IRELAND 1DG (3) WALES 1PG (3) (*Dublin*).
1962–63 **IRELAND** 1G, 1DG, 2PG (14) to 1DG, 1T (6) (*Cardiff*).
1963–64 **WALES** 3G (15) to 2PG (6) (*Dublin*).
1964–65 **WALES** 1G, 1DG, 1PG, 1T (14) to 1G, 1PG (8) (*Cardiff*).
1965–66 **IRELAND** 1DG, 1PG, 1T (9) to 1PG, 1T (6) (*Dublin*).
1966–67 **IRELAND** 1T (3) to 0 (*Cardiff*).
1967–68 **IRELAND** 1PG, 1DG 1T (9) to 1PG, 1DG (6) (*Dublin*).
1968–69 **WALES** 3G, 1PG, 1DG, 1T (24) to 1G, 2PG (11) (*Cardiff*).
1969–70 **IRELAND** 1G, 1DG, 1PG, 1T (14) to 0 (*Dublin*).
1970–71 **WALES** 1G, 1DG, 2PG, 3T (23) to 3PG (9) (*Cardiff*).
(Try upgraded to 4 pts)
1971–72 No match.
1972–73 **WALES** 1G, 2PG, 1T (16) to 1G, 2PG (12) (*Cardiff*).
1973–74 **DRAWN.** IRELAND 3PG (9) WALES 1G, 1PG (9) (*Dublin*).
1974–75 **WALES** 3G, 2PG, 2T (32) to 1T (4) (*Cardiff*).
1975–76 **WALES** 3G, 4PG, 1T (34) to 3PG (9) (*Dublin*).
1976–77 **WALES** 2G, 3PG, 1DG, 1T (25) to 3PG (9) (*Cardiff*).
1977–78 **WALES** 4PG, 2T (20) to 3PG, 1DG, 1T (16) (*Dublin*).
1978–79 **WALES** 2G, 4PG (24) to 2G, 3PG (21) (*Cardiff*).
1979–80 **IRELAND** 3G, 1P (21) to 1P, 1T (7) (*Dublin*).

AGAINST FRANCE

Matches played 53
Wales 35 wins, France 15, 3 drawn

1907–08 **WALES** 3G, 1PG, 6T (36) to 1DG (4) (*Cardiff*).
1908–09 **WALES** 7G, 4T (47) to 1G (5) (*Paris*).
1909–10 **WALES** 8G, 1PG, 2T (49) to 1G, 2PG, 1T (14) (*Swansea*).

1910–11 **WALES** 3G, (15) to 0 (*Paris*).
1911–12 **WALES** 1G, 3T (14) to 1G, 1T (8) (*Newport*).
1912–13 **WALES** 1G, 2T (11) to 1G, 1T (8) (*Paris*).
1913–14 **WALES** 5G, 2T (31) to 0 (*Swansea*).
1919–20 **WALES** 2T (6) to 1G (5) (*Paris*).
1920–21 **WALES** 2PG, 2T (12) to 1DG (4) (*Cardiff*).
1921–22 **WALES** 1G, 2T (11) to 1T (3) (*Paris*).
1922–23 **WALES** 2G, 1PG, 1T (16) to 1G, 1T (8) (*Swansea*).
1923–24 **WALES** 1DG, 2T (10) to 2T (6) (*Paris*).
1924–25 **WALES** 1G, 2T (11) to 1G (5) (*Cardiff*).
1925–26 **WALES** 1DG, 1T (7) to 1G (5) (*Paris*).
1926–27 **WALES** 2G, 5T (25) to 1DG, 1T (7) (*Swansea*).
1927–28 **FRANCE** 1G, 1T (8) to 1T (3) (*Paris*).
1928–29 **WALES** 1G, 1T (8) to 1T (3) (*Cardiff*).
1929–30 **WALES** 2DG, 1T (11) to 0 (*Paris*).
1930–31 **WALES** 5G, 1DG, 2T (35) to 1T (3) (*Swansea*).
1946–47 **WALES** 1PG (3) to 0 (*Paris*).
1947–48 **FRANCE** 1G, 2T (11) to 1PG (3) (*Swansea*).

(Dropped goal revalued to 3 pts.)

1948–49 **FRANCE** 1G, (5) to 1T (3) (*Paris*).
1949–50 **WALES** 3G, 1PG, 1T (21) to 0 (*Cardiff*).
1950–51 **FRANCE** 1G, 1PG (8) to 1T (3) (*Paris*).
1951–52 **WALES** 1DG, 2PG (9) to 1G (5) (*Swansea*).
1952–53 **WALES** 2T (6) to 1PG (3) (*Paris*).
1953–54 **WALES** 2G, 3PG (19) to 2G, 1PG (13) (*Cardiff*).
1954–55 **WALES** 2G, 2PG (16) to 1G, 1DG, 1PG (11) (*Paris*).
1955–56 **WALES** 1G, (5) to 1T (3) (*Cardiff*).
1956–57 **WALES** 2G, 1PG, 2T (19) to 2G, 1T (13) (*Paris*).
1957–58 **FRANCE** 2G, 2DG (16) to 1PG, 1T (6) (*Cardiff*).
1958–59 **FRANCE** 1G, 1PG, 1T (11) to 1PG (3) (*Paris*).
1959–60 **FRANCE** 2G, 2T (16) to 1G, 1PG (8) (*Cardiff*).
1960–61 **FRANCE** 1G, 1T (8) to 2T (6) (*Paris*).
1961–62 **WALES** 1PG (3) to 0 (*Cardiff*).
1962–63 **FRANCE** 1G (5) to 1PG (3) (*Paris*).
1963–64 **DRAWN.** 1G, 2PG (11) each (*Cardiff*).
1964–65 **FRANCE** 2G, 1PG, 1DG, 2T (22) to 2G 1T (13) (*Paris*).
1965–66 **WALES** 2PG, 1T (9) to 1G, 1T (8) (*Cardiff*).
1966–67 **FRANCE** 1G, 2DG, 1PG, 2T (20) to 1G, 2PG, 1DG (14) (*Paris*).
1967–68 **FRANCE** 1G, 1PG, 1DG, 1T (14) to 2PG, 1T (9) (*Cardiff*).
1968–69 **DRAWN.** FRANCE 1G, 1PG (8) WALES 1G, 1T (8) (*Paris*).
1969–70 **WALES** 1G, 2PG (11) to 2T (6) (*Cardiff*).
1970–71 **WALES** 1PG, 2T (9) to 1G (5) (*Paris*).

(Try upgraded to 4 pts.)

1971–72 **WALES** 4PG, 2T (20) to 2PG (6) (*Cardiff*).
1972–73 **FRANCE** 3PG, 1DG (12) to 1DG (3) (*Paris*).
1973–74 **DRAWN.** WALES 3PG, 1DG, 1T (16) FRANCE 3PG, 1DG, 1T (16) (*Cardiff*).
1974–75 **WALES** 1G, 1PG, 4T (25) to 2PG, 1T (10) (*Paris*).
1975–76 **WALES** 5PG, 1T (19) to 1G, 1PG, 1T (13) (*Cardiff*).
1976–77 **FRANCE** 1G, 2PG, 1T (16) to 3PG (9) (*Paris*).
1977–78 **WALES** 1G, 2DG, 1T (16) to 1DG, 1T (7) (*Cardiff*).
1978–79 **FRANCE** 2PG, 2T (14) to 3PG, 1T (13) (*Paris*).
1979–80 **WALES** 1G, 3T (18) to 1G, 1DG (9) (*Cardiff*).

AGAINST NEW ZEALAND

Matches played 10
Wales 3 wins, New Zealand 7

1905–06 **WALES** 1T (3) to 0 (*Cardiff*).
1924–25 **N.Z.** 2G, 1PG, 2T (19) to 0 (*Swansea*).
1935–36 **WALES** 2G, 1T (13) to 1G, 1DG, 1T (12) (*Cardiff*).
1953–54 **WALES** 2G, 1PG (13 to 1G, 1PG (8) (*Cardiff*).
1963–64 **N.Z.** 1PG, 1DG (6) to 0 (*Cardiff*).
1967 **N.Z.** 2G, 1PG (13) to 1PG, 1DG (6) (*Cardiff*).
1969 **N.Z.** 2G, 1PG, 2T (19) to 0 (*Christchurch*).
1969 **N.Z.** 3G, 5PG, 1DG (33) to 2PG, 2T (12) (*Auckland*).
1972–73 **N.Z.** 5PG, 1T (19) to 4PG, 1T (16) (*Cardiff*).
1974 ***N.Z.** 1G, 2PG (12) to 1PG (3) (*Cardiff*).
1978 **N.Z.** 3PG, 1T (13) to 4PG (12) (*Cardiff*).

* *Unofficial Match*

AGAINST SOUTH AFRICA

Matches played 7

South Africa 6 wins, 1 drawn

1906 **S.A.** 1G, 2T (11) to 0 (*Swansea*).
1912–13 **S.A.** 1PG (3) to 0 (*Cardiff*).
1931–32 **S.A.** 1G, 1T (8) to 1T (3) (*Swansea*).
1951–52 **S.A.** 1DG, 1T (6) to 1T (3) (*Cardiff*).
1960–61 **S.A.** 1PG (3) to 0 (*Cardiff*).
1964 **S.A.** 3G, 2PG,1DG (24) to 1PG (3) (*Durban*).
1970 **DRAWN** 1PG, 1T (6) each (*Cardiff*).

AGAINST AUSTRALIA

Matches played 9

Wales 6 wins, Australia 3

1908–09 **WALES** 1PG, 2T (9) to 2T (6) (*Cardiff*).
1947–48 **WALES** 2PG, (6) to 0 (*Cardiff*).
1957–58 **WALES** 1PG, 1DG, 1T (9) to 1T (3) (*Cardiff*).
1966–67 **AUSTRALIA** 1G, 1PG, 1DG, 1T (14) to 1G, 1PG, 1T (11) (*Cardiff*).
1969 **WALES** 2G, 2PG, 1T (19) to 2G, 2PG (16) (*Sydney*).
1973–74 **WALES** 2G, 2PG, 3T (24) to 0 (*Cardiff*).
1975–76 **WALES** 3G, 1PG, 1DG, 1T (28) to 1PG (3) (*Cardiff*).
1978 **AUSTRALIA** 1G, 4PG (18) to 2T (8) (*Brisbane*).
1978 **AUSTRALIA** 3PG, 2DG, 1T (19) to 2PG, 1DG, 2T (17) (*Sydney*).

AGAINST NEW SOUTH WALES

1927–28 **N.S.W.** 3G, 1T (18) to 1G, 1T (8) (*Cardiff*).

AGAINST MAORIS

1888–89 **WALES** 1G, 2T (5) to 0 (*Swansea*).
Note: A goal counted 3 pts., a try 1 pt.

AGAINST N.Z. ARMY TEAMS

1919 **N.Z. ARMY** 2PG (6) to 1PG (3) (*Swansea*).
1946 ***KIWIS** 1G, 2PG (11) to 1PG (3) (*Cardiff*).

* *No caps awarded*

WALES 'B' v FRANCE 'B' RESULTS

1969–70 **FRANCE** 1G, 2PG, 1DG, 1T (17) to 2PG, 1DG (9), (*Paris*).
1970–71 **WALES** 2PG, 1PG (13) to 2PG, 1DG (9) (*Llanelli*).
1971–72 **FRANCE** 4G, 1DG, 1PG (30) to 3PG (9) (*Paris*).
1972–73 **WALES** 4G, 1PG, 2T (35) to 1G (6) (*Cardiff*).
1973–74 **FRANCE** 3G, 2PG (24) to 1G, 2PG (12) (*Toulouse*).
1974–75 **WALES** 1G, 3PG, 2T (23) to 2G, 2T (20) (*Cardiff*).
1975–76 **FRANCE** 1G, 2PG, 3T (24) to 2G, 2PG, (18) (*Rouen*).
1976–77 **WALES** 1G, 2PG, 3T (24) to 1G (6) (*Pontypool*).
1977–78 **FRANCE** 1PG, 3T (15) to 1PG (3) (*Nantes*).
1978–79 **FRANCE** 3G, 3PG, 1T (31) to 1G, 4PG (18) (*Aberavon*).
1979–80 **FRANCE** 2G, 3P, 3T (33) to 4PG (12) (*Bourg.*).

FIVE NATIONS' CHAMPIONS

1883–84	**ENGLAND**
1884–5	—
1885–86	**ENGLAND** **SCOTLAND**
1886–87	**SCOTLAND**
1887–88	—
1888–89	—
1889–90	**ENGLAND** **SCOTLAND**
1890–91	**SCOTLAND**
1891–92	**ENGLAND**
1892–93	**WALES**
1893–94	**IRELAND**
1894–95	**SCOTLAND**
1895–96	**IRELAND**
1896–97	—
1897–98	**SCOTLAND**
1898–99	**IRELAND**
1899–1900	**WALES**
1900–01	**SCOTLAND**
1901–02	**WALES**
1902–03	**SCOTLAND**
1903–04	**SCOTLAND**
1904–05	**WALES**
1905–06	**IRELAND** **WALES**
1906–07	**SCOTLAND**
1907–08	**WALES**
1908–09	**WALES**
1909–10	**ENGLAND**
1910–11	**WALES**
1911–12	**ENGLAND** **IRELAND**
1912–13	**ENGLAND**
1913–14	**ENGLAND**
1919–20	**ENGLAND** **SCOTLAND** **WALES**
1920–21	**ENGLAND**
1921–22	**WALES**
1922–23	**ENGLAND**
1923–24	**ENGLAND**
1924–25	**SCOTLAND**
1925–26	**IRELAND** **SCOTLAND**
1926–27	**SCOTLAND** **IRELAND**
1927–28	**ENGLAND**
1928–29	**SCOTLAND**
1929–30	**ENGLAND**
1930–31	**WALES**
1931–32	**ENGLAND** **WALES** **IRELAND**
1932–33	**SCOTLAND**
1933–34	**ENGLAND**
1934–35	**IRELAND**
1935–36	**WALES**
1936–37	**ENGLAND**
1937–38	**SCOTLAND**
1938–39	**ENGLAND** **WALES** **IRELAND**
1946–47	**WALES** **ENGLAND**
1947–48	**IRELAND**
1948–49	**IRELAND**
1949–50	**WALES**
1950–51	**IRELAND**
1951–52	**WALES**
1952–53	**ENGLAND**
1953–54	**ENGLAND** **FRANCE** **WALES**
1954–55	**WALES** **FRANCE**
1955–56	**WALES**
1956–57	**ENGLAND**
1957–58	**ENGLAND**
1958–59	**FRANCE**
1959–60	**FRANCE** **ENGLAND**
1960–61	**FRANCE**
1961–62	**FRANCE**
1962–63	**ENGLAND**
1963–64	**SCOTLAND** **WALES**
1964–65	**WALES**
1965–66	**WALES**
1966–67	**FRANCE**
1967–68	**FRANCE**
1968–69	**WALES**
1969–70	**FRANCE** **WALES**
1970–71	**WALES**
1971–72	**WALES**
1972–73	5-WAY-TIE
1973–74	**IRELAND**
1974–75	**WALES**
1975–76	**WALES**
1976–77	**FRANCE**
1977–78	**WALES**
1978–79	**WALES**
1979–80	**ENGLAND**

TRIPLE CROWN WINNERS

WALES 16 times — 1892–93, 1899–1900, 1901–02, 1904–05, 1907–08, 1908–09, 1910–11, 1949–50, 1951–52, 1964–65, 1968–69, 1970–71, 1975–76, 1976–77, 1977–78, 1978–79.

ENGLAND 15 times — 1882–83, 1883–84, 1891–92, 1912–13, 1913–14, 1920–21, 1922–23, 1923–24, 1927–28, 1933–34, 1936–37, 1953–54, 1956–57, 1959–60, 1979–80.

SCOTLAND 8 times — 1890–91, 1894–95, 1900–01, 1902–03, 1906–07, 1924–25, 1932–33, 1937–38.

IRELAND 4 times — 1893–94, 1898–99, 1947–48, 1948–49.

GRAND SLAM WINNERS

WALES 8 times — 1907–08, 1908–09, 1910–11, 1949–50, 1951–52, 1970–71, 1975–76, 1977–78.

ENGLAND 8 times — 1912–13, 1913–14, 1920–21, 1922–23, 1923–24, 1927–28, 1956–57, 1979–80.

FRANCE twice — 1967–68, 1976–77.

SCOTLAND once — 1924–25.

IRELAND once — 1947–48.

INDEX

Page numbers in italic refer to the illustrations